PELICAN BOOKS

THE BEGINNINGS OF ENGLISH SOCIETY

Dorothy Whitelock was educated at the Leeds Girls'
High School and at Newnham College, Cambridge,
where she read for the English Tripos. After six years of
research work, in Cambridge and at the University of
Uppsala, she became in 1930 Lecturer, and later
Fellow and Tutor in English language, and Vice-
Principal, at St Hilda's College, Oxford. She was
Elrington and Bosworth Professor of Anglo-Saxon in
the University of Cambridge from 1957 to 1969. She
was an Honorary Fellow of Newnham College,
Cambridge, and of St Hilda's College, Oxford, and
served as President of several learned societies.
Published works include *Anglo-Saxon Wills*, *Sermo Lupi
ad Anglos*, *The Audience of Beowulf*, *English Historical
Documents c. 500–1042*, *Changing Currents in Anglo-Saxon
Studies* (inaugural lecture), *The Anglo-Saxon Chronicle:
A Revised Translation*, and *Sweet's Anglo-Saxon Reader*,
15th edition.

Dorothy Whitelock died in August 1982 and in her
obituary *The Times* wrote of 'her unique combination
of historical judgment, literary sensibility and lin-
guistic skill' and her 'substantial contributions in a
wide area of Anglo-Saxon studies'. With *The
Beginnings of English Society* the article continued; she
'made her mastery of all aspects of Anglo-Saxon
history and culture available to a wide public'.

THE PELICAN HISTORY OF ENGLAND
Edited by J. E. Morpurgo

1. Roman Britain
IAN RICHMOND

2. The Beginnings of English Society
(From the Anglo-Saxon Invasion)
DOROTHY WHITELOCK

3. English Society in the Early Middle Ages
DORIS MARY STENTON

4. England in the Late Middle Ages
A. R. MYERS

5. Tudor England
S. T. BINDOFF

6. England in the Seventeenth Century
MAURICE ASHLEY

7. England in the Eighteenth Century
J. H. PLUMB

8. England in the Nineteenth Century (1815–1914)
DAVID THOMSON

9. England in the Twentieth Century (1914–63)
DAVID THOMSON
with additional material by Geoffrey Warner

DOROTHY WHITELOCK

THE BEGINNINGS OF ENGLISH SOCIETY

PENGUIN BOOKS

PENGUIN BOOKS

Published by the Penguin Group
Penguin Books Ltd, 27 Wrights Lane, London W8 5TZ, England
Penguin Books USA Inc., 375 Hudson Street, New York, New York 10014, USA
Penguin Books Australia Ltd, Ringwood, Victoria, Australia
Penguin Books Canada Ltd, 10 Alcorn Avenue, Toronto, Ontario, Canada M4V 3B2
Penguin Books (NZ) Ltd, 182–190 Wairau Road, Auckland 10, New Zealand

Penguin Books Ltd, Registered Offices: Harmondsworth, Middlesex, England

First published in Pelican Books 1952
Second edition 1954
Reprinted with revisions 1965, 1966, 1968
Reprinted with revisions 1972, 1974
Reprinted in Penguin Books 1991
3 5 7 9 10 8 6 4

Printed in England by Clays Ltd, St Ives plc
Set in Monotype Baskerville

CONTENTS

	PREFACE	7
I	THE HEATHEN ENGLISH	11
II	THE BONDS OF SOCIETY	29
	Loyalty to one's Lord	
	Duty to one's Kin	
III	THE KING AND HIS COURT	48
IV	FINANCE AND ADMINISTRATION	64
	Finance	
	Royal Officials	
V	THE CLASSES OF SOCIETY	83
	The Nobleman	
	The Churl	
	The Slave	
VI	TRADE AND TOWN LIFE	115
	Trade	
	Towns	
VII	THE LAW	134
VIII	THE CHURCH	155
IX	EDUCATION AND LATIN SCHOLAR-SHIP	189
X	VERNACULAR LITERATURE	204
XI	ANGLO-SAXON ART	223
XII	CONCLUSION	241
	SELECT BIBLIOGRAPHY	244
	INDEX	249

PREFACE

THIS book does not set out to give an account of Anglo-Saxon political history, but to assemble from various sources what can be learnt about the ways of life of the English between their settlement in Britain in the middle of the fifth century and their conquest by the Normans in 1066. It examines the principles of society brought from their continental homes, and how these developed in the new land. It deals with the modifications which Christianity introduced and the art and literature which it inspired. A detailed knowledge of political events, of dates, or of kingdoms and kings, etc., is not necessary for the understanding of these chapters. It is enough that the reader should know that Christianity first reached the English in 597 and within a century had spread over the whole country; and that the period can be divided into two, a pre-Viking period, when England consisted of several small kingdoms, and a post-Viking period, when the kings of Wessex were the only English rulers. The Viking raids began with a few isolated attacks at the very end of the eighth century, and became a serious menace between 835 and 878, the year in which Alfred's victory at Edington prevented the extinction of Christian culture in England. By this date the Danes had already begun the settlement of East Anglia, Northumbria, and the North-East Midlands. By 954 these areas had all been recovered for the English crown by Alfred's son and grandsons, but they retained many signs of Scandinavian influence in their language, their place-names and personal names, their administrative divisions and assessment, their law and social customs. A period of peace in the middle of the tenth century, in which took place a great monastic reform and revival of learning, was followed by renewed Danish attacks from 980, which continued throughout the reign of Ethelred the Unready and culminated in the conquest by Cnut. Danish kings, Cnut and his sons, reigned from 1016 to 1042, when the English line was restored in the person of Edward the Confessor. The reader who desires detailed information on these matters is referred to Sir Frank Stenton's *Anglo-Saxon England*, a work to which this present book is deeply indebted.

A few terms used in this book will require explanation. While the names Kent, Essex, Sussex, East Anglia, will occasion no difficulty, it should be noted that Northumbria describes all the lands in English hands north of the Humber, reaching, at the period of their greatest extent, at least as far as the Forth on the north, and to the Irish Sea on the west; that Mercia was in the days of settlement a western outpost in the valleys of the Upper and Middle Trent and its tributaries the Tame and Dove, but, as its kings conquered their neighbours one by one – among them the Middle Angles to the south-east, the *Hwicce* of the Severn valley, the *Magonsæte* about Hereford, the dwellers round the Wrekin – the term Mercia comes to be employed to denote an enormous kingdom bounded by the Humber and the Thames, the Welsh Border and the East Anglian frontier, and from the eighth century it includes London; and that Wessex similarly developed from small beginnings, in Hampshire, Wiltshire, and the Upper Thames valley, until it denotes the southern counties from Surrey to the Bristol Channel and the Cornish border.

Wherever possible, Anglo-Saxon terms have been given modern equivalents; but this is impossible with certain weights and measures. We do not know the capacity of a 'sester' or an 'amber'; a 'mancus' was a weight of gold of about 70 grains, and was considered equivalent to thirty silver pence; a 'mark' was a Danish weight made up of eight 'ores', and there were two systems current in relating it to the native coinage, for we find on some occasions 20 pence reckoned to an 'ore' of silver, and on others 16; the shilling referred to in our records is not usually a coin, but merely a unit of count, denoting 20 pence in early Kent, fourpence in Mercia and early Wessex, fivepence in Wessex in later times; a pound, then as now, contained 240 pence. But all references to money are misleading unless one bears in mind the high purchasing power of the Anglo-Saxon penny (a silver coin), and it is well to remember that 30 pence was the legal price of an ox, fourpence or five-pence that of a sheep. All other terms used in this volume are explained on their first occurrence, except that the nature of the office of an 'ealdorman', the king's highest official, is not discussed until pp. 77-80. In spite of the loss of consistency, I give personal names which are still in use, and those of kings, in their familiar, instead of their Anglo-Saxon form. I retain the well-known nick-name 'the Unready', though I should prefer to render it 'of Evil Counsel', or perhaps 'the Treacherous'.

All workers in this field of study must alternate be-tween thankfulness that so much information from so early a period has survived, and irritation that it is so unevenly distributed, whether as regards period, or locality, or subject. It might have been possible to fill up some of the gaps by imaginative surmise, but I have pre-ferred to restrict myself to what the surviving evidence states or implies.

While it would be impossible to enumerate in brief space all the scholars whose work has been utilized in this book, I should like to take this opportunity of recording my debt to that great scholar the late Professor H. M. Chadwick, who first aroused my interest in the Anglo-Saxons and to whose careful training I owe more than can be expressed; and I wish to thank Professor Bruce Dickins for his constant help and encouragement, and Sir Frank Stenton, whose reading of this book in manuscript was only a final service to a work which his interest over many years has brought into being.

CHAPTER I

THE HEATHEN ENGLISH

ENGLISHMEN in Anglo-Saxon times were aware of the Germanic origin of their race, and most educated men after the first half of the eighth century could probably have added that their forefathers came of three of the bravest nations of Germany, the Angles, the Saxons, and the Jutes, and first landed in the romanized province of Britain in the year 449. They would have derived this knowledge, directly or indirectly, from the writings of the great historian, Bede, whose most famous work, his *Ecclesiastical History of the English Nation,* which he finished in 731, contains a chapter on the origin of his race much used by later writers. It matters little for our present purpose that when chroniclers liked to calculate the number of years that had elapsed since 'the Coming of the English' their choice of 449 as the date of this event went beyond the original statement of Bede; or that the conflicting evidence of our early sources of information makes it impossible to assign a precise year to the beginning of the English settlement in Britain. Neither need we worry overmuch whether Bede's attempted reconciliation of this tradition of threefold origin with the political divisions of his own day can be accepted as accurate in every detail. Slightly older Northumbrian writers do not observe Bede's racial distinctions, but call their own people Saxons, though the Northumbrians are Angles according to Bede. Even Bede himself does not keep during the rest of his work to the division laid down in this one chapter. Although there is enough supporting evidence to show that Bede's division had some basis of fact, it is difficult to avoid the impression that by his day these differences of origin were no longer felt to be important. St Boniface was not excluding Saxons and Jutes when in 738 he addressed a letter to 'all God-fearing Catholics sprung from the race and stock of the Angles', but meant all the inhabitants of England, and King Alfred, a Saxon, uses the term 'Angle-race' in just this sense, and consistently calls his native language English, not Saxon. (In this book, the term English is used to refer to all the Teutonic races in Britain, no matter what their origin, and to their common language.)

What is interesting is that the invaders remained so conscious of their Germanic origin. Bede's older contemporary, St Aldhelm, uses 'our stock' and 'the Germanic race' as parallel expressions, and St Boniface was probably as yet unfamiliar with Bede's historical work when he wrote home from Germany in 738 asking for support for a projected mission to the continental Saxons: 'Have pity on them, because even they themselves are wont to say: "We are of one blood and one bone".' In fact, this strong sense of kinship with the Germanic tribes on the Continent led the Anglo-Saxons to attempt their conversion even before the last strongholds of heathenism in England had fallen. From the remains of their secular poetry we can see that they took an interest in the early history and traditions of all the Germanic peoples, as in their own.

Bede brings the Saxons from the country held in his own day by the 'Old Saxons', that is, the region of the lower Elbe, the Angles from Angeln, on the neck of the Cimbric peninsula, the Jutes, by implication, from the land north of this, now called Jutland. King Alfred (871–99) was familiar with this tradition, for he says 'in those lands dwelt the English before they came hither' after he has mentioned Jutland, *Sillende* and many islands as lying to starboard when the traveller Ohthere sailed down the Cattegat from Norway to Schleswig. It has sometimes been questioned whether Bede was correct in placing the homeland of the Jutes where he does, for the archaeology and institutions of Kent, where the Jutes settled, have affinities, not with Jutland, but with the Frankish territory by the Rhine. Agreement has not been reached regarding the implications of this fact. However, it remains unchallenged that the majority of the invaders of Britain came from North Germany and the Jutish peninsula. The Jutes spoke a language closely related to that of the Saxons and Angles but also akin to Frisian; even if they did come from the Rhineland, they would still come from a Germanic district, though from one more exposed to influences from the Roman empire.

*

It is not necessary to suppose that even in their remoter homes the invaders were entirely unfamiliar with Roman culture. Articles of Roman make found their way to the Baltic shores by trade, and also as loot, for already in the late third century Saxon pirates had become such a menace to the Channel and North Sea coasts that the Romans built a series of forts from the Wash to the Isle of Wight, which were known as the forts of the Saxon Shore. Saxon raiders appear to have penetrated far inland in 429, but the 'Coming of the Saxons', often referred to in later Anglo-Saxon writers, differed from such raids in that it was the beginning of a settlement, at first, if we may accept an early tradition, by peaceful agreement as allies, though a subsequent revolt led to the conquest of the eastern part of the island. Reinforced by a continual stream of immigrants, the invaders pressed further and further west, until eventually they held almost the whole of what is now England, the east of Scotland at least as far north as the Forth, and the Solway Plain.

The newcomers came to a land that differed much from the England of to-day. It was heavily forested, with great stretches of continuous woodland, such as the forests of Selwood, Wychwood, Savernake, Wyre, Arden, Sherwood, Epping, Kinver, Morfe, the Chilterns, and the Weald, all far more extensive than their modern remnants. The Weald stretched from Hampshire to Kent, 120 miles long and 30 broad, according to a late ninth-century writer. The amount of available arable land was reduced also by the presence of large areas of marshland, not only in the eastern counties; Romney Marsh was undrained, and there was a great expanse of fenland in Somerset from the Mendips almost to Taunton. The areas under cultivation were on the whole small, surrounded by woodland and waste; but there was an exception to this: contrary to modern conditions, the chalk and oolite plateaux, such as Salisbury Plain, the Berkshire Downs, and the North Downs, were cultivated as arable. The river valleys in these areas were deserted until the English cleared and cultivated the heavy soils of the lowland valleys. The view that this was because they used a heavy plough previously known only in the areas of Roman Britain where Belgic tribes had settled is no longer generally held.

The land was crossed by a network of Roman roads, connecting the cities and military stations with one another, and with the defences like the great Wall and the forts of the Saxon Shore. Yet it was no flourishing Roman civilization that the invaders found. Long before the Romans withdrew their forces in 410 urban life in Britain had begun to decay. According to Collingwood, it had always been from the economic point of view a luxury, with a political and cultural function. The population in the cities had shrunk and the buildings were falling into disrepair. Few of the villas, which in many areas formed the basis of Romano-British rural economy, had survived the barbarian raids of 368, and subsequent raids had wrought further destruction. The centralized Roman administration had broken down, and petty rulers of native race had established control over areas of varying extent, though, from time to time, one of them may have exercised some sort of overlordship over his fellows. It was one of these, known already to Bede as Vortigern, who invited Saxon allies to settle in the east of the land.

It is not, therefore, greatly to be wondered at that in general the earliest English settlements were not closely related to the Roman road system planned to meet the needs of a centralized administration which was no longer in existence. Left unrepaired, many of these roads would rapidly become unusable over long stretches, though the more important of them were brought back into use as the necessity for intercourse between the settlements increased. Nor did the invaders take naturally to town life. Some Roman cities, Silchester, Caister-next-Norwich, *Viroconium*, Verulam, for example, were never re-occupied, others not immediately. Cambridge was derelict in Bede's day. Even in places where continuous occupation seems likely, important centres like London, York, and Lincoln, the English settlement grew up beside, and not in, the Romano-British town. After all, a population unaccustomed to city life, not possessing a system of economy that enforced centralization of population, would hardly choose to inhabit decaying stone buildings which they did not know how to repair. They themselves were accustomed to build only in timber, or lath and plaster, and it seems clear that they did not retain the services of Britons skilled in masonry, if indeed any such existed by the time of the invasion. After the conversion of the English to Christianity, the early church builders always found it necessary to import masons from abroad. These sometimes re-used Roman masonry for their work; but at the time of the settlement, the invaders could have had little use for buildings whose amenities they did not know how to enjoy.

Nevertheless, even in their partly derelict condition, the monuments of Roman civilization were impressive enough to people unaccustomed to stone buildings, paved roads, and massive ramparts. Small wonder that they called these things 'the work of giants' in their poetry, as, for example, in a gnomic poem prefixed to one manuscript of the Anglo-Saxon Chronicle:

Cities are visible from afar, the cunning work of giants, the wondrous fortifications in stone which are on this earth.

In later days, there was a tendency to build monasteries in disused Roman forts, as at Reculver, *Othona*, Dover, and probably at Coldingham. The Irishman Fursey was given a deserted Roman fortress, probably Burgh Castle, Suffolk, in which to found a monastery. This practice may be accounted for on practical considerations – the protection afforded by the existing walls, the supply of masonry ready to hand – yet one wonders whether any feeling was involved that the continual prayers of men and women devoted to God would put to flight supernatural powers that might inhabit these places.

Educated men like Bede looked with admiration on the remains of the Roman period. He mentions the cities, temples, bridges, and paved roads surviving to his own day. The anonymous writer of the earliest life of St Cuthbert, in telling how the saint saw by second sight the defeat of the Northumbrian forces at *Nechtansmere* in 685, says it was while he and others 'were looking at the wall of the city (Carlisle) and the fountain in it formerly built by the Romans in a wonderful fashion, as

Waga, the reeve of the city, who was conducting them, explained.'

To the Christian Anglo-Saxon poets, these tangible signs of the decay of a civilization more magnificent than their own provided an opportunity for moralizing on the theme of the transience of earthly splendour:

Thus the Creator of men laid waste this habitation, until, deprived of the revelry of the citizens, the old works of the giants stood desolate.

We cannot guess which of the deserted cities gave rise to this poem, but there is another, with a reference to hot springs, which is believed to refer to Bath. The poet's imagination peopled it in the past with men 'glad at heart and bright with gold, adorned resplendently, proud and flushed with wine; they shone in their war-gear; they gazed on treasure, on silver, on cunning gems, on riches, on possessions, on precious stones, on this bright citadel of a spacious kingdom.' All this was changed by 'the mighty fate'.

It is possible that the stone remains of the Roman period did more than inspire the first settlers with super-stitious awe and the Christian moralists with a fruitful theme. It has been suggested that Roman sculptured remains in the north of England formed the inspiration of a school of Christian sculptors, who produced figure sculpture of outstanding merit in the late seventh and eighth centuries, a time when no other part of Europe was producing sculpture in the round.

*

The monuments of Roman Britain remained to impress the invaders. What happened to the native population? Few scholars would now maintain that they were com-pletely massacred or driven out, even from the earliest areas of settlement. More and more, archaeologists are recognizing Romano-British influence on objects found in Saxon cemeteries. In the later settlements, in the West, we find Welsh inhabitants far above the condition of serfdom. A British strain in the personal names of the Anglo-Saxons, especially visible in Northumbria, is witness to a small amount of intermarriage. Yet it would be grossly inaccurate to visualize the invaders as a mere military aristocracy over a large subject population of native origin. The Anglo-Saxon word for a Briton came to be used as a common noun denoting a slave, a fact which tells its own tale of the normal status of the Britons who remained in the parts conquered by the invaders. The influence of the natives on the language of the newcomers was almost negligible; they passed on to them many river-, forest-, and hill-names, and the names of Roman cities, but the invaders gave new names to their own settlements, and, except on the western fringes of the country, no place-name supplies a certain instance of a British habitation name or personal name. A bare handful of words of British origin became part of the English language. All this is incompatible with any view that the invaders were comparatively few in number and were absorbed into the pre-existing population. So also is the desertion of the upland villages on the downlands in favour of the valley sites that the English cleared and worked with their own heavy plough.

There is, in fact, little indication that the invaders' civilization was affected to any appreciable extent by the outlook and institutions of the pre-English inhabitants. The Anglo-Saxons regarded themselves as Germans, and continued to repeat the songs and legends which they had brought over with them – including versified catalogues of the kings and tribes of Germany and the North. The main outlines of English society – apart from those elements introduced later by the adoption of Christianity

– are already distinguishable in the account of the German peoples on the Continent, written by Tacitus in the first century of the Christian era, and can often be paralleled in later accounts of other races of Germanic origin, especially in the rich literature of the Scandinavians. Though neither of these sources can be used unreservedly as evidence for conditions in England, their statements may sometimes allow us to interpret more clearly something that is only hinted at in our own, in some respects, more scanty, records.

*

The Christian religion was established in Britain before the English came, but there is no evidence that any of the invaders deserted in its favour the rites of their forefathers which they brought with them. Thanks to Tacitus, we know something of what these were. He describes a sanctuary of a goddess called Nerthus, which was shared by a group of tribes to be located in North Germany, the Cimbric peninsula and islands, among whom the Angles are specifically mentioned, while the Saxons and Jutes are possibly referred to under other names. He says:

There is on an island in the ocean an inviolate grove, and in it a consecrated car, covered by a robe; only one priest is allowed to touch it. He perceives when the goddess is present in the sanctuary, and accompanies her with great reverence as she is drawn by heifers. Then are days of rejoicing, and festive are the places which she honours with her coming and her stay. Men go not to battle, nor do they carry arms; all iron is locked away; then only are peace and quiet known, then only are they loved, until the same priest returns the goddess to her temple, when she is weary of intercourse with mortals. Thereupon the car and the robes, and, if you wish to credit it, the divinity herself, are washed in a secluded lake. Slaves perform this, who are immediately swallowed up by the same lake. Hence arises a mysterious terror and a pious ignorance, what this may be which is seen only by those about to die.

There is no direct evidence that the English continued to worship Nerthus in Britain. Her cult survived in Scandinavia, where, however, she suffered a change of sex, for her name corresponds exactly with that of the Scandinavian god Njörthr, the father of Freyr and his sister Freyja, all three being fertility gods. But evidence for the heathen religion in England is hard to come by, for our records owe their preservation to Christian writers who had no great interest in heathen religion. There are, however, hints of fertility cults, and we learn most where the writer is probably no longer aware of the original implications of the material he has happened to preserve. For example, the twenty-second letter of the Anglo-Saxon runic alphabet bore the name Ing, and a poem about this alphabet contains the cryptic verse:

Ing was first seen by men among the East Danes, until he afterwards departed east over the waves; the waggon followed. Thus the Heardings named the hero.

It seems a far cry from here to the great god Freyr of Scandinavian mythology, who, in the words of the Icelandic author Snorri Sturluson, 'rules over the rain and the shining of the sun, and over the produce of the earth as well; and it is good to call on him for fruitfulness and peace.' Yet Freyr only means 'lord', and the god is also called Ingunar-Freyr and Yngvi Freyr. The branch of the Germans to which the North German tribes belonged derived its name, Ingvaeones, from him. The waggon in the English poem probably refers to some cult progress like the one Tacitus describes.

An obscure reference like this to a forgotten fertility god would be insufficient to prove the continuance of fertility cults after the invaders left their continental homes and ancient sanctuaries, unless it were supported by other evidence. Some measure of support is given by the existence of a charm for ensuring the fertility of one's land, for it has been only imperfectly christianized, and includes an invocation to Erce, mother of earth. Erce is presumably the name of a goddess, and Bede tells us the names of two other goddesses, Eostre, from whom he derives the name of a spring festival which gave its name to the Christian Easter, and Hretha, of whom nothing further is known. Bede tells us also that the first night of the heathen New Year was called 'the night of the mothers', but what ceremonies are implied by this name we do not know. It is hardly accidental that the boar-emblem, sacred to Freyr in Scandinavian mythology, was regarded by the Anglo-Saxons as having protective powers, even though they may no longer have connected its magical efficacy with the ancient gods of peace and plenty. The emblem was placed on helmets, and one of these is described thus in the Anglo-Saxon epic poem *Beowulf*:

as the weapon-smith made it in former days, adorned it wondrously, encompassed it with boar-figures, so that afterwards no sword or battle-blade could pierce it.

It is also to be noted that the kings of Wessex included in their genealogies a certain Scyld who is mentioned in *Beowulf* and has there some attributes often associated with fertility divinities, e.g. an arrival from and departure into the unknown. The corresponding name is borne in Scandinavian sources by the husband of a fertility goddess, and both English and Scandinavian traditions assign him a son whose name seems to mean 'barley'. It looks, therefore, as if in this figure we have another trace of an old, forgotten, fertility cult.

We are not dependent on scattered references in literature to prove the worship in England of Woden, Thunor, and Tiw, gods already known to the Germans in Tacitus's time, whom Latin writers normally equate with Mercury, Jove, and Mars respectively. These three gods have left their mark on place-names in England. Woden is a frequent first element in these names, as in Woodnesborough and Wormshill, Kent, Wednesbury and Wednesfield, Staffordshire, Wensley, Derbyshire, and the lost *Wodneslawe*, Bedfordshire, *Wodnesbiorg*, Wiltshire, *Wodnesfeld*, Essex, and so on. Thunor occurs in Thunderfield, Surrey, Thurstable, Essex, Thundridge, Hertfordshire, and six times – in Essex, Sussex, Surrey, and Hampshire – before a second element *leah*, which means a wood, or a clearing in a wood. The god Tiw was worshipped in Tysoe, Warwickshire, Tuesley, Surrey, and in the lost *Tislea*, Hampshire, and *Tyesmere*, Worcestershire.

English sources do not tell us what qualities were attributed to these gods, except once, in the case of Woden; for a charm called the *Nine Herbs Charm*, which says:

The snake came creeping, it tore a man to pieces; then took Woden nine glorious twigs, and struck the adder that it flew into nine parts,

for all its obscurity, agrees well with one aspect of this divinity in Scandinavian sources, as the god of knowledge, of intellectual attainment, who wards off evil from mankind by his wisdom. In England, the building of prehistoric monuments was attributed to him; his name is given to the Wansdyke, and one of his by-names to earthworks in different parts of the country called Grim's ditches. In contrast to Woden, Thunor 'the Thunderer' does not figure in English literary sources, but it is to be noted that among the heathen customs that the Church as late as the eighth century was eager to suppress was the observance of the fifth day of the week in honour of Jove (i.e. Thunor).

When the English accepted Christianity, they came to regard their former gods as devils. The Christian poet who drew the contrast:

Woden wrought idols; the Almighty, that is the powerful God, the true King himself, the Saviour of souls, wrought glory, the spacious heavens,

does not suggest that the old gods had never existed. An extant charm claims to be effective against 'the shot of the gods, the shot of the elves, the shot of witches'. Gradually, however, they were forgotten, so that when, at the end of the tenth century, the homilist Abbot Ælfric repeats the normal equation of classical and Germanic deities, he uses the Scandinavian forms of the names of the latter. Presumably the fresh influx of heathen settlers in the Viking age had made these forms more familiar to an English audience than those used in their own, long distant, heathen past.

Words denoting a heathen sanctuary of some kind occur in place-names in all areas of early settlement. Of special interest are Peper Harrow and the lost *Cusanweoh*, Surrey, and Patchway, Sussex, for in all three the second element (*hearg, weoh*) means a sanctuary, while the first is a personal name in the genitive case, so that private ownership is suggested, reminiscent of the position of the Icelandic *goði*, who combined the functions of chieftain and priest. On the other hand, the old name for Harrow-on-the-Hill, Middlesex, which means sanctuary 'of the Gumenings', and the lost *Besingahearh* 'sanctuary of the Besings', Surrey, seem rather to refer to the holy place of a family or group. Some of these places are on hill-tops, whereas the number of place-names with heathen associations that contain a word meaning 'wood' or 'woodland clearing' shows that heathen sanctuaries were often in the woods, and reminds us that Tacitus speaks of sacred groves among the Germans, and that later continental and Scandinavian evidence bears out his statements.

Some of the places which were the meeting-places of

the hundreds in later times have names containing
heathen elements, a circumstance which implies that
people continued after their conversion to Christianity to
meet at the places where they had been accustomed to
carry on their heathen rites. In so doing, they would be
acting in accordance with instructions sent by Pope
Gregory to the missionaries in 601, advocating the conversion of pagan temples into Christian churches, 'in
order that the people may the more familiarly resort to
the places to which they have been accustomed.' There
is, however, little evidence that the missionaries went so
far as to use a heathen building for a Christian church,
though Canterbury tradition believed that St Pancras's
church had once been King Ethelbert's idol-fane; we
read rather of total destruction, as at the great temple at
Goodmanham near York, after King Edwin's council
had decided in favour of the Christian faith in 627, or all
over Essex in 665, when Christianity had been re-estab-
lished after a relapse into paganism in time of plague.
This relapse may have brought it home to the men on
the spot that the continued existence of heathen fanes
had dangers greater than Gregory had realized. King
Aldwulf of East Anglia, a contemporary of Bede, remembered having seen in his boyhood the temple in which
his predecessor King Rædwald – not fully comprehend-
ing the demands of the new faith – had set up an altar to
Christ beside those to his old gods. Bede's account makes
it clear that this was never converted into a Christian
church.

From this passage and other places we learn that
heathen sanctuaries might include temples and images
of the gods. Great sacrifices were held at certain seasons;
a feast was held in the second month of the year at which
cakes were offered to the gods, while the feast after the
autumn slaughtering of the surplus cattle caused Novem-

ber to be known as 'sacrifice month'. These sacrifices were accompanied by ceremonial feastings.

A few scattered details of heathen customs can be garnered. A priest had to observe certain taboos, not being allowed to carry weapons or to ride on anything but a mare; he was believed to be able to bind the hands of his enemies by chanting spells from a high mound. The letters of the Germanic alphabet, runes, were held to have magic powers if used in the correct arrangement; they could, for example, release a prisoner from his fetters. Veneration was paid to trees, wells, and stones, and there was a firm trust in 'incantations, amulets, and other mysteries of devilish art.' The Church preached for generations against these and other superstitions – against the burning of grain 'for the health of the living and the house' after a death, against women who placed their daughters on a roof or in an oven to heal fever. People came to rely on Christian prayers, holy water, and the relics of saints to protect them from the evil powers with which they felt themselves surrounded, and which could be fitted into the Christian scheme of things as the monstrous offspring of Cain, from whom sprang 'ogres and elves and ghouls, and giants who fought against God for a long time.' Place-names afford ample evidence of the prevalent belief in such creatures, for various words for demon and goblin are common in them. The hermit St Guthlac had to fight long and earnestly against the fenland demons whom his coming had displaced. *Beowulf*, the greatest poem in Anglo-Saxon literature, is devoted to the freeing of human habitations from the ravages of supernatural creatures that inhabit the fens and from a dragon residing in a prehistoric burial-mound. The audience for whom the poem was composed would not have felt these themes either fantastic or trivial. The charms which kept away these evil influences were christianized, so that it is rare to find, among those that survive, an uneradicated heathen reference like the ones mentioned above.

From the fragmentary evidence for Anglo-Saxon heathenism, it is not possible to form a clear idea of the pre-Christian views of an after-life, or of the connexion between religion and ethics. Their practice of burying goods with the dead would imply some belief in a future life in which these will be of use, but if we can take at its face-value the speech Bede puts into the mouth of a pagan Northumbrian nobleman, comparing human life to the flight of a sparrow through the king's hall, 'coming in from the darkness and returning to it', this belief was very indefinite, or else it failed to convince the upper classes. No one at the council is reported to have disputed the nobleman's statement. There is certainly no evidence to justify the putting back into this period of the Scandinavian conceptions in the Viking Age of a Valhalla and 'a twilight of the gods'.

The language used on the same occasion by Coifi, the Northumbrian high-priest, suggests that what was expected of the gods was material benefit in this life in return for the due observance of their rites, for he complains to the king:

Not one of your men has applied himself to the worship of our gods more zealously than I, and nevertheless there are many who receive fuller benefits and greater dignities from you than I . . . But if the gods were any good, they would rather wish to help me, who have taken care to serve them the more assiduously.

But it must be remembered that Bede was not in a position to paint a fair picture of the heathen point of view, and it is perhaps best to leave it an open question how far the heathen English connected divine favour with obedience to an ethical code. We may be sure, however, that the breaking of oaths sworn on sacred things was considered to bring down the wrath of the gods, and we are told by Tacitus that the assemblies of the Germans were placed under divine protection, which would make a breach of their peace an act of sacrilege. One of the least Christian features of extant heroic poetry, a feature perhaps inherited from heathen times, is that men seem more concerned with the reputation they will leave behind them than with divine rewards in this world or the next. This view is expressed concisely in *Beowulf*:

> Each of us must experience an end to life in this world; let him who can achieve glory before he die; that will be best for the lifeless warrior afterwards.

The poet's final comment on this hero – and the concluding words of the poem – is that of all men he was 'the most eager for glory.' The poet who wrote this was a Christian, and his hero wins his glory by virtues not incompatible with a Christian code. Yet it emphasizes the difference between this remark and a strict churchman's point of view to note that the tenth-century homilist Ælfric uses an equivalent term to explain what is meant by the deadly sin of pride.

It is often held that Anglo-Saxon poetry is permeated by a strong belief in the power of fate, inherited from heathen times, and some have even seen a conflict between a faith in an omnipotent Christian God and a trust in a blind, inexorable fate. To me, this view seems exaggerated. The word used for fate can mean simply 'event', 'what happens', and though there are passages where some degree of personification is present, such as 'the creation of the fates changes the world under the heavens' or 'woven by the decrees of fate', I doubt if these are more than figures of speech by the time the

poems were composed. If they are inherited from the
heathen past, they may indicate that men then believed
in a goddess who wove their destiny, but the poet who
says 'to him the Lord granted the webs of victory' is un-
conscious of a heathen implication in his phrase. It would
be natural enough that, even while yet heathen, the
Anglo-Saxons should feel that man's destiny is outside
his own control, but stronger evidence would be necessary
before we could assume a belief in the fate-weaving
Norns at the foot of the world-tree Yggdrasil, as described
in the much later, poetic, mythology of the Scandinavians.

CHAPTER II

THE BONDS OF SOCIETY

Loyalty to one's Lord

THE strength of the bond between a man and his lord in the Germanic races impressed Tacitus in the first century, causing him to write some famous words that find an echo throughout Anglo-Saxon literature. Having mentioned that the loyalty is personal, not tribal, for a successful chief may attract to him men from many tribes, and that chieftain and followers vie with one another in showing courage on the battlefield, Tacitus continues:

> Furthermore, it is a lifelong infamy and reproach to survive the chief and withdraw from the battle. To defend him, to protect him, even to ascribe to his glory their own exploits, is the essence of their sworn allegiance. The chiefs fight for victory, the followers for their chief.

In return for their service the men expect horses and weapons, and feasting in the lord's household; they covet the place of highest honour in it.

The acceptance of Christianity made no difference to this attitude, and several centuries after Tacitus it is a very similar picture that is painted in the Anglo-Saxon poetry of Christian date. The lord has his band of followers, often called *gesithas* 'companions', who share 'the joys of the hall' in time of peace and who should be prepared to die for him in time of war. Thus the aged Beowulf looks back with satisfaction on the services he performed for his lord, King Hygelac:

> I repaid him in battle for the treasures which he gave me. ....
> Ever would I be before him in the troop, alone in the van.

The fragmentary poem on the battle at *Finnesburh* tells us that 'retainers never repaid better the bright mead than his young followers did to Hnæf.' Beowulf himself was not so well served, and his young kinsman Wiglaf speaks bitter words of reproach to the men who have failed to come to their lord's support:

He who wishes to speak the truth can say that the lord who gave you those treasures, that war-gear that you stand up in – when he often gave to men on the ale-benches in the hall, as a prince to his thanes, the most splendid helmet and corslet that he could find, far and near – entirely threw away this war-gear, when battle befell him.

Such conduct earned lasting infamy, and Wiglaf goes on to draw a grim picture of the future dishonoured life of the men guilty of desertion.

As in Tacitus, the lord takes the honour of his followers' exploits, and King Hygelac in *Beowulf* is called 'the slayer of Ongentheow', although the deed was done by two of his thanes, whom he richly rewarded. The retainer brings the spoils he has won to his lord. Beowulf gave to King Hygelac the gifts he had been given for his services in Denmark, and on another occasion he expresses his satisfaction that by killing the Frankish champion, Dæghrefn, he had denied him the triumph of bearing in person to his lord, the king of the Franks, the armour of Hygelac, who had been killed in battle, almost certainly by Dæghrefn himself. The minstrel Widsith gave to his own lord on his return to his native land the magnificent ring which King Eormenric had bestowed on him. His lord had given him a grant of land. Grants of land by a king to his thanes are mentioned elsewhere in verse literature.

The bond between lord and retainer went deeper than material benefits on either side. The giving of arms and treasure, which was ceremoniously performed, had a symbolic significance, and it is not mere material loss that inspires the following lament for a dead lord contained in a poem generally known as *The Wanderer*:

All joy has departed. Truly does he know this who must long forgo the advice of his dear lord. When sorrow and sleep both together often bind the wretched lonely man, it seems to him in his mind that he embraces and kisses his liege lord, and lays hands and head on his knee, as sometimes in days of yore he enjoyed the bounty from the throne. Then awakens the friendless man; he sees before him the dark waves, the sea-birds dipping, spreading their wings, frost and snow falling, mingled with hail. Then are the wounds of his heart the heavier, the sore wounds after his dear one; his sorrow is renewed.

The relationship of lord and follower involved the duty of vengeance by the survivor if either were slain – or, at the very least, the exaction of a compensation high enough to do honour to the slain man. A story that told how the followers of a Danish prince Hnæf succeeded in apparently hopeless circumstances in avenging their lord by killing his slayer, the Frisian king Finn, was apparently very popular, for not only is there a fragment of a poem about it among our scanty remains, but also it is told in *Beowulf*, in so allusive and obscure a fashion as to show that the poet expected his audience to be already familiar with it. *Widsith* refers to it also.

It is not only in poetry that we find instances of loyalty to the lord. It was no mere literary convention. The followers of Oswald of Northumbria in the seventh century and of Æthelbald of Mercia in the eighth accompanied their lords in exile, and a little later we find Charles the Great asking the archbishop of Canterbury to intercede with King Offa of Mercia that some English exiles should be allowed to return, now that the lord whom they were accompanying in exile is dead. At the beginning of this century, Bishop Aldhelm of Sherborne wrote to persuade the clergy of Bishop Wilfrid of Northumbria that it was their duty to share his exile, and mentions as a matter of common knowledge that a layman who refused to go into exile with his lord would be an object of scorn and ridicule. Greater sacrifices than voluntary exile were made. In 625 Lilla, a thane of Edwin of Northumbria, thrust his own body between the king and an assassin's stroke, and died in his lord's defence; in 666, Bishop Wilfrid's retinue swore to fight to the death, if need be, against a vastly superior force of heathen South Saxons; in 685 King Ecgfrith fell at *Nechtanesmere*, 'all his body-guard having been killed', and the absence of any comment on or any elaboration of the incident may indicate that it was what was normally expected. An incident of 786 is recorded much more fully; when the thanes of King Cynewulf of Wessex were roused from sleep to find that their king had been killed in a surprise night attack, they refused all offer of terms in spite of their hopeless position, and 'continued to fight until they all lay dead, except for one Welsh hostage, and he was severely wounded.' In their turn, men of the opposing party who were offered quarter on grounds of kinship by Cynewulf's main forces when they arrived on the scene, equally indignantly rejected the suggestion, preferring to stand by their leader to the end. The passage in the Anglo-Saxon Chronicle which records this incident stands out from the annals surrounding it in its fullness and circumstantial detail; it may have been drawn from an oral account handed down for some time before it was written down. The story is told with some measure of narrative art, but there is no reason to doubt the truth of the facts it records. The same annal relates that a swine-herd took vengeance on the slayer of his lord, Ealdorman Cumbra, so we see that it was not only the aristocratic classes that recognized this obligation. The lord's duty to take vengeance or exact compensation for the slaying of one of his men was recognized by the law, which allotted a 'man-compensation' to the lord, in addition to what must be paid to the kindred of a slain man.

It is true that beside these instances of loyalty one must set acts of treachery and violence that sometimes violated the tie between lord and man. In 757, Æthelbald of Mercia was murdered by his own bodyguard – a later generation than those who had shared his exile more than forty years before – and the following year Oswulf of Northumbria similarly perished at the hands of his retainers. In 796 the death of Ethelred of Northumbria was engineered by one of his own nobles, an act that caused Charles the Great to describe the Northumbrians as murderers of their lords. Such incidents were looked on with horror, and Ethelred's death was duly avenged by his thane Torhtmund.

In Christian times the man who took service under a lord swore the following oath over relics:

By the Lord, before whom these relics are holy, I will be loyal and true to N, and love all that he loves, and hate all that he hates, (however) in accordance with God's rights and secular obligations; and never, willingly and intentionally, in word or deed, do anything that is hateful to him; on condition that he keep me as I shall deserve, and carry out all that was our agreement, when I subjected myself to him and chose his favour.

A story in Bede illustrates well the binding force of the oath of allegiance even in heathen times. When Edwin of Northumbria had taken refuge with King Rædwald of East Anglia, he felt that he could not break his pact with this king even on the strong provocation of discovering that he was meditating betraying him to his enemies for money. Rædwald's wife dissuaded her husband from so shameful an act, stoutly declaring that his honour should be more precious than any treasure.

This story shows also that the tie was a personal, and

not necessarily a tribal one. Edwin, it is true, was a fugi-
tive from his own race, but men might voluntarily take
service under the ruler of another tribe. One of the things
that was distressing Bede towards the end of his life was
the danger threatening the defences of Northumbria because of the kings' too lavish and indiscriminate gifts for
religious, or supposedly religious, purposes, for thus their
resources were impoverished and the young men of the
country driven to take service outside where there was
hope of more substantial reward. Besides fugitives and
voluntary guests, even hostages were expected to repay
the host's hospitality with service in time of war. We have
mentioned one instance above, and another occurs in the
late tenth-century poem on the battle of Maldon, where
a Northumbrian hostage fights on with the bodyguard of
Brihtnoth, ealdorman of Essex, after their lord has fallen.

The ideals referred to by Tacitus are still being expressed nine hundred years after his time. In the late
tenth-century *Life of St Edmund*, the author, who claims
to derive his information from St Dunstan, who had it
from the saint's swordbearer, puts into Edmund's mouth
a speech on heroic lines, expressing his determination not
to live after his slain followers, nor to save himself by
flight. A very few years later, the poem on the battle of
Maldon tells how Brihtnoth's retainers fought on, after
his death and the flight of his army, with no hope of
victory, but with determination to avenge his death, as a
due return for his gifts and favours. The heroic code is
nowhere stated more completely or more simply than in
the lines:

Quickly was Offa cut down in the fight; yet he had carried
out what he had promised his lord, when he vowed to his
treasure-giver that both together they should ride safely home
into the stronghold, or fall in the army, die of wounds on the
field of battle. He lay as befits a thane, close by his lord.

Sentiments such as: 'the steadfast men round Sturmer
will not need to taunt me, now my lord has fallen, that I
journeyed home lordless'; or 'he cannot waver who plans
to avenge his lord in the army, nor care about his life';
or 'I will not retire, but I intend to lie by the side of my
lord, of so dear a man' – have been thought to contrast
strangely with the sad tale of treachery and cowardice
told in other sources for the reign of Ethelred the
Unready (978–1016). Yet heroism was not altogether
dead in his reign. In 988, the men of Devon 'who chose
rather to end their lives by a death in battle than to live
ignobly', led by Streonwold, carried the day in spite of
heavy losses; the chief men of the East Angles fell fighting in 1004; the men of Cambridgeshire stood firm at
Ringmere in 1010. The speeches in the Maldon poem,
which was composed for an audience very familiar with
the persons mentioned, probably with the incidents also,
may represent, at the very least, a translation into words
of sentiments to which their deeds had borne ample witness. When they followed men like Brihtnoth of Essex, or
Streonwold of Devon, or Ulfcytel of East Anglia, the
English of Ethelred's day could maintain the heroic
standards.

*

The lord's gift of armour and horses to the man who
entered his service developed into the legal due called
'heriot', which means literally 'war-gear', and which was
paid to the lord on the death of his man, representing
originally the return on the follower's death of the lord's
gift. This payment was remitted when the man fell 'before his lord' on a campaign. To the end of the period it
tended to be paid in kind, a fact which suggests that it
was felt to have symbolic significance. For example, a
tenth-century ealdorman declares:

And I bequeath to my royal lord as a heriot four armlets of three hundred mancuses of gold, and four swords and eight horses, four with trappings and four without, and four helmets and four coats-of-mail and eight spears and eight shields.

A law of Cnut in the eleventh century states the heriot due from different ranks mainly in terms of horses and weapons.

Though the heriot might represent in concrete form a man's sense of obligation to his lord, the principal payment made to a follower in Anglo-Saxon times was in land. Such donations are occasionally mentioned in poetry, more frequently in historical sources. Benedict Biscop, the founder of the twin monasteries of Monkwearmouth and Jarrow, had been a thane of King Oswiu of Northumbria (641–70) before he entered religion at the age of twenty-five, and had received from him a grant of land suitable to his rank; and it is clear from a letter which Bede wrote to Archbishop Egbert in 734 that he considered that a young thane had a right to expect an endowment of land from his prince, to enable him to marry and set up an establishment of his own. Numbers of charters survive in which kings grant land to an individual ealdorman or thane 'on account of his faithful service', but sometimes the words 'and because of his acceptable money' are added, and one cannot be certain that even those without this tell-tale phrase are not in many cases sales masquerading as gifts.

The man got something more than all this from his lord: he got protection. No one would be eager to molest a man who had a powerful lord ready to demand compensation or to take vengeance. The lord took responsibility for the man's acts; he had to produce him to answer a charge in court, or pay the damages himself, and it would be to his interest to defend his man from a wrongful accusation. He was held responsible even for deeds committed before the man entered his service, and would therefore be unwise too readily to accept an unknown man. This may explain why in the poem *The Wanderer* the man bereft of his lord finds it so difficult to find a new protector. The lord's responsibility for his followers is the aspect of this relationship which stands out most prominently in the laws.

*

The Christian Church did not come into conflict with the Germanic principle of loyalty to the lord. It added its sanctity to the oath of allegiance. Vengeance taken for a lord's murder is regarded as a laudable act by no less a churchman than Alcuin himself, whom we find in 801 recommending to Charles the Great a certain Torhtmund, 'a faithful thane of King Ethelred (of Northumbria), a man approved in faith, strenuous in arms, who has boldly avenged the blood of his lord.' But Ethelred was a king foully murdered, and we are hardly justified in assuming from Alcuin's attitude on this occasion that he would in general have approved of acts of vengeance, rather than the alternate procedure, which the Church encouraged, of accepting compensation. How ready the Church was to admit the binding force of a man's duty to his lord can be seen in the *Penitential of Archbishop Theodore*, for this text, unyielding though it normally is in its stern attitude to what the Germanic code regarded as not merely justifiable but laudable homicide, imposes only a slight penance on the man who commits homicide at his lord's command. It placed this act on a level with killing in battle, and considered the lord's command a greater extenuation of homicide than the desire to avenge even a close kinsman.

Moreover, when the claims of the lord clashed with those of the kindred, the idea becomes established during the centuries after the conversion that the duty to the lord should come first. This was expressly stated by the followers of the King Cynewulf mentioned above, for they declared unequivocally that 'no kinsman was dearer to them than their lord' and were willing to run the risk of kindred murder in order to avenge the king's death. The laws of King Alfred allow a man to fight, without becoming liable to a vendetta, in defence of a wrongfully attacked kinsman, but not if this involves fighting against his lord: 'that we do not permit'. This attitude agrees with the tremendous horror at the crime of treachery to a lord expressed by this king in the introduction to his code. Possibly, however, the inclusion of this proviso in the legislation would have been unnecessary if in practice the claims of kinship and affection had not sometimes overridden those of duty to the lord.

The homilists, like the poets, have many passages in praise of loyalty and condemnation of treachery. To Archbishop Wulfstan in 1014 there is a betrayal worse than deserting a lord on the battlefield, or even than plotting his death: 'for the greatest of all treachery in the world is that a man betray his lord's soul' – that is, entice him to sin. The Church taught that other services than vengeance could be rendered for a departed lord, i.e. the taking of alms to Rome, or the making of grants to religious houses, for the good of his soul. A paragraph that sums up the Christian view of loyalty occurs in Cnut's laws and is probably from the pen of Archbishop Wulfstan. It concludes:

> For all that ever we do, through just loyalty to our lord, we do to our own great advantage, for truly God will be gracious to him who is duly faithful to his lord.

Duty to one's kin

The bond of kinship may at times have had to yield before the claims of the lord, but it was nevertheless very important in Anglo-Saxon society. Every individual depended on the support of the kindred in all the affairs of life, and the poetry shows that the position of the kinless man was regarded as wretched indeed. Beside the lament for a dead lord quoted above could be placed a dirge in *Beowulf* by the last member of a kindred. He placed his ancestral treasures in the grave-mound and 'sad at heart he uttered his grief, alone after them all he wandered wretchedly, day and night, until the surge of death touched his heart.' Another poem speaks with sympathy of the man who must be alone – 'better would it be for him that he had a brother.' This poet is thinking of the everyday affairs of life, but usually, both in literature and in the laws, it is in connexion with the vendetta that we hear most of the claims and obligations of the kindred.

If a man were killed, it was the duty of his kindred to take vengeance on the slayer or his kindred, or to exact compensation. The fear of the action of the kindred was originally the main force for the maintenance of order, and to the end Anglo-Saxon law regarded homicide as the affair of the kindred, who were entitled to receive the 'wergild', i.e. 'man-price', for any of their members slain. Vengeance was no mere satisfaction of personal feeling, but a duty that had to be carried out even when it ran counter to personal inclination, and a favourite theme in Germanic literature was provided by any situation when this duty clashed with other feelings, such as friendship or marital affection. The duty was incumbent on both paternal and maternal kinsmen, and the kinsmen of the slayer were all liable to it unless they repudiated the slayer and thus dissociated themselves from responsibility. But in that case they could not afterwards carry on a vendetta for him or receive compensation if he were slain; they had renounced their rights to claim kinship with him.

A composition, in money or property, could be accepted without loss of honour provided it was adequate to the rank of the slain man. This was so already in the time of Tacitus, but it was always open to the injured kindred to refuse settlement and carry on the vendetta if they preferred. Alfred's laws seem to have tried to change this, but without success. Fixed compositions for homicide, in proportion to the rank of the slain man, were established early, at first expressed in numbers of oxen; and the rate at which a man must be paid for if he were killed, i.e. his wergild, became so much the most important mark of rank that the various social classes were sometimes described by terms derived from it, e.g. (men) of two – or six, or twelve – hundred (shillings). It was a great grief and humiliation if a kinsman lay 'unavenged and unatoned for'. In such a situation the old King Hrethel in *Beowulf* found life unbearable; he took to his bed and died when one of his sons accidentally killed another, for there could be no vengeance nor compensation within the kindred:

That was a fight unatoned for by money, though grievously committed, weighing heavily on the spirit; yet the prince had to lose his life unavenged.

The vendetta was not a wild act of lawlessness; the conditions under which it was carried on, and the details of the procedure, were carefully regulated by law. There were definite rules as to the division of the financial responsibility between the slayer, and his paternal and maternal kinsmen, the latter being responsible for only half as much as the former. In the same proportion as they paid for the act of one of their members, they received if they were the injured party. A portion of the wergild went to a group of very close relations, and the law was specific as to the amount of this and the limit of time in which it must be paid. In Kent it had to be paid 'at the open grave' and the rest of the wergild within forty days. There were strict regulations regarding the circumstances in which vengeance was permissible. It was illegal to carry on a vendetta against a man who had committed homicide when defending either his lord, his man, or his kinsman from wrongful attack, or who had killed a man whom he had caught in the act of violating his wife, daughter, sister, or mother, provided he killed him on the spot.

Similarly it was illegal to wage a vendetta on behalf of a man who had met his death as a convicted thief, or perpetrator of some other capital crime. His kinsmen were bound to give an oath that they would take no steps to avenge him. If they held that he had been unjustly executed, they must bring an action to prove this before they could legally take vengeance or exact compensation. The *Beowulf* poet compares Hrethel's grief for the loss of his son with that of an old man who sees his son's body swing on the gallows, for both were debarred, though for different reasons, from the consolation of an effective vengeance or an adequate compensation, and their dead lay dishonoured. Finally, a slayer's guilt had to be proved before vengeance could legally be taken. A man accused of homicide had the right to deny it by oath, with the support of oath-helpers, according to the normal procedure of the courts. Probably a homicide would usually admit his act, for attempted concealment turned it into murder, to be classed with slaying by secret means, poison or witchcraft, which could not be expiated by money payments. Among the local abuses of law that the legislation of the reign of Ethelred the Unready (978–1016) aimed at correcting was a practice that had grown up in the North which regarded as valid an accusation of homicide if made on the day of the slaying, apparently regardless of whether proof were forthcoming that it was directed against the proper person or not.

*

When the English were converted to Christianity, it was unavoidable that there should be a clash between Christian and pre-Christian ethics in this matter of vengeance. It may be this that lies behind an incident reported by Bede, in which King Sigeberht of Essex was killed by two of his heathen kinsmen because they were angered by his habit of forgiving his enemies the wrong done to him. They may have felt that by this leniency he was failing in his duty to protect his kindred. However that may be, the *Penitential of Archbishop Theodore* states in unambiguous language:

> If anyone kills a man in vengeance for a kinsman, let him do penance as a homicide, seven or ten years.

This attitude must have come as a shock to the early converts to Christianity, and even this penitential yields a little by assigning a shorter penance if the vengeance taken was for a brother.

The Church was eager to encourage settlements by composition. This was, of course, no new thing, and already in heathen times attempts were sometimes made to secure more lasting reconciliation of opposing families by means of diplomatic marriages, though the hero of *Beowulf* makes the comment:

> Normally it happens but rarely that the slaughterous spear lies quiet even for a short time, after the fall of men, though the bride be fair.

The Church threw its authority on the side of compensations, remitting, according to the penitential already mentioned, half the penance to the homicide who is willing to pay the wergild to the injured kindred. Bede relates how Archbishop Theodore used his influence to bring about a settlement after King Ecgfrith's brother had been killed by the Mercians. But this way out of the dilemma was not always open. There remained the problem of dealing with the slayer who either would not, or could not, pay the wergild. It is this which keeps the vendetta alive throughout the whole Anglo-Saxon period. The law could try to bring pressure on the slayer and his kindred to make them pay, but homicide was an expensive matter, and the man of a poor family could not be allowed to get off scot-free.

The Church took care to fit its own members into the scale of wergilds, equating a priest with a thane. But a man left his kindred when he entered religion and compositions were paid to his monastery. The *Dialogue of Archbishop Egbert of York* concerns itself with the position that arises when the slayer of an ecclesiastic cannot pay the wergild, and declares that he is to be handed over to the king for punishment 'lest the slayers of the servants of God should think that they can sin with impunity.' The natural inference is that he assumes that, when the slain man is a layman, the kindred will carry on the vengeance, if no compensation is obtainable. The Church cannot do this; so the king must act for it. We have already seen that in some circumstances Alcuin considered vengeance a praiseworthy act.

The modifications in the laws of successive Anglo-Saxon kings of the regulations governing the blood-feud are themselves adequate evidence of its continued existence. King Alfred forbade violent action against an adversary before justice had been demanded of him; King Edmund (939–46) prevented the slaying in vengeance of anyone except the actual perpetrator of the deed. He laments the prevalence of feuds:

The illegal and manifold fights which are among us distress me and all of us very greatly.

His laws go into detail on the elaborate precautions to be taken when a slaying is being compounded, showing how easy it was for enmity to flare up again if the parties were brought face to face. First, the slayer is to deal with the kindred of the man he has slain through a go-between, who is to obtain for him, under security, a safe conduct, so that he can come forward and give pledges and securities for the wergild. After that, if anyone attacks him, it is regarded as a breach of the king's protection, punishable by a heavy fine.

The prevalence of feuds in King Edmund's time was probably in part due to the influx of Danish settlers into the north and east of England at the end of the previous century, for in all the Scandinavian lands vendettas were very common, and there was an opinion current that to pursue vengeance was a more manly course of action than to accept compensation. It is certainly from the north of England that we get the most vivid account of a feud, one that lasted for three generations, on until after the Norman Conquest. Earl Uhtred of Northumbria roused the enmity of Thurbrand, a member of a rich landed family in Yorkshire, and he engineered the murder of Uhtred in 1016, as he entered the hall at *Wiheal* to make his submission to Cnut. Uhtred's son Aldred avenged his father by killing Thurbrand, and the feud descended to the latter's son Carl, but by the intervention of friends a settlement was made, and mutual reparations were paid. It seemed so complete, that Aldred and Carl became sworn brothers and planned to go together on a pilgrimage to Rome; but they were hindered by a storm, and, while they were together at Carl's house at Rise, something – we are not told what – must have caused Carl to remember old grudges, for he slew Aldred in Rise wood. The feud then lay dormant for a long time. It was not until 1073 that Earl Waltheof, the son of Aldred's daughter, avenged his grandfather's murder by sending assassins who killed all Carl's sons and grandsons as they were feasting at the house of the eldest son, Thurbrand, at Settrington – all except two, one whom they spared for his excellent disposition, and one who was not present.

Conditions in the North after the Viking Age were undoubtedly much wilder than elsewhere, yet even in the more civilized South the blood-feud survived till quite late, as is shown clearly by an incident as late as the episcopate of Bishop Wulfstan of Worcester (1062–95), in whose diocese the five brothers of a slain man refused to come to terms even though the slaying had been accidental; they said that they preferred to be excommunicated rather than fail to avenge their brother, and it required a miracle to make them change their minds.

*

Though the laws concern themselves principally with the kindred in its relation to the blood-feud and the wergild, people depended on their kinsmen for many other kinds of support; but the obligations within the family were known by custom and are rarely expressly stated in our sources. We know that close kinsmen, at any rate, arranged marriages and settled the terms of marriage agreements for their members, and that a woman's kindred continued to watch over her interests after her marriage. The nearest kinsmen looked after the estate of a child whose father died while it was a minor. Kinsmen were responsible for seeing that an accused member came forward to answer a charge, and if he did not, and became an outlaw by default, they were forbidden to harbour him under pain of heavy penalties. It is possible that at one time they acted as oath-helpers to support his oath of his innocence.

There are some signs that in the later Saxon period the kindred was no longer an adequate force to maintain order, either from the point of view of the state or of the individual. Homilists complain bitterly of the decay of this bond:

Now too often kinsman does not protect kinsman any more than a stranger, neither a father his son, nor sometimes a son his own father, nor one brother another.

On the other hand, the laws have from time to time to deal with the abuse of power by a too powerful kindred, which tries to prevent the proper operation of the law in relation to its own members. King Athelstan (924—39) ordered the transportation to another district of persons of a kindred so powerful that they could not be restrained from crime or from harbouring criminals. The kindred's responsibility for producing its members to answer a charge proved insufficient to bring men to justice, so an artificial association was imposed from above for this purpose. According to a law of Cnut which may be quoting an older source, every adult free man was to be in a 'tithing', that is, a group of ten men who acted as sureties for one another's behaviour, 'and his surety is to hold him and bring him to answer any charge.' Men also formed voluntary associations of a semi-religious, semi-social character, called gilds, which reinforced the kindred in some of its protective functions. Statutes of such gilds have survived from the late tenth and the eleventh centuries from Exeter, Bedwyn, Abbotsbury, Woodbury, and Cambridge. The thanes' gild in Cambridge took on the responsibility of carrying on the vendetta after a wrongfully slain gild-brother, and also undertook to support any of their members who slew a man in a necessary feud, and to help him to pay the wergild. If, however, any member killed a man without good reason, 'foolishly', he had to bear the feud alone. These statutes thus supply evidence, if such were needed, that the blood-feud was still prevalent in late Anglo-Saxon times. A rather similar organization was formed in London already in King Athelstan's time. It seems to have concerned itself primarily with common action to suppress cattle-lifting, but it also declared its members to be 'all in one friendship and one enmity', that is, that they would avenge one another's wrongs.

CHAPTER III

THE KING AND HIS COURT

THE Anglo-Saxons were familiar with the institution of kingship already in their continental homelands, and long after they settled in Britain they continued to tell stories of kings who reigned in continental Angeln as far back as the fourth century, one of whom, Offa, reigning twelve generations before his famous Mercian namesake and descendant, was remembered as the king who established the Eider as the boundary between the Angles and the *Swæfe*, their southern neighbours in their homeland. Most royal families in England claimed to be descended from gods, Woden in most instances, Saxneat, a god worshipped also by the continental Saxons, in the case of the royal house of the East Saxons. It is probable that in very early times the heathen kings had some priestly functions.

Until the great Danish invasion of 865–78, England was divided into several kingdoms, though for long periods those south of the Humber were united under an overlord known, according to a ninth-century authority, as a *Bretwalda* 'ruler of Britain'. This was no mere empty title; subject kings paid tribute to their overlord, they attended him from time to time at his court, they obtained his consent to their grants of land, they fought under his leadership in time of war. An Anglo-Saxon poet may well have contemporary parallels in his mind, of a *Bretwalda* calling his subject kings to his standard, when he describes the gathering of Pharaoh's host in the following words:

He had chosen the flower of the nations, two thousand famous men of noble birth, kings and kinsmen. . . . Therefore each of them led out his men, every warrior whom he could assemble in time.

By the time Bede was writing his *Ecclesiastical History* this overlordship had been held in turn for single reigns by Sussex, Wessex, Kent, and East Anglia, and for three successive reigns by Northumbria. Wulfhere of Mercia held similar power in the late seventh century, and during the greater part of the next century Mercia, under its kings Æthelbald and Offa, was supreme over all the lands south of the Humber. The supremacy of the West Saxon kings, which was established early in the ninth century, proved permanent because the other kingdoms were destroyed by the Danes. When the kings of Wessex had reconquered the Danelaw in the tenth century, they became henceforward rulers of a united England.

The richly furnished ship-burial at Sutton Hoo suggests that even the kings of heathen days had considerable wealth at their disposal, and, as the smaller kingdoms became absorbed into those of more powerful rulers, the kings' dignity increased and their courts became more impressive. Bede speaks of the pomp upheld by King Edwin of Northumbria:

> Even in time of peace, as he rode with his thanes between his cities, villages, and provinces, his standard-bearer was wont always to go before him; and also if he walked anywhere along the streets, that kind of standard which the Romans call 'tufa' and the English 'thuuf' was borne before him.

Eighth-century poets, who are clearly drawing on their knowledge of contemporary courts when they speak of the kings of ancient Scandinavia or of Israel, describe a somewhat elaborate court-etiquette, and refer to the material splendour of gold-inwrought tapestry, tessellated pavements, drinking-cups of precious metals. Later kings were no less concerned with their visible splendour; in the midst of all his many activities, King Alfred found time to supervise the building of halls and chambers and the production of objects of beauty, inviting to him craftsmen from many nations to this end. His great-grandson King Edgar showed by his impressive coronation ceremony at Bath in 973 that he grasped the political value of external magnificence.

*

The king was in a unique position at law. His mere word was incontrovertible, and he need not support it with an oath. An attempt on his life, whether directly, or by harbouring his enemies and outlaws, cost life and all possessions. It is obvious, therefore, that the slaying of a king by any of his subjects was a crime that could not be compounded for, and thus when documents mention the amount of the king's wergild – that is, the price to be paid for him if he were killed – they must be concerned with settlements between warring factions or nations, such as the occasion when the men of Kent paid to King Ine of Wessex in 694 the sum of thirty thousand (pence), to obtain peace after they had burnt Mul, a member of the West Saxon reigning house, and his followers some years previously. In a text dating from the post-Viking period and written in the north of the country, a king's wergild is set at fifteen times that of a thane, and half of it is to be paid to his kindred, half to the people. Mercian law only demanded a wergild approximately six times that of a thane, but this evidently refers only to what was paid to the kindred, for an equal amount, called a 'royal payment', is to be paid in addition. We have no direct evidence for Wessex, but the amount paid for Mul is the wergild of a Mercian king, without the 'royal payment'. This would not be called for in this instance, for Mul was, at most, only a sub-king.

If anyone fought in the king's house, he forfeited all that he possessed, and his life was at the king's mercy.

Increasing importance was attached to the sanctity of the king's person as the period advanced. King Edmund (939–46) decreed that no man guilty of bloodshed was to presume to come into the king's neighbourhood until he had done penance for his crime and undertaken to make reparation to the kindred. This king, as we have seen, was greatly concerned to decrease the number of blood-feuds, and a regulation which in effect forbade the appearance at court of anyone concerned as a principal in a feud must have been effective in the desired direction. Later codes extend this prohibition to other categories of offenders, and state also that if an excommunicated man comes into the king's neighbourhood, he is to forfeit both life and goods. Popular tradition interpreted the king's neighbourhood as extending on all four sides of the gate of the house in which he was residing 'three miles and three furlongs and the breadth of three acres, and nine feet and nine "spear-hands" and nine barley corns.' Men liked to be precise on such matters.

A very heavy fine, 120 West Saxon shillings, a sum equivalent to twenty oxen, was due to the king for various crimes regarded as a breach of his protection, and for forcible entry into his house, while lesser offences had smaller fines. He might give his special peace to particular individuals or places or occasions, and if he did, the penalty for breach of this peace varied according to whether it had been given by the king in person, or through a subordinate. The homilist Ælfric draws the following parallel to illustrate and bring home to his hearers the difference between the old dispensation, given by God through his prophets, and the new, given by Christ himself:

One thing is the ordinance which the king ordains through his ealdorman or his reeve; quite another is his own command in his presence.

The law draws a distinction between a breach of the king's peace, 'given with his own hand', which incurs the death penalty, and a breach of the peace given by the ealdorman or the king's reeve, which can be compensated for by fines. These increase in size with the importance of the assembly in which the peace was pronounced, and in the northern Danelaw they were so heavy that they must have been beyond the capacity to pay of any but the wealthiest of men. It seems probable, therefore, that the responsibility for payment lay with the whole district if it failed to produce the disturber of the peace, or if, having produced him, it chose to redeem him from death. Such arrangements were in force elsewhere: at Dover in the Confessor's time there was a special king's peace from Michaelmas until St Andrew's day 'and if anyone broke it, the king's reeve took a fine from all in common.' In dealing with corporate acts of violence or disobedience, kings sometimes used more summary methods than levying fines: they ravaged the district concerned. King Eadred ravaged Thetford in 952 when an abbot had been murdered there, and King Edgar ravaged Thanet in 969 because of the ill-treatment there of some York merchants. Similar violent measures were taken by the unpopular kings Ethelred the Unready (978–1016) and Harthacnut (1040–2), but it is clear that respected and efficient rulers on occasion took this line of action.

*

The Church made its contribution to the idea of the dignity and sanctity of kingship. Kings state in their regnal styles that they reign by the grace of God, and towards the end of the eighth century the practice of an ecclesiastical coronation was introduced from the Continent. It grew in importance, special emphasis being laid on the anointing of the king. A coronation order was composed by Archbishop Dunstan for Edgar's delayed coronation at Bath in 973, and this order later influenced the forms used abroad. The ceremony at Edgar's coronation made a great impression, and a Latin writer some thirty years later gives a full account of it, including the oath sworn by the king. There also survives a vernacular version of this, as given by King Ethelred at his coronation at Kingston, and it is as follows:

> In the name of the Holy Trinity! I promise three things to the Christian people subject to me. First that God's Church and all Christian people of my dominions shall keep true peace. Secondly, that I forbid to all ranks robbery and all injustice. Thirdly, that I promise and command justice and mercy in all judgements, that the gracious and compassionate God, who liveth and reigneth, may through that grant us his eternal mercy.

By the early eleventh century it could be declared that 'A Christian king is Christ's deputy among Christian people.' We can see the influence of this theory. Whereas in 757 a West Saxon king was deprived of his kingdom 'on account of his unjust deeds' by the West Saxon council, and Alhred of Northumbria was deposed in 774, Ælfric at the end of the tenth century can state as an accepted fact that a king cannot be deposed. He says:

> No man can make himself king, but the people has the choice to elect whom they like; but after he is consecrated king, he has authority over the people, and they cannot shake his yoke off their necks.

Archbishop Wulfstan considered the expulsion of King Ethelred in 1013 as 'a very great treachery', second only to the betrayal of one's lord's soul.

Though the king was elected, the choice was normally limited to members of the royal family. In early times, any man who could trace his descent back to the founder of the royal dynasty considered that he had a claim to the throne, and much conflict was occasioned in some kingdoms by rival claims. It became increasingly the custom to elect the eldest son of the last king. This custom was broken when King Alfred was chosen to succeed his brother in 871, but his predecessor's sons were young, and, with an invading army in the country, it was hardly the time to elect a child. On King Alfred's death, his eldest son was chosen, and an attempt by the son of Alfred's elder brother and predecessor to obtain the throne was foiled. After this we hear of no further suggestion that a king should be chosen from this elder branch, though it included men of standing and capacity. Even after the murder of Edward the Martyr in 978, when his brother Ethelred was still a minor, there seems to have been no thought of passing over a descendant of Alfred in favour of an adult descendant of a more distant king.

The election of a king was frequently nothing more than the acknowledgement of the obvious successor, but when such was lacking, some decision among various possibilities might have to be made. The body responsible for the appointment was the king's council of 'wise men', which was made up of the archbishops, bishops, the abbots of the greater abbeys, the ealdormen, the more important king's thanes, and sometimes the king's priests. They were not always in unison regarding the succession to the throne; when Cnut died in 1035 one party wished to elect his son Harthacnut, absent in Denmark, but another wished to postpone decision until his arrival, and appoint Cnut's illegitimate son Harold as regent meanwhile, and this party prevailed. A more remarkable disagreement occurred in 1016, under abnormal conditions. King Ethelred died while Cnut's Danish army was attempting the conquest of England, and in the disordered state of the country an assembly at Southampton chose Cnut as his successor, whereas another at London elected Ethelred's son Edmund.

The king's council advised him on important matters of policy, on the issue of laws and the alienation of land by charter to religious houses and others. Bede has left us a vivid picture of the deliberations of the Northumbrian council over the acceptance of the Christian faith. Offa of Mercia, as overlord of the south of England, held councils that were attended by all the greater ecclesiastics south of the Humber, but only by Mercian laymen. When all England was united under one rule, ecclesiastical and lay magnates came to the council from all parts, but after the reign of Athelstan (924–39) those from the extreme north seem rarely to have been present, and it may be that they were summoned only when matters of deep importance were to be discussed. A council at London of 989 or 990, which is unusual because of the presence at it of several northern dignitaries, is called 'the great synod', 'the great assembly', in the document that mentions it, and was probably felt to be abnormal. The king summoned his council 'from far and wide' when he needed it; the great festivals of Christmas, Easter, and Pentecost were favourite times for large gatherings, and several surviving law-codes we know to have been issued by councils that sat at these seasons, Athelstan's fifth code at Exeter at Christmas, Edmund's first code at London at Easter, Cnut's laws at Winchester at Christmas. In these three cases the meeting took place in an important borough, but the council often met at royal estates in places of no particular significance. To house so great a company with their retinues the royal residences must have been of considerable size, and Asser, King Alfred's biographer, tells us that this king gave much attention to building and improving various royal vills. Some of the company may have lived in tents. Bishop Ælfsige of Chester-le-Street had presumably made the long journey south to attend a council

when his companion, Aldred the Provost, added some
collects into the ritual book the bishop had with him,
with the note that he did so 'south of Woodyates at Oakley
(Down) in Wessex, on Wednesday, St Lawrence's Day,
for Ælfsige the bishop in his tent, when the moon was
five nights old, before tierce.' But we cannot be certain
that Woodyates was actually the place of assembly –
though a council had met there a century earlier; it may
merely have been a halting place on the way to or from
the council. In any case, St Lawrence's day is in August;
the attenders at winter councils can hardly have been
housed in tents. Others, besides Bishop Ælfsige, possessed tents. A certain Ælfric Modercope bequeathed to
a bishop 'my tent and my bedclothing, the best that I
had out on my journey with me' and tents are mentioned
in other wills.

Men journeying to and from councils and assemblies
were protected by a special peace, which meant that
heavier penalties were attached to offences committed
against them on their way. Travellers to the king's court
could claim hospitality en route; occasionally we hear of
royal grants of estates to serve as halting-places on oft-
made journeys, such as the grant of Crayke in Yorkshire
by King Ecgfrith of Northumbria to St Cuthbert, as a
resting place on his way to York, if we are to believe the
Durham tradition. A late, but probably reliable, authority says that King Edgar gave estates in England to
Kenneth of Scotland, so that he could stay at them on his
way to court.

*

Even apart from occasions on which the council was
meeting, the king was accompanied by a large company.
Ælfric divides the court of a secular ruler into officials
and thanes, and King Eadred's will shows that his
highest court officials were his 'dish-thanes' or seneschals,

his 'wardrobe-thanes', perhaps the same official as one called elsewhere a 'bower-thane', i.e. chamberlain, and his butlers. Below these he had stewards, and he refers in general terms to other office holders, among whom would probably be 'horse-thanes', or marshals. These offices were held by men of the highest class, and added to their prestige. The court included also king's thanes who had no special office, men who corresponded to the lord's followers mentioned by Tacitus. Old English poetry divides a king's following into 'tried men' and 'young men', and this division agrees well with one distinguishable in the writings of Bede between older men with an establishment of their own, who spend only part of their time at court, and young followers who have not yet received a landed endowment. Similarly, King Alfred's court consisted of the sons of the nobility who were being brought up there and king's thanes who spent only part of their time there. Alfred had organized these so that they served him in regular rotation, one month at court and two at home looking after their own concerns.

When the Dane, Cnut, became king, his court was guarded by his 'house-carls', a term of Scandinavian origin applied to military retainers organized as a gild or fraternity, with strict rules regulating their relations with the king and with each other. They had an assembly of their own, in which were judged offences against their code. It is only in later, Scandinavian, sources that we are told about the details of their organization, of the order of precedence at banquets, of the penalties for various misdemeanours. At first they formed a guard for a king of foreign race, but they were retained by Cnut's successors, even after the English line was restored. Moreover English noblemen copied the royal court and kept house-carls of their own. The expense of maintaining the royal house-carls was met by a tax. The boroughs of Dorset and Devon, in the reign of Edward the Confessor, contributed for this purpose at the rate of one mark of silver from ten hides. By this reign, at any rate, it had become common also to reward house-carls with land.

After the conversion to Christianity, kings were accompanied by their chaplains, who acted also as secretaries. From quite early times, the business of government required some men of education at its centre, and only the ecclesiastical order could supply them. King Alfred divided his whole income into fractions earmarked for special purposes, and this would have been impossible without at least some rudimentary form of royal treasury. The king's priests were in charge of his archives also, at any rate from the tenth century, when we begin to hear of documents kept with the king's relics. Certainly by the time of King Athelstan (924–39), and probably long before, there was a royal chancery in fact, though not in name, that drew up the charters issued in the king's name. We know the name of one of the secretaries of King Alfred's father, King Æthelwulf; he was a Frank, called Felix. King Eadred left in his will fifty mancuses of gold and five pounds to each of his priests 'at his relics', five pounds to each other priest. In the eleventh century it was not uncommon for a king's priest to be rewarded for his services with a bishopric.

*

The king moved from one royal estate to another, accompanied by his court. It can have been no light matter to offer hospitality to such a company. When King Athelstan had promised to visit a lady of royal rank, called Æthelflæd, his purveyors came the day before to inspect her provisions for the royal visit, and reported all in order except that the supply of mead was inadequate. The hostess prayed to the Virgin, with the result that the mead never failed, although the butlers served the guests all day with drinking-horns, goblets, and other vessels, 'as is the custom at royal banquets.' Feasting and drinking at the king's court are alluded to frequently in the poetic literature. The company was entertained by minstrelsy and song, and men told tales of their experiences. In *Beowulf* the aged king himself entertained the court in this way; at Athelstan's court the young Dunstan heard an old man, who claimed to have been the sword-bearer of King Edmund of East Anglia, tell the story of that king's martyrdom at the hands of the Danes. It may have been before the assembled company that the travellers Ohthere and Wulfstan gave King Alfred the accounts of their voyages in northern waters and the Baltic which were incorporated into the translation of Orosius.

Foreign visitors were frequent at the courts of English kings. In the days when England contained several kingdoms, the court of the overlord was attended by the kings of subject provinces, and there were friendly visits and marriage alliances between the various royal houses, and an interchange of envoys on business of different kinds. Not all of these came in good faith; King Edwin of Northumbria nearly lost his life by receiving without suspicion the envoy of a treacherous West Saxon king. The precautions, described in *Beowulf*, before the newcomers are allowed into the king's presence – the herald's enquiry into their business and antecedents, and his consultation with the king before he permits them to proceed, leaving spears and shields outside – are doubtless drawn from life. Intercourse with foreign courts across the Channel existed even in heathen times, when Ethelbert of Kent married the daughter of the Frankish king Haribert, and it increased as time went on. Pippin sent letters and gifts to King Eadberht of Northumbria (737–58), and Charles the Great and Offa (757–96) were in constant communication, exchanging gifts and discussing the common interests of the lands they governed. Charles at one point went so far as to interfere in the succession to the throne of Northumbria. Alfred's father maintained a connexion with the Carolingian court, and married a Frankish princess as his second wife, while Asser says that Alfred's court was visited by Franks, Frisians, Gauls, pagans (i.e. Scandinavians), Welsh, Irish, and Bretons, and claims that embassies from foreign nations were a daily occurrence. We may allow a little for exaggeration, but much of what he says receives confirmation elsewhere; his information that letters and gifts came from as distant a personage as the patriarch of Jerusalem is supported by the survival of some medical recipes sent to Alfred from this source. Royal guests at Alfred's court included the Welsh king Anarawd of Gwyneth, son of Rhodri Mawr, who came in order to secure Alfred's support and was confirmed while at the court, Alfred standing sponsor and presenting him with generous gifts, as he did also the Danish king Guthrum at his baptism, which was agreed on after the Danish defeat at Edington in 878.

We hear more of visits from the non-English kings of Britain in the next century. Most of them acknowledged King Athelstan's authority and some of his charters are witnessed by the rulers of Wales, and of Strathclyde, and (once) of Scotland, present at his court when the documents were drawn up. They attest as sub-kings. Kenneth, king of Scotland, was escorted to King Edgar's court by the bishop of Chester-le-Street and the earl of Northumbria, where he received the grant of Lothian in return for his homage; and in the same king's reign a scene was enacted at Chester in 973 that impressed itself deeply on men's minds. Post-Conquest writers declare that Edgar was rowed on the Dee by eight subject-kings visiting his court. Whether this is true or not, we may be sure that something spectacular took place from the words of Ælfric, an almost contemporary authority:

And all the kings who were in this island, of the Cumbrians and the Scots, once came to Edgar, eight kings on one day, and they all submitted to Edgar's direction.

King Alfred married his youngest daughter to a count of Flanders, and several of his granddaughters were married into continental ruling families. It would be tedious to list all the references to foreign embassies and visitors that occur in the sources for the later part of our period, but some scenes are more fully reported. Hugh, duke of the Franks, sent an embassy led by Athelwulf, son of Baldwin of Flanders and Alfred's daughter, to King Athelstan to ask for his sister's hand in marriage. The mission was received before an assembly of magnates at Abingdon, and it brought an impressive set of gifts,

perfumes such as never before had been seen in England, precious stones, especially emeralds, in whose greenness the reflected sun lit up the eyes of the onlookers with a pleasing light; many fleet horses; . . . a certain vase of onyx, carved with such subtle art by the engraver that the cornfields seemed truly to wave, the vines to bud, the forms of men to move, and so clear and polished that it reflected like a mirror the faces of those gazing on it; the sword of Constantine the Great, on which the name of the original possessor could be read in letters of gold, and in whose pommel above thick plates of gold you could see fixed an iron nail, one of the four which the Jewish faction prepared for the crucifixion of our Lord's body; the spear of Charles the Great, which, when that most invincible emperor, leading an army against the Saracens, hurled among the enemy, never failed to secure the victory; it was said to be the same which, being driven by the hand of the centurion into our Lord's side, opened by the gash of that precious wound Paradise to wretched mortals;

and so on through a list of further relics, including part

of the true cross and of the crown of thorns. The suitor had taken the trouble to study Athelstan's tastes; this king was a great collector of relics and apparently not very critical of what he was told about them.

Very different gifts were brought by another embassy. This came from Harold the Fairhaired, king of the Norwegians, and the envoys, Helgrim and Osfrid, were received at York in royal fashion, and given rich gifts. Harold had sent to Athelstan a ship with a golden beak and a purple sail, surrounded within with a dense wall of gilded shields. We are not told of the political purpose of their visit.

Incidents of this kind may have been rare, but the arrival of foreign messengers and the return of English envoys were common. Foreign ecclesiastics and scholars came also, from the time of the Irishman, Adamnan, who has left us a reference to two visits to the court of King Aldfrith of Northumbria at the end of the seventh century, to the days of Edward the Confessor (1042–66), when Norman and Lotharingian ecclesiastics sought their fortune in England. To single out a few from many instances, we may mention the sensational visit to Alfred of three Irishmen who had set out without oars or rudder and with food for seven days and arrived in Cornwall after a voyage of just that length; the foreign scholars invited by Alfred to help his educational reform; the monks of St Bertin's in St Omer who came to King Edmund (939–46) when dissatisfied with a reforming abbot at home, and were given by him a monastery at Bath; the monks from Fleury and Ghent who came to help King Edgar draw up a common rule of observance for English monasteries; the Danish priest Gerbrand who came in 1022 to be consecrated bishop of Roskilde by the archbishop of Canterbury. Throughout the period, there were envoys coming backwards and forwards from the papal curia, and occasionally the important event of the visit of a papal legate.

Finally, we can add the visits of merchants bringing rare goods from abroad. The Norwegian Ohthere brought walrus tusks to King Alfred, and, if we can trust the evidence of the Icelandic sagas, it was the habit of Icelanders on trading ventures to visit the court and perhaps enter into the service of the king for a time. Thus Gunnlaug Ormstunga came to the court of Ethelred the Unready, and sang before him a panegyric singularly inapplicable to that monarch.

All the host of the generous and warlike king fears England's lord as a god; and the race of men bows to Ethelred.

We naturally need not assume that all the business of these visitors took place before the assembled court. Yet they would receive hospitality along with the members of the court and hand on news of the outside world and the tales of their own lands. As there would also be a constant coming and going of the king's messengers who bore his writ and seal to the shire-moots and to the individual magnates in all quarters of his land, one may believe that after attendance at court its members might return to their own localities with something to recount.

CHAPTER IV

FINANCE AND ADMINISTRATION

Finance

THE king derived his income partly from royal estates, which were scattered over the whole country, each in the charge of a king's reeve. Another important source of revenue was his 'farm', a food-rent paid to him by all the lands in his realm that had not been freed from this charge by special exemption. It was rendered at the royal estates, and the lands from which it was due were grouped together into units, each of which was to supply annually the 'farm of one night', that is, the provisions originally considered adequate to support the king and his court for a day. Though sometimes it was commuted into a money payment, it was normally paid in kind, in ale and corn, malt, honey, dairy-produce, and livestock. The king drew income also from the tribute of subject kings, from inheritance after foreigners, from tolls, and from fines and forfeitures incurred in the law-courts. The king's reeves presided over these and collected what was due to the king. Even when grants of the profits of juris- diction were made to private individuals, the fines for some of the more serious offences were reserved for the king.

Besides his actual income, whether in money or in produce, the king had many rights that he could claim from his subjects. He did not need to spend his resources on the equipment or payment of an army, or on the hir- ing of labour to build fortifications and bridges. These obligations, like the king's farm, were distributed over the estates of the land; exemption from them was so rare that a charter that claims such exemption is immediately suspect. The king is more ready to grant – for a consideration – exemption from some of his other rights, from the duty of supplying hospitality to his messengers, his huntsmen, and falconers, or of feeding his dogs or his hawks. A bishop of Worcester in 855 paid three hundred shillings to get an estate freed 'from feeding any hawks or falcons or any huntsmen of king or ealdorman, likewise from the feeding of those men whom we call in English "the Welsh expedition" (a term of uncertain meaning), and from giving lodging to them or to mounted travellers, whether English or foreign, whether nobles or commoners.' Certain places, because of their position, were liable to special services. Thus an estate on the coast of Cornwall supplied maritime guard instead of bridgework; Dover was responsible for giving aid to the king's messengers crossing the Channel; the priests of the king's three churches in Archenfield bore the king's embassies into Wales; Wallingford owed carrying services by land or water, as far as Reading, Blewbury, Sutton Courtenay, and Bensington; at Torksey, 'if the king's messengers should come thither, the men of the same town should conduct them to York with their ships and their means of navigation, and the sheriff should find the messengers' and the sailors' food out of his farm'; if the king visited Shrewsbury, the sheriff supplied him on his departure with twenty-four horses to accompany him as far as Leintwardine, or as far as the first house in Staffordshire; and so on. A variety of local arrangements about guarding the king's person and helping him in his hunting when he came on a visit are mentioned in Domesday Book, and similarly, his rights to customary payments varied from place to place. Six counties, Worcester, Warwick, Oxford, Northampton, Leicester, and Wiltshire each paid him ten pounds for a hawk, twenty shillings for a sumpter-horse; Oxfordshire and Warwickshire paid twenty-three pounds for dogs; three royal manors in Bedfordshire paid sums from 130 to 65 shillings for dogs; the city of Norwich supplied a bear and six dogs for bear-baiting.

We know from his life by Asser that King Alfred reorganized his finances. Alfred gives us his views on the subject of royal expenditure in a passage which he inserts into his translation of Boethius's *Consolation of Philosophy*:

> I desired tools and materials for the work that I was charged to perform, namely that I might worthily and fittingly steer and rule the dominion that was entrusted to me. . . . This, then, is a king's material and his tools for ruling with, that he have his land fully manned. He must have men who pray, and soldiers and workmen. Lo, thou knowest that without these tools no king can reveal his power. Also, this is his material, which he must have for those tools – sustenance for those three orders; and their sustenance consists in land to live on, and gifts, and weapons, and food, and ale, and clothes, and whatever else those three orders require. And without these things he cannot hold those tools, nor without these tools do any of the things that he is charged to do.

The division of mankind into the three orders is common medieval doctrine, and Alfred may have learnt of it from Frankish sources, for references to it begin in these about the same time, though it happens that Alfred's statement is fuller and more complete than any other known to me from so early a date.

It is interesting to compare Alfred's actual division of the income that reached his treasury. Half of it he devoted to religious uses, that is, to the men who pray. The other half he subdivided into three portions, one for the soldiers and thanes who served him in turn at his court, one for his workmen, whom he had gathered from many races, and the third for visitors who came to him from every race, far and near. The soldiers mentioned in this connexion are the king's bodyguard; the bulk of the men who fight, the rank and file, were not recompensed from the king's treasury, any more than were the largest class of the men who work, the tillers of the soil; these gave their services in return for the land they held. Alfred makes no provision in this division for the royal officials in the shires or on the royal estates, for these derived their income from a share of the royal income before it was handed over to the king, and from lands allotted to them. Grants of land lie outside the subject of this chapter in Asser. The queen and the princes were also provided for by estates assigned to them. The evidence for this is later than Alfred's time, but does not suggest that it was an innovation. The king's council about 975 took away from the abbey of Abingdon some estates which King Edgar had given there, because they were estates belonging to the king's sons. The king's wife received a gift of lands at her marriage: Emma is said to have been given Winchester, Exeter, and Rutland by Ethelred, and the last-mentioned place appears in the possession of Edward the Confessor's queen also. It is, in fact, highly probable that it became a separate county by reason of its having been a queen's dower. The Confessor's queen is shown by Domesday book to have had very extensive lands, but we cannot tell how many came to her from her own family. The same source shows that there were customary gifts to the queen in many places by the end of the Anglo-Saxon period, and they may be of ancient date. For example, she received a hundred shillings from each of the counties of Worcester, Warwick, Northampton, and Oxford, and sums from two to four ounces of gold from the Bedfordshire royal estates of Luton, Leighton Buzzard, and Houghton Regis.

*

The royal revenue so far described was planned to meet normal demands; any abnormal need for money had to be met by a special tax levied on the country. Over most of the country the unit of assessment on which it was raised was the hide, originally the amount of land felt sufficient for a peasant household, though from the beginning, Kent was assessed in 'sulungs', i.e. areas which could be worked by an eight-ox plough, while in the parts of England settled by the Danes in the Viking Age the hide was replaced by the Danish 'ploughland' which Latin sources render 'carrucata'. All over the country estates were assessed in these measures for fiscal purposes in round figures which even in the beginning could only roughly have approximated to the actual area of the individual estate. The process seems to have been as follows: a large district was given an assessment reckoned in multiples of a hundred hides or ploughlands, and this number was then divided locally among the component estates of the district in units of five or multiples of five (in the Danelaw, which calculated by the long hundred of 120, the units are usually of six, or multiples of six, carrucates). As the assessment remained fixed over very long periods, while the actual conditions might alter greatly, it tended to move further and further from any correspondence with the real size of the estates. We hear most of this assessment in relation to a tax known as 'Danegeld', but it is much earlier than the introduction of this tax, and was probably first laid down in connexion with the payment of the king's farm.

Greater sums of money than could be obtained from the normal revenue were required for the tribute to buy off Danish raids. Already in 865 the East Angles 'made peace with the Danes', and doubtless made it at a price, but even at that time the notion of buying off an invader was not new. Oswiu of Northumbria had attempted to

buy off Penda of Mercia in 654, apparently from the
royal treasure. After 865 the practice became only too
common, and the requisite sums were obtained by
special taxation. This is shown clearly by a document in
which a bishop of Worcester leases one of the estates of
his see in return for twenty mancuses of gold, in order to
meet his church's contribution to 'the immense tribute
of the barbarians in the year in which the pagans occupied London' (i.e. 872). When the Danish king, Swein,
was accepted by a large part of England and resided at
Gainsborough in 1013, he imposed a tribute, and seems to
have employed the existing machinery in its collection;
for it was a local magnate, Thurcetel, surnamed 'Salmon',
who collected it from the hundred of Flegg, Norfolk, and
who, learning of Swein's death as he was riding to deliver
the money, brought it back and re-paid it to the con-
tributors. In 1040 another Danish king, Harthacnut, sent
his own house-carls to collect a heavy tax for the payment
of his ships' crews, and at Worcester the populace rose
against two of them and killed them.

King Eadred, who died in 955, left in his will sixteen
thousand pounds to his people 'that they may be able to
buy relief for themselves from famine and from the
heathen army, if they need.' Certain prominent ecclesiastics were to hold it in trust for the benefit of groups of
counties in the south of England and in Mercia. In 991 a
Danish army was bought off for the sum of ten thousand
pounds, and in the years that follow repeated and ever-
increasing payments are made. A treaty of 994, which survives, was bought for twenty-two thousand pounds, and
by 1012 the amount had risen to forty-eight thousand.
It was in this year that Archbishop Ælfheah of
Canterbury, held prisoner by the Danes, refused to allow
the people to be burdened any further by paying a
ransom for him, and died a martyr's death at the hands

of his incensed captors; and in the same year also, King
Ethelred took into his service ships of Danish mercenaries, who had left their own side because they were
shocked by the murder of the archbishop. An annual tax
was levied to pay for them, and a standing force of house-
carls was kept through the reigns of Cnut and his sons,
and paid by a tax known as 'army-payment'. It was
stopped by Edward the Confessor in 1051. After the
Norman Conquest it was referred to as 'Danegeld'.

*

Meanwhile another charge had become incumbent on
the land, the upkeep of a fleet. Some early kings, such as
Edwin and Ecgfrith of Northumbria, had fleets, but we
are not told who paid for their building and their manning, nor for Alfred's fleet, which he enlarged with new
and larger ships, built 'neither according to the Frisian
nor the Danish pattern, but as it seemed to him that they
would be most useful.' They were manned partly by
Frisians, and it is possible that ship-builders were among
the craftsmen whom Asser tells us the king invited to
work for him and paid out of his revenue. But it is probable that the bulk of the cost of providing and maintaining ships was borne by the land as in later times. A fleet
plays a part in the campaigns of Alfred's successors,
Edward and Athelstan, and Edgar's fleet was at Chester
in 973 when he received the submission of the Welsh and
Scottish kings. A post-Conquest writer assigns to this
king three thousand six hundred ships, and speaks of an
annual circuit of the whole island. Without accepting his
statements in full, we may reasonably suppose that the
possession of a strong fleet was one of the reasons why
Edgar overawed the foreign kings of Britain.

More information on the provision of ships is available
for Ethelred's reign (978–1016). He demanded both a

land-army and the furnishing of ships in 999, but owing to delays and incompetent leadership 'at the end it effected nothing except oppression of the people and waste of money and the encouragement of the enemy.' In 1008 the order went out that ships were to be built throughout England, 'a warship from 310 hides and a helmet and a coat-of-mail from eight hides.' They were ready the following year:

> There were more of them than there had ever been before in England in any king's day, according to what books tell us, and they were brought all together to Sandwich, and were to lie there and defend this land against every raiding army. But yet we had not the good fortune nor the glory that that naval force was of any use to this land, any more than it had been on many previous occasions.

Once again, 'they let all the nation's labour thus lightly come to naught.' According to the laws of this reign, warships were to be ready every year soon after Easter.

About 1005, an archbishop of Canterbury left to the king his best ship with its sailing tackle along with sixty helmets and coats-of-mail, and about the same time a bishop of Crediton left to the king a sixty-four-oared ship. The archbishop bequeathed also a ship to each of the counties of Kent and Wiltshire, obviously to lessen their burden of supplying ships. There are traces in some counties of an arrangement of hundreds in groups of three, each group to provide one ship, and Domesday Book gives sporadic information on ship service at various places. Maldon for example supplied one ship; more often, we read of contributions in men, goods, or money: Warwick sent four boatswains or four pounds when the king led a sea expedition; an annual charge of sixpence a house at Colchester could be devoted either to provisioning the king's mercenaries or to an expedition by land or sea; if the king went against his enemies by

sea, the burghers of Leicester must send him four horses
to London, to carry weapons or other things where they
were needed; vague references to service by land or sea
are sometimes found. A document from about the year
1000 describes how St Paul's apportioned over its estates
its obligation to supply forty-five seamen.

From 1012, when Ethelred took into his service forty-
five Danish ships, a standing fleet was kept, and charged
for at the rate of eight marks (i.e. over four pounds) to
the rowlock. This amounted to a heavy burden, and the
fleet was disbanded by Edward the Confessor in 1049 or
1050. By the end of his reign some of the Channel ports
had responsibilities for sea-defence; thus at Lewes 'if the
king sent his men to guard the sea, without going himself' all the men of the borough, no matter on whose land
they dwelt, paid twenty shillings, which was given to
'those who had charge of the arms on the ships.'

*

The king's rights with regard to the calling out of the
army are not specified in detail in the laws. These give
the penalties for disobeying a summons, and for desertion
from the army, and state that all penalties for crime are
increased when the army has been called out; but they
do not say if there was a limit to the number of men
whom the king could demand, nor do they specify the
minimum equipment in weapons and provisions that
each man must bring with him, though King Athelstan
legislates to ensure that shields shall be of a proper
quality. He forbids the covering of them with sheepskin
(instead of ox-hide). In times of crisis, it is probable that
every able-bodied man could be summoned to the host.
This was done in 1016, but the mere fact that the
chronicler troubles to state this expressly implies that it
was not the normal proceeding. It is only when we reach
Domesday Book that we are told how many men must go

from estates of a certain size. A normal rate in Edward the Confessor's time seems to have been one man from five hides, but there are differences in local custom as each place made its own bargain with the king. In Berkshire, a man went from five hides with provisions for two months or four shillings from each hide instead; at Malmesbury, the king had the right to one man from five hides, or a pound; Oxford ought to send twenty men, but could buy itself free at the rate of a pound a man; at Warwick 'when the king went by land', ten burgesses went on behalf of all the others; Leicester supplied twelve. We are told that Exeter performed the same service as five hides of land, and the three small Devonshire boroughs, Totnes, Lidford, and Barnstaple, together performed the same service as Exeter. This seems to let the Devon boroughs off lightly, but between them they also paid annually a mark of silver for mercenaries. The Dorset boroughs pay at exactly the same rate, a mark of silver for ten hides, 'for the needs of the house-carls', and nothing is said of obligations to the host when it was summoned. We cannot be sure that any of these arrangements are of great antiquity. A law of Athelstan's, in the first half of the previous century, ordering every landowner to have two well-mounted men for each plough in his possession, suggests, if it applies to the obligation of military service, a very much heavier demand, and it is possible that later kings aimed at smaller contingents in order to improve the quality of their equipment. The traditional armament of the Anglo-Saxon churl, spear and shield, had become inadequate for changed conditions of warfare.

Domesday Book occasionally tells us something of the arrangements made locally as to who was to perform the military service due from an estate, as in this passage relating to land in Lincolnshire:

The men of the Wapentake of Candleshoe, with the consent of the whole Riding, testify that in the time of King Edward Siwate, Alnod, Fenchel, and Aschil divided their father's land among them equally and share and share alike, and held it in such wise that if there were a call to the king's army, and Siwate could go, the other brothers assisted him. After Siwate, a second went, and Siwate and the rest assisted him; and thus with respect to them all.

We may perhaps see a glimpse of a village council deciding who shall answer the king's summons in the specific words which Abbot Ælfric uses to translate a vaguer Latin original:

The township was ordered to equip two soldiers for the army. Then the two boys (i.e. two foundlings brought up in the village) were chosen for that military service.

King Alfred introduced the innovation of dividing the forces he could call on into two sections, only one of which was on service at any time, to be relieved by the other contingent when they had covered a set period. The Chronicle records one occasion when the serving force came to the end of its term and, having used up its provisions, disbanded before the relieving division arrived on the spot, but in general the system seems to have worked well. Certainly in the reign of Alfred's son Edward the English army proved a most effective force for the offensive warfare of reconquering the land ceded to the Danes.

Anglo-Saxon kings often led their armies in person. Indeed, at one point in 1016, the assembled host refused to act, and disbanded because the king was not present; but the circumstances were unusual, and they may well have suspected that the king's son who had summoned them was playing a lone hand. Desertion from the army was a much more serious offence if the king himself were leading it than otherwise. In this event, it was punishable by death, unless the culprit could redeem himself by payment of his own wergild; in the king's absence, desertion from the army was punished by a fine of 120 shillings. While the laws state the general penalties for such offences, Domesday Book shows that there could be local variations even in matters of this kind. Thus while the fine for neglecting a summons to the army was five pounds (which equals 240 West Saxon shillings) in Oxford and Warwick, the same offence in Berkshire and in Worcester might cost all one's lands.

*

The assembly of the army took time, and so it did not provide an adequate defence against sudden attack. This became very obvious in the era of Viking invasions, for the Danes could land a powerful force on the coast, or on the banks of navigable rivers, do great damage, and sail away with their plunder before the forces of the district could be mustered. Alfred began therefore to surround his territories with a ring of fortresses, manned and kept in repair by the surrounding districts. Long before Alfred's time, the kings had the right to demand work on fortifications as one of the three public charges on all estates, those charges which from the middle of the eighth century are almost always reserved whenever any grant of exemption from dues or services is being made. The labour for the great earthwork built by Offa on his Welsh frontier would be forthcoming under this charge, and before Alfred's time early ninth-century charters make mention of the fortification of strongholds 'against the pagans', in a few cases enlarging the obligation to include the destruction of (enemy) fortifications. Alfred's 'burghal system' was new, therefore, only in its scale, and perhaps in making more permanent arrangements for the upkeep of the strongholds. Asser complains

of the failure of the people to co-operate willingly with
the king in this work, which meant that in some places
the forts he had ordered were incomplete, or not begun,
when invasion came. It may be that the charge of making them fell heavily on some already burdened districts.
It is clear that the systematic defence of his realm by this
means was not completed until the reign of his son
Edward, from whose time comes a document known as
the *Burghal Hidage*, which gives the number of hides of
land allotted to the maintenance of the individual fortresses. Edward also consolidated his advance into
Danish-held territory by similar fortifications, and his
sister Æthelflæd, the Lady of the Mercians, followed the
same plan in the area under her control. The type of
fortification differed according to local conditions; sometimes it was merely a question of repairing existing walls
of Roman origin, whereas at other places an earthwork
and stockade were thrown up at some previously unforti-
fied site; a fort at Towcester was surrounded with a stone
wall. It was reckoned that a fortress would require as a
garrison four men to every pole of wall, and the allotment
of a definite number of hides of land to the maintenance
and manning of a fortress is based on the assumption that
one man would come from each hide, and that eighty
hides would be responsible for keeping in repair twenty
poles of the wall. The laws of the next reign enjoin that
the repairing of fortresses must be completed a fortnight
after the Rogation days. In the reign of Edward the Confessor the demand of one man from each hide was still
being made at Chester, where the reeve summoned a
man from each hide in the county to repair the wall and
bridge. The lord of any man who failed to appear paid
to the king and earl a fine of forty (Norman) shillings,
which was equivalent to 120 Mercian shillings.

The repair of bridges is associated with military

service and fortress work to make up the three public dues. One surviving document shows how this duty might be apportioned. It consists of a list of the estates whose business it was to repair Rochester bridge, with the number of piers for which each was responsible, in terms such as:

The second pier belongs to Gillingham and to Chatham, and they have to provide planks for one pole and put three beams in position.

Royal Officials

As King Alfred remarks, 'the affairs of the kingdom' were 'various and manifold', and a reference we get to his dealing with an appeal to his judgement in a law-suit, as 'he was in his chamber, washing his hands', suggests a very busy man with no time to waste. The king needed deputies who could deal with the routine business of government in the various parts of the kingdom. This deputy was called an ealdorman, until in the eleventh century this term was superseded under Scandinavian influence by the name earl, which had previously been used in this sense only in the parts of England densely settled by the Danes. In English territory the word earl had had, as we shall see later, a different meaning, denoting, not an official, but merely a man of the upper class, but this usage was obsolete long before the eleventh century, and the way was open to adopt the term earl to replace the native term ealdorman.

The ealdormen were appointed by the king. Sometimes they were related to the royal house; one mentioned in a charter of King Beorhtwulf of Mercia in 852 is called 'his uncle's son' in the boundaries attached to the charter, and the descendants of Alfred's elder brother are sometimes ealdormen of the Western Provinces in the late tenth and early eleventh centuries. Sometimes in the eighth century ealdormen belong to the family that had ruled the province as kings before its absorption into a larger kingdom. Most often they were drawn from the king's thanes. Their office was not hereditary, but it became usual in the tenth century to choose ealdormen from a few outstanding families, and the same ealdormanry frequently remained in one family for more than one generation. The sons of Ealdorman Athelstan 'Half-King' (c. 932–58) succeeded him in East Anglia, and Mercia was regarded as belonging to the house of Leofric in the eleventh century.

Until the tenth century an ealdorman south of the Thames was normally in charge of a single shire, but later several shires are united under one ealdorman; Æthelweard, for example, was Ealdorman of the southwestern shires at the end of the tenth century. The south of England had been arranged in its modern shires much earlier than the rest of England; Kent, Sussex, Essex, and probably Middlesex represent originally independent kingdoms, and Surrey is the 'south region', the land south of the Thames that once belonged to the Saxons north of it. Norfolk and Suffolk represent ancient divisions of East Anglia. But the shires of Wessex, except for Devon and Berkshire, took their names from their chief settlement, Somerset from Somerton, Hampshire from Southampton, and so on, and probably arose from a very early administrative arrangement. This superseded the conditions of the age of settlement, when the land was divided into smaller regions, separated from one another by stretches of forest and waste in which precise boundaries were unnecessary.

It is less easy to discover what was the area under an ealdorman's control in Mercia and Northumbria. The

modern shires here are of later growth, hiding to a great
extent the older division into regions, though we know
the names of the tribes of some of these. Our shires of the
East and North Midlands and of York have developed
from the areas attached to Danish boroughs after the
Viking settlement, while the shires of the South-West
Midlands, which are similarly named from a single
borough, probably owe their origin to a tenth-century
reorganization which may have taken the West Saxon
shires as its model. By this time it was no longer customary for each shire to have its own ealdorman, and
Mercia is sometimes treated as one large ealdormanry,
though sometimes smaller ones are carved out of it; but
when Mercia was a separate kingdom, it seems to have
had as many as eight, or even ten, ealdormen in office
concurrently. We do not know how Northumbria was
divided among its ealdormen in its independent days.
When it became part of the kingdom of England it was
sometimes under a single ealdorman, whereas sometimes
Yorkshire was treated as a distinct area.

Within his own area of operations, the ealdorman was
the king's representative. He led the forces of his district
in war, and presided at its judicial assembly. Like the
king, he had official estates, and rights of claiming
hospitality for his officials and messengers. A charter of
836 which frees a bishop's estate from, among other
things, hospitality to the king or ealdorman has an en-
dorsement that shows that the ealdorman's rights had
had to be bought out, for it says: 'and the bishop gave to
Ealdorman Sigred six hundred shillings in gold and to
Ealdorman Mucel ten hides of land at Crowle.' The
ealdorman received a proportion, perhaps a third, of the
fines due to the king at the law-courts, and a third of the
revenues from the boroughs within his province, at any
rate by the end of the period. He was entitled to a fine of

120 shillings if anyone fought at an assembly where he was presiding, and he had higher compensations than other men of the same class for breach of his protection, fighting in his house or violent entry into it. In the North, the only area for which evidence exists, his wergild was four times that of a king's thane. A Surrey ealdorman in Alfred's reign uses the expression 'my two wergilds', which suggests that, like a Mercian king, he may have been entitled to a wergild by reason of his office as well as the normal wergild of a man of his class.

Royal grants of land to individual ealdormen are common, but one cannot distinguish gifts in gratitude for service from sales. The wills of several ealdormen have survived from the ninth and tenth centuries, and show that they had extensive lands, but nothing at all comparable to the enormous accumulation of landed property by the families of Earl Godwine and Earl Leofric in the eleventh century that is revealed by Domesday Book. Many of the estates bequeathed in the wills can be shown to have been acquired by inheritance, and others may have been. It is difficult to judge therefore whether in general the holding of this office was highly profitable.

*

When the area under an ealdorman came to consist of several shires, we begin to hear of an official called the 'shire-reeve', that is, the sheriff. He is first mentioned in the latter part of the tenth century, but men who hold this office are sometimes referred to under the wider designation of 'king's reeve'. It is possible that the office of sheriff may have existed for some time before the first use of the specific title, but there would be little need for it while the ealdormanries were small, and in the ninth century the laws assume that a man in need of assistance will apply direct to the ealdorman, not to a sheriff. The latter was appointed by the king and took charge of his rights in the shire. He presided at the shire-moot in the absence of the ealdorman; it was the sheriff who as the king's representative took Archbishop Dunstan's oath in a land-suit in Kent between 964 and 988. When the king wished to communicate with the shire, he sent a writ addressed to the bishop, the earl, and at times the sheriff. Sometimes estates were attached to the office; by the end of the period the practice was not unknown by which the sheriff paid an agreed sum to the king as the proceeds of the shire and made what profit he could out of the actual receipts.

The term 'king's reeve' does not necessarily, nor usually, refer to the sheriff, but is in frequent use before that office came into being. It normally refers to the man in charge of a royal estate and responsible for the collection of the king's farm from the surrounding area. He presided at the 'folk-moot' mentioned in Alfred's laws; a trader had to bring the men he was proposing to take up country with him 'before the king's reeve in the folk-moot'; he collected the fines and forfeitures due to the king, and in some circumstances he had to keep prisoners at the king's estate.

The towns were similarly in charge of a king's reeve, called a *wic-* or *port-*reeve. A town-reeve of Winchester was an important enough person for the Anglo-Saxon Chronicle to record his death in 896, while that of the reeve of Bath is entered in 906. The town-reeve is mentioned by name when the king addresses a writ to a town. The duties of these reeves included the control of the tolls paid by traders to the king. The king's reeve of Dorchester rode out to find out the business of the first ships of Danish men to reach the coast of Wessex (789–802), for if they were traders it was his business to exact toll; his enquiry cost him his life. Toll had even to be paid

when slaves were purchased for the purpose of manumitting them, and so the Exeter manumissions often
mention that the town-reeve took the toll on the king's
behalf. The town-reeve's duties would be increased when
it was forbidden to buy outside a town. He had to be
present as a witness, and at the proceedings when
property was attached. He had duties of supervision with
regard to the mint in his town.

In the reign of Ethelred the Unready, we read of fric-
tion between an ealdorman and the king's reeves. In 995
two brothers had been killed while illegally defending
one of their men who had stolen a bridle. Æthelwig, the
king's reeve in Buckingham, and Winsige, the reeve in
Oxford, gave them Christian burial. Ealdorman Leofsige
complained to the king, because the brothers had forfeited their right to this. But the king, who says 'I did
not wish to sadden Æthelwig, who was dear and
precious to me', not only refused to take action in the
matter, but also granted to this reeve the brothers' forfeited estates. Later, Ealdorman Leofsige was banished
for slaying another favourite reeve of the king, a man
called Æfic, in his own home. If Ethelred made a practice of upholding his reeves without enquiry into the
legality of their actions, this may help to account for
the lack of good service and support from his ealdormen
that is one of the features of his unhappy reign.

CHAPTER V

THE CLASSES OF SOCIETY

In the eyes of the law, the chief mark that distinguished one class of society from another was the price that had to be paid in compensation for the slaying of one of its members, which was called the wergild. There was a different scale in force in Kent – at any rate in the early period – from that current in the rest of England. A Kentish nobleman is called an earl in the seventh-century laws of that kingdom – a term which carried no connotation of office at that date – and his wergild was three hundred Kentish shillings, probably the sum originally equivalent to three hundred oxen, which was just three times the wergild of the ordinary free man, the churl. In the other parts of the country the word earl is used in this way, to denote a man of the upper class, only in poetry and in the rhyming formula 'earl and churl'; it has otherwise become obsolete, and men of this class are called *gesithas* 'companions', or in later times thanes – a word which once meant 'servant' but later went up in the world, because of the dignity involved in serving the king; or they might be referred to by a name derived from the amount of their wergild, men 'of twelve hundred', for this was the number of shillings to be paid if one of them were slain. In Wessex, by Alfred's time this amount is exactly equivalent to that paid for a Kentish earl, for a West Saxon shilling contained at that date five pence, while in Kent the shilling had twenty pence; in Mercia, and probably in Wessex in early times, the shilling only contained four pence, so that the thane's wergild was rather lower. Both in Wessex and in Mercia it was six times that of a churl, for in these areas the churl's wergild was only about half that of his Kentish counterpart. In Northumbria there was probably a similar ratio between the wergilds of the nobleman and the churl, but the position has been obscured by the fact that the only record on the subject gives the thane a wergild exactly equivalent to that of a late West Saxon thane, but seems to have reckoned the churl's wergild in terms of Mercian shillings, of fourpence to the shilling instead of fivepence. In Wessex – evidence for other areas is lacking – there was up to the time of Alfred an intermediate class of men, with a wergild of six hundred shillings. These were of the *gesith*, not the churl class, and there is some evidence to suggest that they were not entitled to the highest wergild because they possessed less than five hides of land. As there is no later mention of this intermediate class, and the phrase 'of twelve hundred and of two hundred' is used to cover the whole free population, we may assume that the six-hundred wergild was abolished. Perhaps the class entitled to it was never a large one.

The wergild was not the only line of demarcation between the various classes of free men. Similar variations existed in the compensations due to them for other injuries, such as offences against persons or places under their protection, forcible entry into their houses or fighting on their premises. The oath of a man of a higher class was valued at more than that of a churl. On the other side, the higher ranks paid greater fines when convicted of crimes; for some offences, such as the harbouring of fugitives, the offender had to pay the amount of his own wergild; for some others, the neglect of military service, for example, the man of the highest class paid 120 shillings, the intermediate class 60 shillings, and the churl 30 shillings, in Alfred's time.

The Nobleman

To the eleventh-century writer of a private treatise on the management of a large estate, called 'The Rights of Various Classes', the rights and obligations of a thane were that he held his lands by title-deed, that is to say, free from dues and services to the king except for the three public charges of military service, construction of fortifications, and repair of bridges, and with the right to bequeath them to whom he wished. The writer admits, however, that on some estates, the thane may be liable to some other services at the king's demand, watch over his person, maritime guard, guard duties in the host, provision of the equipment for a ship, the building of deer-hedges at the king's estate. Domesday Book supports him. It tells, for example, how from some lands in Kent the king has a bodyguard for six days at Canterbury or Sandwich and it is supplied by the king with food and drink.

There survive a few other private dicta as to what were the qualifications that entitled a man to be a thane. One says that a churl who throve so that he possessed five hides of land on which he paid the royal dues, should, if killed, be paid for with the wergild of a thane; it adds :

And even if he thrive so that he have helmet and coat-of-mail and a gold-plated sword, if he has not the land, he is nevertheless a churl.

Even if he had the necessary five hides, his children were not, according to this writer, born to the rank of thane; the rank became hereditary only if his son and his son's son similarly held this amount of land; otherwise they were to be paid for at the churl's rate. Another document, written probably in the eleventh century, in a somewhat nostalgic mood about things that had 'at one time' been the practice, says:

> If a churl prospered, so that he had fully five hides of land of his own, a church and a kitchen, a bell-house and a castle-gate, a seat and a special office in the king's hall, then was he henceforth worthy of the status of a thane.

So also was a merchant who had thrice crossed the sea in his own ship.

This writer does not tell us in what way things have changed. Has it become too difficult for a deserving man to receive the coveted recognition? Or are men with inadequate qualifications becoming members of the higher class? Perhaps both things are happening; the writer may feel that thaneship is now granted for other things than honest merit. On general grounds we may be sure that this rise in status would not be automatic: some ceremony, or at least some public notification, would be essential, for the community must know how much a man's oath is worth, and what it would cost to kill him. There was room for no vagueness or difference of opinion about individual cases. There is an interesting passage in an eleventh-century manuscript that shows that a churl was made a thane by an act as definite as that by which an owner manumitted his slave, or the king appointed his ealdorman – by this date called an earl. We are told in a context that shows that we are dealing with an actual fact, not merely somebody's theory as to what once was, or ought to be, the practice, that a churl became a thane 'by the earl's gift'.

Some men of the upper class possessed extensive estates, scattered over a wide area. The thane Wulfric Spott, the founder of the monastery of Burton-on-Trent in 1004, possessed seventy-two estates in addition to an unspecified number in South Lancashire and the Wirral;

lously preserved. Building in stone was, however, the exception. Byrhtferth of Ramsey, writing in 1011, describes the building of a house as follows:

First, one examines the site, and also hews the timber, and fits fairly the sills, and lays the beams, and fastens the rafters to the ridge-pole, and supports (it) with buttresses (?), and afterwards adorns the house pleasantly.

The hall was furnished with trestle tables and fixed benches, which were strewn with mattresses and pillows when the hall was used as sleeping quarters. It was hung with tapestries; *Beowulf*, which mentions gold-inwoven tapestry, implies that in early days hangings were used only on special occasions, even in a royal hall, but they doubtless became more common later, and are quite frequently mentioned in tenth- and eleventh-century wills. They could be used for sinister purposes, as when the assassins of Earl Uhtred hid behind them in the hall at *Wiheal* in 1016 and murdered him when he came in to make his peace with Cnut. The Bayeux tapestry has survived to show us what could be the quality of English work at the end of the period, and it is probable that a tapestry presented to the monastery of Ely by Ealdorman Brihtnoth's widow was something similar; on it were depicted the deeds of her husband, presumably including his heroic death at the battle of Maldon. The wills supply further information about those furnishings that were valuable enough to be handed down, as they contain clauses like:

I grant to St Peter's monastery at Bath . . . the best dorsal that I have and a set of bed-clothes with tapestry and curtain and with everything that belongs with it.

or:

And to Eadgifu two chests and inside them her best bed-curtain and a linen covering and all the bed-clothes that go with it.

The objects found in the graves of the heathen period show us that already then drinking cups and elaborately decorated horns were made, and that the Anglo-Saxon chieftains valued beautiful table-ware enough to import glass from across the Channel and silver-ware from as far away as the Eastern Empire. There is no reason to suppose that their standards in this respect deteriorated in later centuries, and such objects are often bequeathed: e.g. 'a cup supplied with a lid', 'two silver cups', 'her gold-adorned wooden cup', 'two ornamented horns', 'a bowl of two and a half pounds', 'the drinking horn which I bought from the community of the Old Minster' and so on.

*

Life in a nobleman's hall was very like that at court, on a smaller scale. Like the king, lay and ecclesiastical lords had their officials: the prince Athelstan speaks of his seneschal, a bishop of Elmham of his cup-filler; Ealdorman Brihtnoth's chamberlain fought beside him at Maldon; the seneschal of the abbot of Ely held an estate of the abbey in Cambridgeshire; an eleventh-century testatrix makes bequests to two stewards. All great households included one or more domestic chaplains, whose functions were secretarial as well as religious. Great ecclesiastics, as well as laymen, kept a large retinue of retainers, and in the seventh century Bishop Wilfrid's was so large that it aroused the envy and enmity of the queen.

In the hall men amused themselves with feasting and drinking, often beyond measure. Abbot Ælfric writes reproachfully to an Oxfordshire thane who has plied him too heartily with strong drink when he was his guest. The picture given in the devil's speech in the poem *Juliana*, of men ready to renew old quarrels when they have drunk too much, and the graphic account of a riotous feast in the poem *Judith*, may have been drawn from life. Over their cups men made boasts of what they would perform, and this was regarded not only as excusable, but to be admired, provided the boast was lived up to. Brihtnoth's men, faced with certain defeat at Maldon, were reminded of the vows they had often made about stern battle, when drinking on the benches in the hall: 'Now can be tested who is brave.' A wise man will take thought before he utters a vow, but a man who promised nothing, who refused to commit himself, would probably not have been admired.

Harp-playing and song helped to pass the long evenings, and certainly the performers were not always professionals. In *Beowulf* the king himself performs to the harp, and a king's thane supplies entertainment on another occasion. St Aldhelm, who was of royal descent, was a skilled performer, and King Alfred saw to it that his sons and daughters should be taught Saxon songs. Some of the professional minstrels may have been of aristocratic rank. In the early period, at any rate, they went from hall to hall, as described by the poet of *Widsith*:

So go the singers of men, destined to wander through many lands. They tell their needs, they speak words of thanks, ever south or north they find someone wise in songs, generous in gifts, who wishes to exalt his fame before the company.

Other indoor amusements included dicing and a game akin to chess.

A thane's life was not spent between the hall and the battlefield, as one might almost imagine from poetic sources alone, nor in the sports of the field, important though these were. Stag-hunting, fox-hunting, and hawking were favourite pastimes for kings and nobles. All such men had their huntsmen and their fowlers, and it is common for services in connexion with these sports to form part of the terms by which landowners let out their lands. Trouble was taken to secure fine dogs and hawks. A king of Kent writes to the missionaries in Germany, requesting, in addition to their prayers, that they should procure for him some falcons of a kind unobtainable in his own country, and dogs of a specially fine breed were sent by King Alfred as a present to the archbishop of Reims when he wished to obtain his help with his educational reforms. A Kentish thane, late in the tenth century, bequeathed to the king two hawks and all his staghounds, and it was while stag-hunting that King Edmund was almost carried over a precipice, and made a vow, as his horse was hovering on the brink, to recall Dunstan from exile. A picture of a deserted hall in *Beowulf* includes the lines: 'No good hawk flies through the hall, nor does the swift horse stamp in the courtyard.' A verse in the *Runic Poem* gives us a glimpse of men discussing the points of a horse, and both *Beowulf* and Bede supply vignettes of young men testing the speed of their horses by horse-racing as they go on a journey.

These were the pastimes of men of rank, but they had their more serious occupations also, military duties in time of war, legal duties of attendance at assemblies, of assisting in the suppression of crime, of riding out on the track of stolen cattle. They had to keep order in their households, for whose offences they were legally responsible, having to bring the accused to answer to a charge or themselves pay the compensations; probably they were often concerned in litigation on behalf of themselves or their men. The more important of them had duties at court, and all had their obligations to the Church. When we add to all this the supervision of their estates, we realize that 'the joys of the hall' so extolled in verse can have occupied no disproportionate amount of the thane's time.

Some men of this class were literate. Alfred planned that all young men of free birth and adequate means should learn to read English. How far this dream was realized is uncertain, but laymen who could read were no rarity in the late tenth century. Bishop Ælfwold of Crediton left a copy of a theological treatise to a layman, and a casual reference to 'books and such small things' in a woman's will perhaps suggests that it was no remarkable thing for lay households to have some books. Ælfric wrote theological treatises for Wulfgeat of Ilmington and Sigeferth of Asthall, both of them ordinary men of the thane class, of no particularly distinguished position; while his patron, Ealdorman Æthelweard, was himself the author of a Latin chronicle. Byrhtferth of Ramsey assumes that some laymen may want learned matters explained to them. He says, in 1011, that priests must fully understand the 'moon's leap'; otherwise they may be put to shame 'before the king's nobility'.

*

We are less well-informed about the activities of the women of this class, but we may assume that the mistress of the house was occupied in supervising the running of it, no small matter when baking, brewing, spinning, and weaving were all done at home. A small tow-chest is one of the articles bequeathed in a woman's will. The qualities that the author of a gnomic poem regards as desirable in a queen can be taken to apply to noble ladies in general, for the poem was composed at a time when courts were small and domestic:

A woman shall prosper, be loved among her people, shall be cheerful, keep counsel, be liberal with horses and treasure; always, everywhere, greet first at the mead-drinking the protector of nobles before the band of retainers, give the first cup promptly into her lord's hand, and study the benefit of both of them in their housekeeping.

The mistress of the house herself attended to the needs of important guests, and she and her daughters presented the wine-cup to those persons whom they wished to honour; as it says of the king's daughter in *Beowulf*:

Sometimes Hrothgar's daughter bore the ale-cup before the retainers, to the nobles in turn; I heard the company in the hall call her Freawaru, as she gave the studded goblet to the warriors.

A *gesith's* wife who Bede says was healed by Bishop John of Beverley 'presented the cup to the bishop and to us, and continued to serve us with drink as she had begun till the meal was over.'

Little is said in our records about the upbringing of children in Anglo-Saxon times, and I know no evidence that there was any general habit of letting them be fostered away from home, though youths of noble birth might be brought up at court, and those destined for the Church be placed early in episcopal households. When a man died leaving a child, the law held that 'it was right that the child accompany the mother' while the kindred administered his property during his minority. It is perhaps worth noting that the gnomic poetry reveals an attitude to the education of the young which we tend to regard as modern, for it says:

One shall not rebuke a youth in his childhood, until he can reveal himself. He shall thrive among the people in that he is confident.

The activity of an Anglo-Saxon lady was not confined to her own home. She could hold land in her own right, dispose of it freely, and defend her right in the courts. She could act as a compurgator in law-suits. She could make donations for religious purposes and she could manumit her slaves. She was, in short, very much more independent than were women after the Norman Conquest. Thus we read in Domesday Book of a certain Asa in Yorkshire, who 'held her land separate and free from the domination and control of Beornwulf her husband, even when they were together, so that he could neither give nor sell nor forfeit it; but after their separation she withdrew with all her land, and possessed it as its lady.'

*

That the upper classes cared for fine apparel we know mainly from the homilists' diatribes against it, especially against priests, monks. and nuns who emulated the laity in this respect. Men wore a mantle over a knee-length tunic and trousers, and sometimes bequeath silken robes and fur cloaks. The mantle was fastened by a brooch, often of beautiful workmanship and great size, the tunic held by a belt that might have richly ornamented clasps and mounts. Gold and silver finger-rings, armlets, and collars might be worn, and much interest was taken in the elaborate ornamentation of weapons and of horse-trappings. The verse literature, which never describes clothes, can spare several lines to depict a helmet, a sword-hilt, or a coat-of-mail, and men speak with loving precision of such things in their wills, when they specify who shall have 'the silver-hilted sword which belonged to Ulfcetel', 'the sword with the pitted hilt', 'my round shield', 'the inlaid sword which belonged to Withar', 'the sword worth 120 mancuses of gold with four pounds of silver on the belt', 'a spear inlaid with gold.' How long such things could be treasured and handed down as heirlooms is shown by the bequest made by the prince Athelstan to his brother in 1015 of 'the sword which King Offa owned.' The latest king of this name, and presumably the one meant, was the great Mercian king who died in 796. One would like to know if the sword so treasured was the Avar sword sent to Offa as a gift from Charlemagne. As for horse-trappings, they are often included in heriots; gold-plated bridles and saddles adorned with precious metals occur in poetry, and we need not take this to be exaggeration. Just after the Norman Conquest the reeve of Saham, Norfolk, transferred to a man of Earl Ralf the service of five sokemen, paying between them 10s. 8d. a year, in exchange for a bridle; and the bridle whose theft, as we saw above, led to such trouble in the reign of Ethelred may have been a valuable article. One is often struck in reading documents of the period by the very great value of articles of adornment, when considered in relation to the purchasing power of money. A necklace of 120 mancuses of gold, such as one reads of in the tenth century, would have purchased 120 oxen, or 600 sheep, or fifteen male slaves, at the price assigned to them by the laws; a mancus seems fairly frequently to have bought three acres of land in the East Midlands about the same period, but naturally the price of land varied with its nature, and, as the recorded sales are usually to churches, it may be that the seller hopes to get spiritual benefits by letting it go cheaply. Nevertheless, such comparisons show that quite a few articles of adornment might constitute a large capital.

Women wore a kirtle reaching to the ground, a tunic, and a mantle, fastened by brooches that were often worn in pairs, one on each shoulder. They wore rings, armlets, and necklets, and also diadems or circlets of gold. Their wills show more interest than those of menfolk in their garments and jewellery, referring to linen and woollen kirtles, to 'her best dun tunic', 'her old filigree brooch worth six mancuses', 'a necklace of forty mancuses', 'a headband of thirty mancuses of gold.' No testatrix, however, gives the impression of having an extensive wardrobe, but probably only those garments of especial value, used for great occasions, are thought worthy of mention.

The Churl

The ordinary freeman is most commonly called a churl. In Wessex and Mercia his wergild was only one-sixth of that of a nobleman of the twelve hundred class, and he is therefore sometimes called 'a man of two hundred (shillings.' A Kentish churl had a wergild of double this amount, of one hundred Kentish shillings, a sum equivalent to four hundred West Saxon shillings, and was a man of substance, whose normal holding was the amount of land that an eight-ox plough could keep under cultivation, with pasture and woodland in addition. Below him in the social scale was a class called *læt*, with a wergild that varied from four-fifths to two-fifths of that of a churl, whose members have been thought to be a subject population, for a corresponding term was used among some continental German tribes to denote a class intermediate between freemen and slaves. Over the rest of England, the churl's holding was probably originally a hide of land, for this term means 'household' and once denoted the land that was considered adequate for one family. The acreage considered necessary varied in different parts of the country, 120 acres being reckoned to the hide in the East Midlands in the tenth century, though in the west country hides were much smaller – barely half this number of acres. By the later part of the period, by a rough equation, a Kentish ploughland was reckoned as two hides. Below the churl in Wessex were classes of Welsh peasants with lower wergilds than Englishmen of the same status.

Though he apparently lived at a lower economic level than his Kentish counterpart, the churl in the other kingdoms of the Heptarchy was nevertheless a man with the full rights of a freeman, and often held land that he had inherited from his ancestors and would leave to his children. He paid a freeman's dues to the Church, attended the popular assemblies, fulfilled his military obligations, claimed compensation for trespass into his homestead, or for fighting inside it, and was not bound to the soil – he could 'go whither he would'. He might well own more than one hide of land, for there was a widespread feeling that a property of five hides was necessary before a man began to be regarded above his class as a churl. A charter of King Ethelred in 984 mentions a 'rustic' who had had eight hides of land near the Kennet.

It is generally agreed that the position of the churl deteriorated as time went on. Even in the early days there were churls who did not own land that they could live off; by about 700, and perhaps long before, there were men who took their land at a rent from a lord, and, if they also accepted a homestead from him, he had a right to agricultural services as well as rent. When King Alfred made his treaty with the Danes late in the ninth century, peasants (churls) who occupied land for which they paid rent were set level, for the purpose of compensation by wergild if they were slain, only with the Danish freedmen, i.e. manumitted slaves. A tenth-century testatrix bequeaths along with an estate peasants (*geburas*) of whose tenure she uses the phrase in Alfred's treaty. Some late tenth- or eleventh-century entries in a Gospel-book from Bedwyn imply that occupiers of *geburland* cannot leave it at will, as the following example will show:

This is Ecgwynn's witness, that Edwin granted her that she might bring herself out of the *geburland*, free to journey into every land, in return for ten mancuses of silver, when Ælfsige held office and Wynstan was his deputy, in their witness and that of Ælfheah the priest and of all the servants of God at Bedwyn and of all the people.

We are expressly told in an eleventh-century document

THE CLASSES OF SOCIETY

dealing with the management of a large estate that there were great varieties in local custom with regard to the rights of the various classes of men, and we can never hope to get into a simple formula the differences between the minor categories of the peasant class up and down the country. This document tells us nothing about churls who lived on land of their own, for these lie outside its theme. From Domesday Book we suspect that such men existed, but apparently they were not very numerous in the South and West in late Anglo-Saxon times. Many an independent freeman may have had to purchase protection and financial help in times of stress and disorder at the cost of relinquishing some of his rights. Not all powerful men were scrupulous in observing the rights of weaker individuals, and Archbishop Wulfstan includes the lessening of the rights of freemen among the abuses of his day: 'Freemen are not allowed to rule themselves, nor to go whither they would, nor to deal with their own property as they would.' Cnut's laws complain of overbearing men who defend their followers at law either as freemen or bondmen, whichever seems easiest to them. Through one cause or another, the average peasant in the south and west of England was in this matter of personal freedom below the majority of the peasantry in the areas settled by the Danes.

The document on estate management deals with various classes that hold their land from a lord. Highest come men called *geneatas*, 'companions', who pay rent and render services mainly of a non-agricultural kind – riding services, bodyguard over their lord's person, watch over his horses, escort duties for his guests, services connected with his hunting, and so on. They seem to be represented in the Domesday survey of several counties, especially in the West Midlands, by men called *radcnihts*. The bishops of Worcester leased out a number of the estates of their

see on terms very similar to these, and we may note that
it was a *geneat* that a landowner in 896 sent to ride round
the boundaries of a disputed estate with the claimant's
representative.

We learn also what could be demanded from the
gebur, a peasant who had been given his holding – a
quarter of a hide – by the lord, and supplied with two
oxen, one cow, and six sheep as initial stock, seven acres
already sown, tools for his work and utensils for his
house. In return, after the lapse of a year, he is to give
two days' work every week, and three days at harvest
time, and from Candlemas to Easter, unless he should be
using his horses on the lord's service. He is to pay a rent
of tenpence at Michaelmas, twenty-three sesters of barley
and two hens at Martinmas, a young sheep, or twopence,
at Easter. In rotation with others of his kind, he is to keep
watch at his lord's fold in the period between Martinmas
and Easter. In addition, he must plough one acre a week
in the autumn ploughing, fetch the seed from the lord's
barn, and plough three acres extra as 'boonwork', two
acres in return for his pasture rights. As part of his rent, he
ploughs a further three acres and sows them with his own
seed. He joins with one of his fellows in keeping a stag-
hound for his lord, and he gives six loaves to the latter's
swineherd when he drives his herd of swine to the mast
pasture. On his death, his lord inherits his goods.

Similar demands were made from men of this class at
Tiddenham, from which an eleventh-century survey
survives, but local conditions cause variation in detail.
Fish-weirs on the Severn and Wye were an important
source of income on this estate, so here the *gebur* must
provide rods and help in the building of the weirs. At
Martinmas he gives a ball of good net-yarn. Wherever
there were special industries separate arrangements of
this kind would be made.

The demands are heavy, but definitely limited by custom. These men are not the lowest in the scale of freemen. There is a class of *cotsetlan* 'cottage-dwellers', who may hold as little as five acres and who do services for their holding, but pay no rent; and there are free labourers without homes of their own, whom the lord is to supply with food, shoes, and gloves.

The lord did not depend entirely on the services of his tenants; he had his specialist workmen, his overseers, his herdsmen, his dairymaids, etc. Such persons were sometimes slaves, but often free. They received their perquisites by custom: the sower has a right to a basketful of every kind of seed he sows; the oxherd may pasture two oxen or more with his lord's oxen on the common meadow, and his cow may go with the lord's oxen; the cowherd is to have the milk of every grown cow for seven days after it has calved; and his cow may go with the lord's cows; the shepherd has twelve nights' dung at Christmas and one lamb of those born in the year, and a bell-wether's fleece, and the milk of his herd for seven days after the equinox, and a bowl of whey or of buttermilk throughout the summer; the woman who makes the cheeses has all the buttermilk except the herdsman's portion; the overseer of the grain gets all the corn that falls at the door of the barn; every tree blown down in the wood belongs to the woodman. Special allowances or feasts are customary on certain occasions, varying according to the custom of the district, such as Christmas, Easter, the time of 'boonwork' in the harvest, or at the ploughing; a 'rick-cup' may be given at the bringing home of the corn.

A good example of an estate very much of the type the author of this treatise had in mind is afforded by the Domesday Book account of Queen Edith's estate at Leominster, Herefordshire. It had 30 ploughs on the

demesne, and 230 others, and there were 8 reeves,
8 beadles, 8 *radcnihts* (corresponding to the *geneatas* of the
treatise), 238 villeins (corresponding to the *geburas*), 75
bordars (corresponding to the *cotsetlan*) and 82 persons
of unfree birth. The villeins ploughed 140 acres of the
lord's land and sowed it with their own wheat seed; they
paid eleven pounds and 52 pence. The *radcnihts* gave 14
shillings and fourpence and three sesters of honey. There
were eight mills, worth 73 shillings and 30 sticks of eels.
The woodland rendered 24 shillings in addition to pan-
nage. In its general make-up this great estate agrees
closely with the treatise, though naturally Domesday
Book cannot go into minute detail on local customs.

*

There was also much local variation in the system of
working on the land. Our documents mainly give us information about the open-field system and we are told
little about the estates where owners held their arable land
in blocks, or about the isolated farms in the clearings that
were being steadily won from the waste throughout the
period. When the open-field system was in use, all the
available arable was not cultivated in any year; part,
a half or a third, was left fallow, and the part under cultivation was further divided among winter-sown and
spring-sown crops. It was distributed among the various
holders in strips, each strip representing a day's ploughing, and an individual holder did not receive adjacent
strips, but scattered over the fields as they fell to him by
rotation. Meadow was similarly divided, and each man
had his definite rights in the common pastures – whether
these were permanent or formed by the part of the arable
that was lying fallow – in the woodlands, that were important for pasturing of swine as well as for the provision
of timber and firewood and for the hunting of game, and

in the fisheries or any other sources of profit belonging to
the vill. Such appurtenances are often specifically mentioned in grants of land, as, for example, in a charter of
822, which gives an exhaustive list – 'fields, woods,
meadows, pastures, waters, mills, fisheries, fowling-
places, hunting-grounds, and whatever is contained in
it.' At one time the Weald of Kent was used as unen-
closed swine-pasture by the large communities which
made up the Kentish people, communities whose territories became the lathes of Kent; but before long portions
were assigned to individual manors. Each man had his
rights in proportion to the size of his holding, and he also
had his duties and obligations. We see him about 700 in
association with his neighbours in the laws of Ine of
Wessex, which fix the responsibilities for fencing the
common fields and meadows, and discuss the amount to
be paid for the hire of another's yoke of oxen. The plough
was drawn by oxen, and it was assumed that a team
would normally consist of eight; few churls would be
wealthy enough to possess a full team, and most would
have to combine with their fellows to get their land
ploughed.

Under the methods of agriculture current, the land
would not easily be made to produce a livelihood; it
needed steady work all the year round. To quote C. S.
and C. S. Orwin: 'Autumn sowing on the fallow was
followed by winter cultivation of the stubble and spring
sowing, after which fallow cultivation and hay-making
occupied the farmer until the corn harvest finished the
farming year.' Wheat and barley were the principal
crops, the latter being necessary not only for bread but
also to provide malt for brewing; rye, beans, and peas are
mentioned sometimes, and flax was cultivated also. Owing to the shortage of feeding stuffs, only a minimum of
stock could be kept throughout the winter; many beasts

had to be slaughtered in the autumn and the flesh salted
for winter consumption. Most men would have a small
croft in which they could grow the few vegetables then in
use, and the herbs required for seasoning and medicinal
purposes. A much more important activity was bee-
keeping, for honey was not merely their sole means of
sweetening, it was the major ingredient of mead; in some
parts of the country rents continued to be paid in sesters
of honey after the remaining dues had been commuted
to a money payment.

After a bad season, food could become very scanty before the next year's crops were garnered. The poorer men
had few reserves, and a succession of bad years or the
dislocation caused by wars and invading armies brought
about serious famine. The destitute depended on the
alms of the charitable; a testator may leave by will that
a hundred poor men are to be fed annually at Ely on
St Audrey's day; a king can order his reeves to supply
one poor man on each of his estates every month with
an 'amber' of meal, a flitch of bacon, or a wether worth
fourpence, and with clothes for a year; but such mitiga-
tions were occasional and haphazard. The chroniclers
and homilists speak frequently of famine, and Abbot
Ælfric accepts the fact that men die of hunger as part of
the divine scheme of things:

The Almighty Ruler sometimes withdraws sustenance from
men on account of sins, but nevertheless we believe that he
whom hunger kills goes to God unless he was particularly
sinful.

*

Not all men of the churl class were engaged in tilling the
land and minding the flocks. It was men of this class who
carried on the necessary crafts, often in the service of a
lord. Asser mentions King Alfred's goldsmiths and craftsmen of all kinds, his falconers, hawkers, and dog-keepers.

The king's huntsmen and foresters occur frequently in our records, and are sometimes rewarded for their services with estates of considerable size, as when in 987 Ethelred gave three hides and three perches at Westwood and Farnley to his huntsman Leofwine. In the Latin dialogue composed by Abbot Ælfric to exercise his pupils in Latin vocabulary, the king's huntsman is made to say: 'He clothes and feeds me well, and sometimes gives me a horse or armlet, that I may the more joyfully ply my craft'; and in one manuscript he is made to add: 'I hold the first place in his hall.' The fowler discusses whether it is preferable to tame new birds every season or to feed the trained birds throughout the summer, and in an Old English poem we are given a sketch of his methods:

One man shall tame the proud wild bird, the hawk on the hand, until the bird of prey becomes gentle; he puts jesses on it, feeds thus in fetters the creature exulting in its w'ngs.

Similar sketches survive of the builder, the seaman, the merchant, etc. There was an opinion current among some people at any rate, that the latter's trade, successfully carried out, ought to entitle a man to the status of a thane, and seamen such as King Edward's steersmen, who held land in Domesday Book, may not have been churls. The goldsmith also plied a much honoured craft; if he were the man of a 'mighty king' he received 'broad lands in recompense' – the poet's statement is supported by charters and Domesday Book, where several of King Edward's goldsmiths are mentioned as holders of lands, one of them, Theodric, with estates in three counties, Oxfordshire, Berkshire, and Surrey. Private persons also rewarded their goldsmiths with land; for example, the Cambridgeshire thane Ælfhelm Polga gave half a hide to his goldsmith, for him to alienate as he pleased. Goldsmiths occur as donors, not recipients, in an entry in a Gospel-book from Thorney: two, called Ælfric and

Wulfwine, who served a lady by name Eadgifu, gave two ounces of gold which, the entry says, 'is on the outside of this same book in filigree work', but which, alas, is there no longer. We hear also of the weaponsmith, who 'can make many weapons for the use of men, when for men's battles he works a helmet or a dagger or a coat-of-mail, a bright sword or a shield-boss, firmly fitted to repel the flying javelin.' The young prince Athelstan, whose will of 1015 betrays a great interest in his weapons, kept a sword-polisher. Another very skilled craft is mentioned in the Wiltshire section of the Domesday survey: a certain Leofgyth is holding in 1086 land held by her husband in King Edward's day; we are told: 'This Leofgyth made and makes orphreys for the king and the queen'. This sort of gold-embroidery was also done by Ælfgyth 'the maid' to whom Godric the sheriff gave in the Confessor's reign half a hide of land in Buckinghamshire on condition that she should teach his daughter to make orphreys; a lady, Æthelswith, practised this art at Coveney, Cambridge-shire. This shows that it was an accomplishment for a high-born woman, not merely a means of earning one's bread.

Much less exalted craftsmen are the blacksmith, who makes ploughshare and coulter, goad and fish-hook, awl and needle, the carpenter, responsible not only for various tools and utensils, but for houses and ships, the fisherman who sells his catch in the towns and could sell more if he had it, the tailor, the salter, the baker, and the cook. Sometimes these people were of unfree birth – a female weaver, a sempstress, and a male cook are be-queathed in wills and a male weaver is granted his free-dom in a manumission – but often they were free folk of the churl class.

Finally, we have the trades that catered, not for men's needs, but for their pleasures, minstrels of a humbler type than those mentioned in a previous chapter, who were probably of the thane class. These gleemen sang their lays in the market-places and the ale-houses, and their method was imitated by St Aldhelm, if William of Malmesbury's tale is true, when he stood on the bridge to attract an audience to him by his songs, later turning to more edifying matter. In the eleventh century, priests are forbidden to be 'ale-minstrels' or gleemen. Occasional glimpses are to be had of other entertainers; a buffoon figures in an account of a tenth-century miracle, and some sort of acrobat or tumbler is described in the words of the poem: 'One is agile, he has a skilful art, the gift of giving entertainment before the retainers by his actions, light and flexible.'

The churl was not, any more than his betters, entirely dependent on professionals for his entertainment; the men on an estate of Whitby Abbey in the seventh century were able to perform each in his turn with the harp – all except Cædmon. Bede speaks elsewhere of men drinking and making merry together, and listening to a traveller's account of what had befallen him on his way. Ale-houses are sometimes mentioned, in which quarrels arose only too easily and gave rise to bloodshed; vigils over the dead were seized on as an opportunity for conviviality, to the scandal of the Church, which complained also that men used the Church holidays for feasts instead of religious observance. It was not easy to prevent riotous behaviour in the churchyard, or even in the church itself. Among outdoor amusements men had bull-baiting, and perhaps cock-fighting. But in general, the routine of daily work, and its interruptions by attendance at assemblies, or the hue and cry after a thief, or the tracking of stolen cattle, or other legal duties, would probably leave men of this class with little leisure on their hands.

One knows but little of the conditions in which they

lived. The house of the average peasant was a simple affair, with a main all-purpose room and some out-buildings. The fire burned in an open hearth and the smoke found its way out through a hole in the roof, which was often of thatch, the house itself being of wood or lath and plaster. If we could take as typical the few Anglo-Saxon villages whose sites have been discovered and ex-cavated, we should be forced to assume that the peasants in the heathen period lived in extreme squalor, in cramped huts whose floors they used as refuse heaps. But these, later deserted, sites may have been occupied by unusually poverty-stricken sets of men, while richer sites remained in continuous occupation, or the huts may have belonged to slaves; in any case, it is hardly legitimate to use this evidence for the standard of living of the average churl in Christian times.

The Slave

The slave had no wergild. He was a chattel, and if any-one killed him, he had merely to pay his value to the owner. The usual price of a slave was a pound, the equivalent of eight oxen, and the sale of a slave took place, like that of cattle or other goods, before proper witnesses, so that the purchaser could vouch the seller to warranty if later anyone claimed that the slave had been stolen. Toll was paid on the transaction, as on any other sale; in the Rape of Lewes in the reign of Edward the Confessor the toll was fourpence. Slaves are sometimes included in inventories of stock, as, for example, 'thirteen men cap-able of work and five women and eight young men and sixteen oxen, etc.' As a slave had no property of his own in the eyes of the law, it followed that he could not be punished by fines when convicted of crime, and he was therefore liable to flogging for minor offences, and to mutilation and death for serious crimes, unless the owner were willing to redeem him by paying the fines and compensations involved. If the owner himself ill-treated or even killed his slave, he incurred ecclesiastical penalties, but it was not the concern of the law.

Christian influence worked to mitigate the lot of the slave, preaching 'We are all God's bondmen, and so he will judge us, as we judge those over whom we have authority.' Stories were told of the intervention of saints to prevent harsh treatment of slaves. The slave obtained certain rights by custom. His right to earn for himself in his free time was admitted, and Alfred's laws ordain that slaves are to be allowed the four Wednesdays in the Ember weeks in order that they may sell what has been given to them or what they have been able to earn in their leisure time. Similar injunctions are met with elsewhere, and Archbishop Wulfstan considers the disregard of these rights as one of the abuses that have brought down on his countrymen the wrath of God, in the form of the Viking invasions. There was also a fixed standard – with, of course, local variations – of what was due to a bondman for his labour. An unfree swineherd received a little pig and his chitterlings, 'and otherwise the rights which belong to bondmen.' A bondwoman was to receive as yearly provisions eight 'pounds' (i.e. the large pound, approximating to a hundredweight) of corn, a sheep, or threepence, as winter relish, a sester of beans as Lenten relish, whey, or a penny, in the summer; while a man got twelve 'pounds' of good corn, two sheep, one good cow, and the right to cut wood. Moreover 'to all bondmen belong a Christmas and an Easter food-allowance, a plough-acre and a harvest handful, in addition to their essential right.' Slaves were sometimes able to buy their freedom, which is a further indication that in practice their right to have possessions was acknowledged.

The ploughman in Ælfric's *Colloquy* describes a hard lot:

> I go out at dawn driving the oxen to the field and yoke them to the plough. It is never so harsh a winter that I dare lurk at home for fear of my master, but when the oxen have been yoked and the ploughshare and coulter fastened to the plough, I must plough each day a full acre or more. . . . I must fill the oxen's manger with hay, and water them, and clear out the dung.

To his questioner's remark 'Alas! it is heavy work,' the ploughman replies: 'Yes, it is heavy work, because I am not free.'

Slaves often ran away. The law tried to put a stop to this by harsh penalties if the runaway were caught. According to the laws of King Athelstan (924–39), he is to be stoned to death. Anyone who abetted him, even unintentionally, was to recompense the owner. The loan of a weapon to a slave was regarded as giving him a chance to get away:

> If anyone lends a sword to a man's servant, and he runs away, the lender is to pay a third (of his price). If he provides him with a spear, he is to pay half. If he lends him a horse, he is to pay the full price.

It proved particularly difficult to prevent slaves from running away to join the Danish forces during periods of Viking ravages. The two treaties which are extant between English and Danish armies, one from Alfred's reign, one from Ethelred the Unready's reign, each contain a clause stating that neither side shall receive the runaway slaves of the other. The English slave who joined the Viking forces ravaging his district might seize the opportunity to turn the tables and pay off old grudges on his former master; Wulfstan laments that 'often a thrall binds very tight the thane who was formerly his master, and makes him a slave'; or it might happen that the slave killed his former lord in a fight, and no wergild was paid to the kindred.

*

The unfree class consisted of persons of different origins. Some were the descendants of the British population, as the use of the word for 'Briton' to mean simply 'slave' testifies. The menial tasks described in some Anglo-Saxon riddles are performed by 'Britons'. Some slaves were captives taken in the wars between the different English kingdoms. Thus the Mercian captor of a Northumbrian thane sold him to a Frisian slave-merchant in London, from whom he was ransomed by the Kentish king, son of the sister of the queen whose thane the captive had once been; and there is extant an interesting letter from Archbishop Berhtwald of Canterbury to Forthere, bishop of Sherborne, written between 709 and 712, asking him to persuade an abbot of Glastonbury to release in return for a ransom of three hundred shillings a captive girl, whose relatives have asked for his mediation, 'in order that she may pass the rest of her life with her kindred, not in the sadness of servitude, but in the delights of liberty.' The *Penitential of Archbishop Theodore* shows that it was not uncommon for people to be led off into slavery, for he found it necessary to permit remarriage after a lapse of five years to the husband or wife of anyone led into captivity who could not be redeemed.

In times of great dearth, men might be reduced to the extremity of selling their children or other kin into slavery. Wulfstan writes in 1014:

Also we know full well where that miserable deed has occurred that a father has sold his son at a price, or a son his mother, or one brother another, into the power of foreigners.

They might even relinquish their own freedom in order to be fed, as a manumission states in vivid words: a woman sets free 'the men who gave her their heads to obtain food in the evil days.' But the commonest type of English slaves were the penal slaves, persons enslaved as a punishment for certain specific crimes, or because of their inability to pay the fines and compensations which they had incurred. The kindred of a slave of this kind must redeem him within a year, or they lost all subsequent right to his wergild if he were slain; after a year, his wife could marry again. The offspring born in slavery to slaves of any origin would be themselves unfree.

There was originally some doubt whether the Church ought to own penal slaves, and, though Archbishop Theodore pronounced in the seventh century that it could, the Council of Chelsea of 816 made their manumission on the death of a bishop obligatory. Other landowners than bishops give instructions in their wills that all the penal slaves on their estates are to be set free, and perhaps people were not altogether comfortable at owning slaves of their own race. Except in Kent in very early days, it was strictly forbidden to sell people of English race across the sea, or into the control of foreigners, by which phrase the heathen Danes are primarily meant; yet, in spite of the laws, a foreign slave trade persisted, and Bishop Wulfstan II of Worcester tried to put an end to it at Bristol after the Norman Conquest.

The redemption of captives and the manumitting of slaves were Christian acts of mercy much encouraged by the Church. Most surviving wills contain instructions for the freeing of some slaves, penal or otherwise, sometimes mentioning them by name, sometimes speaking in general terms, such as: 'and all my men are to be free, and each is to have his homestead and his cow and his corn for food.' Separate manumissions were entered on the flyleaves or other blank spaces of gospels and service books, and have come down to us from Bath, Bodmin, Lichfield, Bedwyn, Exeter, Durham, and St Augustine's, Canterbury. Here is a typical example:

Here it is made known in this gospel that Godwig the Buck has bought Leofgifu the dairymaid at North Stoke and her offspring from Abbot Ælfsige for half a pound, to eternal freedom, in the witness of all the community at Bath. Christ blind him who ever perverts this.

The ceremony often took place at the altar, but it might instead be performed at cross-roads, to symbolize the freedom of the manumitted slave henceforward to choose his or her own path; for example:

Eadgifu freed Wulfric at the cross-roads, three weeks before midsummer, in the witness of Brihtstan the priest and of Cynestan and of the cleric who wrote this.

The essential thing was that the act should be done before adequate witnesses, who would prevent its infringement if any person were bold enough to attempt this in defiance of the ecclesiastical anathema with which most manumissions are provided. A particularly interesting manumission is one performed by King Athelstan, probably on the day of his coronation, which runs:

King Athelstan freed Eadelm immediately after he first was king. Ælfheah the priest and the community, Ælfric the reeve, Wulfnoth the White, Eanstan the prior, and Byrnstan the priest were witness of this. He who perverts this – may he have the disfavour of God and of all the relics which I, by God's mercy, have obtained in England. And I grant the children the same that I grant the father.

The manumitter retained certain rights over the man he had freed. He had the inheritance after him, and his wergild if he were killed. This was a necessary protection for the freedman, for it might easily happen that he had no free kinsmen and therefore no one to exact compensation if he were injured or slain. It was his former owner's duty to claim the compensation, otherwise the freedman could have been molested with impunity. It is an application of the same principle that makes the king the receiver of the wergild of a foreigner, who, like the freedman, will be unlikely to have kinsmen in the land to act for him. Manumission does not, therefore, put a man at once exactly on the level of a man who is freeborn, and it may be that the term half-free which is occasionally met with in our records was applied to manumitted slaves.

CHAPTER VI

TRADE AND TOWN LIFE

Trade

TRADE did not play a very large part in the activities of the early English communities, for these were to a considerable extent self-sufficing for the necessities of life; yet from the beginning most settlements had to import two very important commodities, salt and metals, the former necessary for preserving meat and fish for winter consumption, the latter essential for the tools with which a livelihood was obtained. Salt was obtained from saltpans in coastal areas, and from the salt districts of Worcestershire and Cheshire as soon as the English invaders pressed so far west. Express mention of saltpans as an important adjunct of an estate occurs fairly early in charters; for example, King Cynewulf of Wessex gave one at Lyme Regis in 774 to the bishop of Sherborne, mentioning the need of salt for ritual uses as well as for the seasoning of food; already in 716–7 King Æthelbald granted to the church of Worcester 'a portion of land on which salt is wont to be produced, at the south side of the river which is called Salwarp . . . for the construction of three salt-houses and six furnaces', in exchange for 'six other furnaces in two salthouses in which likewise salt is made, namely on the north side of the said river.' Domesday Book allows us to see something of the organization of the salt industry by the latter part of the Saxon period. It mentions 285 saltpans in Sussex alone. The chief salt town of England, Droitwich, appears as a very specialized community, in which, while the majority of the saltpans belonged to the king or the earl, many other persons had interests; the estates of lay landowners, even as far afield as Oxfordshire and Buckinghamshire, sometimes have saltpans in Droitwich attached to them, and others are possessed by the churches of Westminster, Coventry, St Peter of Gloucester, St Guthlac of Hereford, and St Denis of Paris, besides the nearer churches, Worcester and Pershore. A fuller and more interesting account is given of the industry in Cheshire, for we learn not only of the ownership of the salthouses, but also details relating to tolls, etc. Thus it is stated that if the earl sold any of the salt from one salthouse which supplied his manor of Acton all the year round, two-thirds of the toll went to the king, one-third to himself, whereas other owners had their salt for their own consumption free of toll only from Ascension Day to Martinmas. The rate of payment varied a little from place to place, but was normally fourpence on a cart drawn by four oxen, twopence on a horse-load, or on eight men's loads. There were preferential rates for those dwelling within the hundred or in the county, and we get a glimpse of the salt pedlars: men from the same hundred, who carried salt about the country to sell it, had to pay a penny for each cart; if, however, they carried it on a horse, they paid a penny at Martinmas. Landowners who possessed saltpans of their own were a minority; most people must have been dependent on pedlars such as these for their supplies.

Iron-working was carried on on a small scale at various places, in Kent, Sussex, Northamptonshire, Lincolnshire, Yorkshire, etc., and it was an important industry in the forest of Dean, with the result that estates in Gloucestershire and Somerset often pay part of the king's farm and of their rents in blooms of iron. In this form, iron was traded over the country, to be made into ploughshares, fishhooks, and tools of all kinds by local smiths, but probably from very early times there was specialization in the production of the finer goods of the weaponsmith, so that ornamented helmets, coats-of-mail, and inlaid swords would be obtained by trade, for only the wealthiest of magnates could employ workmen of such expert skill. The ordinary local smith could no doubt supply the plain spear-heads and simple shield rims and bosses required by the common man. As we have seen, specialist craftsmen were employed by the king and great nobles; it was natural also that they should be found in places where there were markets and a general concourse of people. There were eight smiths at Glastonbury in the Confessor's reign, and six at Hereford, each of whom made annually for the king a hundred and twenty horseshoes; Gloucester supplied the iron for the rivets of the king's ships.

The most important source for the supply of lead was Derbyshire. Thus in 835 Wirksworth was rendering annually to the archbishop of Canterbury lead to the value of 300 shillings, and in the reign of Edward the Confessor a group of royal manors in the county included in their farm five cartloads of lead, consisting of fifty slabs. Building-stone was another article of commerce after it became customary to build in this material, but our records reveal little about methods of quarrying and distributing it. As far as possible material of such weight would be conveyed by water, and it was thus that the brothers of Ely set out to fetch stone for St Audrey's coffin; they did not, however, seek a quarry, but found what they wanted in the deserted Roman site of Cambridge. Only sporadic mention is made of quarries, as, for example, four quarries, one for millstones, in Sussex with annual values from ten and tenpence to four shillings.

*

One must not exaggerate the self-sufficiency of the individual settlements even with regard to foodstuffs and
clothing materials. It cannot have been long before
certain well-placed communities found themselves able
to produce supplies of this or that commodity in excess
of their own needs, and to trade their surplus for necessities in which they were less supplied, or even for luxury
goods. Instances that leap to one's mind are the dairy
produce, especially cheese, of the Vale of the White
Horse, and the manufacture of sheep-milk cheese in the
Essex marshlands; here and in many other sheep-farming
areas the yield of wool would be more than could be used
up at home.

Very frequent references can be found to the importance of fisheries in the assessment of the value of an
estate, and in many cases the yield is far too great for
home consumption. The rent from the sea fisheries along
the coasts is normally expressed in herrings; Southease,
Sussex, rendered 38,500, and Dunwich, Suffolk, 60,000.
Eels were the most important product of inland
fisheries and were caught in great numbers, especially in
the fenlands; at Wisbech alone seventeen fishermen paid
a rent of 59,260 eels. It is less common to find mention of
other kinds of fish, but a fishery belonging to Earl Edwin
at Eaton by Chester paid a thousand salmon, Petersham,
Surrey, paid a thousand lampreys as well as the same
number of eels, and Southease paid four pounds 'for
porpoises'. Ælfric is probably describing contemporary
conditions when he lets his fisherman say that he sells his
catch in the towns and cannot catch as many as he could
sell.

There is evidence as far back as heathen times of some
trade in luxury articles. Archaeology shows that elaborate jewellery from Kent, glassware from the Rhineland,
silver vessels from as far afield as the eastern Mediter-

ranean, found their way gradually into the houses of Anglo-Saxon royal and noble families. Wine was imported also, though it may not have flowed so freely in real life as it appears to do in poetic descriptions of life in royal halls. It was one of the products brought by merchants from Rouen at the end of the tenth century, and in the eleventh an estate of Hyde Abbey was paying as a yearly rent six sesters of wine. It occurs also in the list of imports given by the merchant in Ælfric's *Colloquy*, which runs: 'Purple robes and silk, precious stones and gold, rare apparel and spices, wine and oil, ivory and brass, copper and tin, sulphur and glass, and many such things.' Furs were imported also, and at Chester the king's reeve had a right of pre-emption on any marten pelts brought into the port. A document relating to London in the reign of Ethelred the Unready mentions incidentally the following goods brought in at this port: timber, fish, wine, and blubberfish; it is not said that the first two items came from abroad.

Less can be said about exports; English cloaks are the subject of correspondence between Charles the Great and Offa; wool, cloth, and cheese are mentioned as exports, and the code of about 1000 which deals with the trade of London allowed foreign traders to buy in London wool and fat, besides three live pigs for their ships. They could buy the wool only after it had been unloaded, which I presume to be a regulation to force them to buy from the Londoners, instead of buying the whole cargo direct from a ship bringing it to the city. But the earliest commodity to be mentioned as an export from England is slaves – not necessarily because it was the most important, but because it evoked most interest for other than commercial reasons. In the late sixth century Pope Gregory assumed that boys of English race could be bought in Gaul, and gave instructions for their purchase, that they might be reared in the Christian faith and help to convert their countrymen; Bede and his contemporaries thought it likely that English slaves should be sold in a Roman market in the sixth century; about 679 a Mercian nobleman sold to a Frisian merchant in London a Northumbrian prisoner of war. As late as the eleventh century, an Anglo-Danish great lady was trading English girls to Denmark, according to an accusation levied by William of Malmesbury. We have already seen that attempts to put an end to the overseas traffic in slaves were unavailing, and that it was being carried on at Bristol in the latter part of the eleventh century.

Merovingian coins are found in English deposits of the seventh century, and late in this century coins were struck in England. A few early Kentish coins are in gold, but gold coins are rare in Anglo-Saxon times. Early silver coins, which numismatists call *sceattas*, have no certain king's name, for it is no longer held that a few with PADA or EPA in runes can be assigned to Penda of Mercia or Eorpwold of East Anglia. About 775 two obscure Kentish kings began to issue larger, thinner coins, which numismatists call pennies, on a Frankish model, and from about 785, when Offa of Mercia took over the Canterbury mint, pennies of such excellent workmanship and design were issued in his name that some were imitated on the Continent. In his reign a few pieces have the name and portrait of his wife, Cynethryth, and archbishops of Canterbury begin to issue coins. So do East Anglian kings, and Offa's son-in-law Beorhtric of Wessex, though his successor, Egbert, did not follow his example until after his conquest of Kent in 825. Meanwhile Mercian kings used mints at Rochester and probably at London, while a copper coinage, known as *stycas*, was begun in Northumbria about 830, to be superseded by silver pennies after the Scandinavian settlements.

The good relations between mid-ninth-century kings of Mercia and Wessex are shown by their combining to issue coins, especially when Alfred and Ceolwulf II (whom the Danes allowed to rule in Mercia from 874) each issued a coin with the same reverse. Alfred had coins minted at London when he occupied it in 886. In the reigns of his son and grandsons, as they became rulers of all England, more and more mints were opened all over the country. Towards the end of Edgar's reign (959–75) a great reform produced a type of penny which was to be standard over all England, with dies supplied from one centre, and designs changed at fixed intervals, at first probably of six, then of three years. Current money would then have to be exchanged for the new issue. From this time there were a great number of mints. In its main features this system remained unchanged throughout Saxon times, and it was taken over by the Normans.

*

Trade was certainly not inconsiderable by the eighth century, as can be seen by the care with which kings guarded their rights to receive tolls. The remission of the toll on a single ship for the benefit of a religious house was a matter of enough moment to call forth a royal charter. Æthelbald of Mercia was addicted to gifts of this kind, and charters of his survive which remit the dues on ships at London for the abbess of Minster and the bishops of Rochester, Worcester, and London. Eadberht of Kent freed a ship at Fordwich for the abbot of Reculver and ships at Sarre and Fordwich for the abbess of Minster. In some of these documents it is specified that if the ship is lost or wrecked, it can be replaced by another on the same terms. References in general terms to the payment of toll, or to grant of the right by the king to private persons, are common throughout the period, but it is mainly in Domesday Book that we are given details. It is there that we learn that in the Confessor's time the ferries across the Humber at South Ferriby and Barton-on-Humber were valued at three pounds and four pounds a year respectively; that at Lewes both buyer and seller paid a penny on a horse, and the toll on an ox was a halfpenny, on a man fourpence; that at Southwark no one had any right to toll on the strand or in the water-street except the king. His rights here were valued at £16, but this figure included fines paid by those who committed a crime in these places.

Kings issue trade regulations of various kinds. They may interfere to forbid the export of certain goods, as when King Athelstan forbids the export of horses and various kings prohibit the sale of men across the sea; they establish prices – a wey of wool is not to be sold at more than 120 pence according to Edgar's law; the same code standardizes weights and measures 'as one observes in London and Winchester'; a careful supervision of the mints is maintained; the Church's veto of trading on Sundays and certain festivals is enforced by the secular authorities. Precautions at the ports were necessary to prevent the entry of hostile ships; we know something of the arrangements at Chester, where a ship must await a licence to enter. If a ship arrived or departed without the king's permission, each man on board was liable to a fine of forty shillings to the king and the earl; the ship, crew, and cargo were confiscated if the ship came in in spite of a royal prohibition. But most of all, laws are concerned to see that all trading takes place before proper witnesses, so as to make the sale of stolen goods difficult. Ine's laws, about 700, state the necessity of witnesses, and in the early tenth century Edward the Elder tries to insist that all trading must take place in a town; this innovation was not kept up, but his grandson Edgar enjoined the appointment of a standing body of witnesses in every borough and every hundred, before whom all purchases were to be made.

There was also another problem to be dealt with, namely the possibility of misdemeanours and offences by or against traders as they moved about the country. They must not behave in a suspicious fashion; thus the laws both of Wihtred of Kent and Ine of Wessex contain, by what must have been an agreement between the kingdoms, the clause:

> If a man from a distance, or a stranger, journey away from a road, and he then neither shouts nor blows a horn, he is to be assumed to be a thief, to be either slain or redeemed.

An earlier Kentish law made a man who entertained a trader or other stranger more than three days responsible for any injury he might commit, and later King Alfred enjoined that every trader was to bring the men he was taking into the country before the king's reeve at a public meeting, and was to take only such men as he could bring to justice if necessary. Precautions were particularly necessary if trade was to be carried on between men of different kingdoms or different nationalities; already the early laws of Kent protect the Kentishman buying in London, and Alfred's treaty with Guthrum stipulates that hostages must be given as security for peaceful dealings and honest intentions before trading takes place between English and Danes. Similar regulations were necessary for traffic between the English and the Welsh.

Finally, kings might interest themselves in the conditions of trading across the sea. Offa entered into an agreement with Charles the Great by which each undertook to protect the traders of the other country when within their realm, and again, in the eleventh century, Cnut on a pilgrimage to Rome took the opportunity of obtaining from the Emperor and other rulers he met there greater security and reduction of tolls for his subjects, traders and others, travelling in their lands. These instances show that foreign trade was not exclusively in the hands of the foreign traders, and there is other evidence in the same direction. Already in the eighth century an English merchant called Botta was settled at Marseilles, perhaps as an agent for collecting goods to be sold in England. The Viking raids of the late eighth and the ninth centuries disrupted trade on the Continent, but Englishmen may well have taken part in the Baltic trade opened up about this time. At least, there is no reason to deny English nationality to a certain Wulfstan who described to King Alfred a journey taken to the Frisches Haff; he has an English name. In the late tenth century, Ælfric remarks casually that English merchants go to Rome, and Sir Frank Stenton has noted that King Ethelred's treaty with the Danes assumes that English ships will be met with in foreign harbours.

On the other hand, we hear of foreign traders in England from early times. Bede speaks of London as 'the mart of many nations, resorting to it by sea and land', and mentions the purchase of a captive by a Frisian merchant in London. The existence of a Frisian community at York in the eighth century is indicated in the life of a Frisian saint, and at the end of the ninth century Alfred's fleet was partly manned by men of this race. But perhaps the strongest evidence for the amount of sea-traffic in Frisian hands is the assumption of an Anglo-Saxon poet that a seaman is likely to have a Frisian wife:

Dear is the welcome guest to the Frisian woman when the ship comes to land. His ship is come and her husband, her own bread-winner, is at home, and she invites him in, washes his stained raiment and gives him new clothes, grants him on land what his love demands.

Men from other lands came also. At the end of the tenth century a document dealing with trade in London speaks of men from Rouen, Flanders, Ponthieu, Normandy, France, Huy, Liège, Nivelles, and the territories of the Emperor; from about the same date comes a description of York as the resort of merchants from all quarters, especially Danes. Irish traders visited Cambridge about this time. We learn of this because a certain priest called Leofstan stole a cloak from them; the incidental nature of this reference should serve as a reminder of how piece-meal and fragmentary our evidence is on this subject as on many others. Nevertheless, the bulk of the internal trade in England was probably in English hands. It will be enough to illustrate this by reference to the freedom from toll over all England claimed by the men of Dover, or to the incident in 969 when King Edgar took venge-ance on the men of Thanet for ill-treating some York merchants.

The merchant and seaman plied an honoured trade. The poets speak with appreciation of the seaman 'who can boldly drive the ship across the salt sea' or 'can steer the stem on the dark wave, knows the currents, (being) the pilot of the company over the wide ocean', and it was at least a current opinion in the early eleventh century that the merchant who had crossed the sea three times at his own cost should be entitled to a thane's rank. The merchant in Ælfric's *Colloquy* stresses the dangers of his lot:

I go on board my ship with my freight and row over the regions of the sea, and sell my goods and buy precious things which are not produced in this land, and I bring it hither to you with great danger over the sea, and sometimes I suffer ship-wreck with the loss of all my goods, barely escaping with my life.

Towns

The places first mentioned as centres of trade had been
towns in the Roman period. Whether or not there was
unbroken continuity at such places, it was natural that
population should begin to congregate at places con-
veniently situated for meeting-places, and, throughout
the Saxon period and beyond it, new towns spring up on
harbours, navigable rivers, at the junction of important
roads, or where such roads crossed the greater rivers. For
example, at the date of Domesday Book, a Berkshire
place called *Ulvritone* is said to have 51 'haws' (town-
houses), and it was doubtless this circumstance that
caused its old name to be ousted by Newbury, 'the new
borough', recorded from about 1080. Or some more accidental circumstance, such as the requirements of an important royal estate, as at Reading, Windsor, or Bedwyn,
or of a large monastery, might cause the congregation of a
group of tradesmen and artisans. By 1066 there were 46
burgesses at St Albans, 28 at Pershore, while the population of Barton near Abingdon included ten tradesmen
dwelling in front of the door of the church. Many
other monasteries had towns springing up around them.

Many of the places which are ancient boroughs by the
time of Domesday Book may have started from similar
small beginnings in a distant past, for which our evidence
is woefully scanty. What there is relates mainly to Kent,
and Sir Frank Stenton has shown that there was town-
life at Rochester and Canterbury by the ninth century.
London was an important trading centre already in
Bede's time; while it was still under the kings of Essex,
the Kentish kings possessed a hall in it; in 857 a bishop of
Worcester obtained a house there, not far from the west
gate, with certain commercial rights, and a later bishop

carried out a similar transaction in 889. It is not likely that
this church was the only distant landowner to find it
convenient to secure a footing in this city. There is also
early evidence for a trading community at York and
there were doubtless a number of other places that were
something more than agricultural settlements in the
period before the Viking invasions.

To combat these invasions, King Alfred inaugurated
his 'burghal system', i.e. the provision of fortified centres
that could protect a tract of country against enemy attack, a policy continued under his son Edward, from
whose reign comes a document known as the *Burghal
Hidage*, which gives the names of the boroughs thus
formed in the area under West Saxon rule. Some of the
boroughs were places which already had some concen-
tration of population and were now supplied with new
or improved defences; others, as we are expressly told
by Asser, were new, that is were founded at places of little
previous importance. Oxford and Wallingford, each
founded on eight yardlands of land, seem to belong to
this class, and the account in Domesday Book suggests
that population had been attracted to them by favourable conditions of tenure. In any case, the security
afforded by the new defences of the boroughs would draw
traders and craftsmen.

Although by the end of the Saxon period other persons
might own property and rights in the boroughs, in
general the burgesses held their tenements at a fixed rent
from the king, who also had other 'customs', the details
of which varied from place to place. The profits arising
from the jurisdiction in the borough were usually divided
between the king and the earl, two-thirds to the king and
one-third to the earl; but there is not complete uniformity, for the king seems to have retained the whole at
some places, for example in the Wiltshire and Somerset

boroughs, whereas at others he granted some of his rights away: two-thirds of the profits of Fordwich went to the abbey of St Augustine's, the bishop had a third of those at Worcester, the archbishop had all the king's dues in one ward at York. Moreover in most boroughs there were owners who possessed the profits of jurisdiction arising from offences committed on their property or by their men. If there ever was any simple or uniform plan it has been complicated by many private arrangements before the period for which any considerable information is available.

The process by which many landowners acquired property and interests in the boroughs is mainly hidden from our sight. As we have seen, bishops of Worcester were acquiring houses in London at an early date. From the tenth century we get many references to country estates which included among their appurtenances one or more properties, called 'haws', in a neighbouring borough. For example a lease of an estate at Kilmiston, Hampshire, in 961, includes 'the haw in the *port* (market-town) inside the south wall, which belongs to that estate', and similar statements become increasingly common. An eleventh-century bishop of East Anglia disposes by will of a haw in Norwich and another in London. It is no longer usual to connect the ownership of such town-houses by country landowners with the duty of garrisoning and repairing the borough, laid on the shire. They are always spoken of as sources of profit to their owners. It would obviously be convenient for a landowner to possess a house in a trading centre nearby, and the thanes of North Berkshire tend to possess houses in Oxford, while those of South Oxfordshire regard Wallingford as their centre, thus cutting across the shire system. Many Surrey estates are connected with Southwark, not with Guildford the county-town. But it is obvious that the convenience of

a town-house for obtaining supplies for the estates, or as
a residence during visits to town, will not explain the
number of cases when we find a landowner in possession
of a great number of houses in a borough. To take a few
by no means extreme instances, the archbishop of Canterbury could not have required six houses in Wallingford,
or the bishop of Chester fourteen in Stafford, or the
abbess of Barking twenty-eight in London, and it cannot
have required ten houses in Bristol to supply the manor
of a certain Ælfgar in Bishopsworth. It can hardly be
questioned that some landowners have been investing in
house-property in the boroughs. A document of 975-8
suggests that land in Winchester had become expensive,
for the community at the Old Minster was content to
relinquish a country estate of twelve hides which they
were holding at an annual food-rent, in order to obtain
a plot of only two acres, with the stream adjacent to it,
in the city.

According to Tait, there are seventy-one boroughs in
Domesday Book, apart from those that had grown up on
royal estates, or on those of ecclesiastical or secular lords.
It is not easy to estimate the size and population of any
of these places, and two of the most important, London
and Winchester, as well as some others such as Bristol,
Tamworth, Hastings, Romney, Hythe, are not surveyed
in this record. A law of King Edgar (959-75) made a
rough division of boroughs into two classes; large, which
must have a body of thirty-six standing witnesses, and
small, with only twelve; King Ethelred, probably between
991 and 1002, divided 'ports', that is trading places, into
'principal', to which he allows three moneyers, and
'others' which are to have only one. The greatest places
must lie outside this division, for both before and after
they have many more moneyers than this, working at the
same time. King Athelstan (924-39) had allowed eight

to London, seven to Canterbury, six to Winchester, but towards the end of the Saxon period there were over twenty at London and more than ten at York. The evidence of existing coins and of Domesday Book establishes as front-rank boroughs London, York, and Winchester, Lincoln, Chester, Canterbury, Oxford, Hereford, Thetford, Gloucester, Worcester, Norwich, and Ipswich. Domesday does not state the population, but only the number of burgage tenements, and it is uncertain how many persons inhabited each. The figure five usually taken as a basis for calculating the population is almost certainly too low; it gives not much over eight thousand to York, and though a writer about 1000 may be greatly exaggerating when he says York had a population of thirty thousand adults, would he be quite so wildly out as that? Even retaining this conservative estimate of 5 persons to a tenement, Norwich had a population of 6,600 persons in 1066, Thetford of nearly five thousand; Lincoln seems about the same size as Norwich. All other boroughs are smaller, except, of course, London and Winchester, for which there are no figures.

*

The boroughs and towns possessed arable fields, common pastures, and meadows, but not in a quantity to make them to any degree self-sufficing communities, nor must it be supposed that each burgess cultivated his share; in some places the arable was let out to a few individuals. The majority of the population must have depended for food and other supplies on the produce brought from outside to their markets. One remembers Ælfric's fisherman, who sold his catch in the towns, and we hear also of women who sold butter and cheese in London and of boat-loads of fish, hampers of eggs and of hens, brought to the London market; one of the earliest recorded street-names is that of the vendors of meat. Nevertheless the average Anglo-Saxon town probably presented a some-what rural aspect; there were crofts and gardens within and around the walls, and many citizens possessed cattle which they pastured on the common of the town. There were also several corn mills inside the towns; fourteen are mentioned in the Domesday record of Derby, and the tenth-century boundaries of a small site in Winchester include the west mill, the east mill, and the old mill.

One of the features of a town of the later Saxon period that would have struck a modern observer was the very great number of churches in proportion to the size of the place. Our evidence is incomplete, for Domesday Book mentions them only incidentally; yet we know of about twenty in Norwich and over a dozen in Lincoln. Eight besides the minster are clearly referred to in the Domes-day survey of York, and Derby had at least six. A comparatively small place like Wallingford had three churches of sufficient antiquity for them to be mentioned in the early twelfth century in a charter purporting to come from 948, and five churches at Oxford occur in Domesday. The churches were probably not the only stone-built buildings in the towns in the later period. Royal residences were being built in stone already in Alfred's time, and this material would be most likely to be used for them in towns, where the risk of fire was great. The king's hall is referred to in many towns, and some-times there were halls of other great personages; Queen Emma had one in Winchester, and the Confessor's queen, Edith, in Stamford, Toki, son of Outi, in Lincoln, Thurbert in Colchester, Earl Godwine in Southwark. The majority of the houses were, however, still built of wood, and hence the laws were strict about the responsi-bility for fire. At Chester the man in whose house it started had to pay three ounces of pence, and two shillings to his nearest neighbour.

Mention has been made in an earlier chapter of the voluntary associations, the gilds, into which men were forming themselves in the later Saxon period; a 'knights' gild' at Canterbury occurs as early as the mid ninth century, though it is uncertain what was meant by a knight at that time; it may already have borne its late Old English meaning of an armed retainer of a lord. London had a 'knight's gild' by the eleventh century. Gilds are mentioned at Canterbury and Dover in Domesday Book, and in the reign of Edward the Confessor, according to a survey drawn up in Henry I's reign, there were two 'knights' halls' in Winchester, of one of which we are told that it was 'where they drank their gild and they held it freely under King Edward.' Other Winchester evidence speaks of a chapmen's hall, and later we hear of a hall 'where the good men of Winchester drank their gild.' At a much earlier date, in the reign of Athelstan (924–39), there is a document concerning a 'peace-gild' of the London district, which under the presidency of the bishops and reeves of the area is active for the suppression of theft. Besides its police duties, it has both religious and secular obligations to its members, and it has a somewhat elaborate organization and a common purse. Its officials meet once a month, usually when the butts are being filled, and have their meal together, 'and they shall feed themselves as they themselves think fitting' – an early instance of a civic banquet. The size of London made its organization peculiar; it was divided into wards, each with a ward-moot presided over by an ealdorman, and had a meeting called a husting for settling its civil cases as well as a great open-air folk-moot for maintaining order. Some other towns were divided into wards, but there is no evidence that any had more than one form of assembly, the borough-moot that according to a law of King Edgar was to meet three times a year. The boroughs were under a royal official usually called a port-reeve, and in some of the bigger places, like London and Winchester, there were more than one at a time.

When all is said, it must be admitted that we have inadequate evidence to form a clear picture of how life was lived in an Anglo-Saxon town, but it is worth looking at the so-called Winton Domesday, the text which supplied information about the gilds mentioned above, and which helps to make up for the omission of this city from Domesday Book. In the reign of the Confessor Winchester has a *balchus* of the king where thieves lay in prison. Not only the holders of houses are recorded, but also those who had stalls and shops, some of which had belonged to Queen Edith, and a storehouse which was rented by a reeve from King Edward. The burgesses also possessed storehouses which had since been turned into forges. Among the householders of the town at that time were several priests; a number of moneyers held houses, including a master moneyer, and so did a goldsmith, a shoemaker, a park-keeper, a 'brand-wright', a hosier, a turner, a soap-maker, and some beadles. More than one reeve of Winchester is mentioned. But most of the names occur without any occupations attached. Street-names include tanners' street, shoemakers' street, flesh-mongers' street, and shield-makers' street, showing the tendency of men of the same trade to congregate together. Many of the persons were distinguished by nick-names, which show that the citizens of Winchester were fertile in invention; they include names meaning Clean-hand, Bit-cat, Fresh-friend, Soft-bread, Foul-beard, Money-taker, Penny-purse, and Penny-feather.

CHAPTER VII

THE LAW

THE English tribes came over from their continental homes already possessing an elaborate and developed legal system, whose basic principles were shared by other Germanic nations, though in the course of time modifications made in the various systems caused them to move apart. In England the Christian influence to which the law was exposed from the end of the sixth century caused some alteration, especially in relation to family law, but it left the structure unchanged.

It was owing to the influence of the Church that the law began to be put in writing. The first Christian English king, Ethelbert of Kent, 'established, with the advice of his councillors, judicial decisions, after the Roman model; which are written in the language of the English, and are still kept and observed by them.' What brought this about in the first place was the necessity to add to existing law injunctions relating to the Church. These laws survive, and they begin: 'God's property and the Church's – twelve-fold payment', i.e. what is stolen must be repaid at twelve times its value. They continue, however, to deal with secular matters, among other things putting on record the tariff of compensations to be paid for all types of bodily injury.

After this other kings promulgated laws, when there was occasion either to add new statutes or modify existing ones, or to re-state old law that was being disregarded. Ethelbert's seventh-century successors in Kent issued codes, and so did Ine of Wessex (688–726), probably inspired by his contemporary, Wihtred of Kent. The laws of Offa (757–96), the greatest of Mercian kings, were known to King Alfred, but have not come down to us. Alfred himself issued a long code, with the laws of Ine as an appendix to it, and after his day most of his successors issued codes.

Yet, although the surviving body of written law fills a formidable volume, Anglo-Saxon law was never codified in full in pre-Conquest times. In addition to the enactments of kings we possess a few short private treatises on individual subjects, but a great mass of customary law was handed on orally, and no attempt seems to have been made to codify it until the days of the Norman legists, when much was forgotten or misunderstood. There is no evidence that the English possessed, as did the Scandinavian races, an official law-speaker, whose business it was to keep alive the knowledge of the law by reciting it at public gatherings at regular intervals, but it is worth noting that a poem known as *The Gifts of Men* enumerates among the men whom an all-wise Deity endows with special faculties one who 'knows the laws, when men deliberate' as well as one who 'can in the assembly of wise men determine the custom of the people.' In later times, this expert knowledge was sometimes possessed by the clergy. The aged Æthelric, formerly bishop of Selsey, was brought to the judicial enquiry at Penenden Heath in 1075–6 to answer questions on Anglo-Saxon law, and as late as the reign of William II we find the king recommending that a certain priest called Ælfwig should continue to hold the living of Sutton Courtenay, which he now granted to Abingdon, because he was learned in the law. Something is added to our knowledge of Anglo-Saxon law in the working by the survival of records of law-suits, generally relating to land, and by occasional references in literary sources, and finally, by many statements in Domesday Book on the customs in force in the reign of Edward the Confessor.

These sources reveal variety of custom in various areas. The Norman lawyers recognized three great divisions of Anglo-Saxon law, the law of Wessex, the law of Mercia, and the Danelaw, that is, the law current in those parts of the country ceded to the Danes at the end of the ninth century, including not only Northumbria and East Anglia and the area of the Danish Five Boroughs of Lincoln, Stamford, Nottingham, Derby, and Leicester, but also Northamptonshire, Rutland, Huntingdonshire, Cambridgeshire, Bedfordshire, Hertfordshire, Buckinghamshire, Middlesex, and Essex. When the English kings brought this area back under their rule, they did not greatly interfere with its legal customs. King Edgar states expressly:

Moreover it is my will that among the Danes such good laws shall be valid as they best appoint; and I always conceded this to them and will concede it as long as my life lasts, on account of your loyalty, which you have always shown to me.

He insists strongly on this right to local differences in general, while imposing a universal measure aimed at the suppression of theft. Some differences between Wessex and that part of Mercia that was never under Danish rule are of older origin, dating from the days when they were separate kingdoms. This threefold division, however, by no means covers all the varieties of local custom revealed in our sources, and we have already noted in previous chapters some instances where the general injunctions laid down in the laws have been modified in individual areas as each of these made special and separate terms with the king.

The king legislates with the advice of his council – in fact, some enactments seem to have gone out in the name of the latter alone. The measures agreed on were put into final form by one of the ecclesiastical members present. In the reigns of Ethelred and Cnut it was Archbishop

Wulfstan of York who framed most of the enactments. Copies were sent to the ealdormen in charge of the various provinces, as is stated at the conclusion of one of Edgar's codes:

Many copies of this are to be written and sent both to the Ealdorman Ælfhere (of Mercia) and Ealdorman Æthelwine (of East Anglia), and they are to send them in all directions, so that this measure be known both to the poor and the rich.

The duty of the Northumbrian earl had been mentioned in a previous chapter of the code. Copies would also be sent to the greater ecclesiastics; the bishop of the diocese, who presided beside the ealdorman at the shire-moot, to deal with cases in which the interests of the Church were involved, would need to keep himself informed of any developments in the law. It is to the Church that we owe the preservation of the laws; the official law-books of the administration have not survived, and our knowledge of Anglo-Saxon law would be poor indeed but for the preservation of the archives of the cathedrals of Rochester, London, and Worcester.

*

Law-suits were brought forward in a public assembly which the early laws call vaguely a folk-moot. There is no suggestion in King Alfred's laws that there was any higher court than this, and an appeal from it was made direct to the king. In the tenth century there appears to have been a reorganization by which the land was divided into areas called 'hundreds' (except in the northern Danish counties, where the term used is 'wapen-take'), which had a court that met every four weeks, while above this there was a shire-moot, which met twice a year. A law of Cnut's suggests that appeal can be made from the hundred to the shire, for it forbids recourse to self-help until justice has been refused three times in the hundred and once in the shire. The division into hundreds has a recent and artificial look in the Midlands, for the areas there are often neatly assessed at just one hundred hides; in the South, however, there is little sign of such neat assessment, which suggests either that the name was given to areas that had never consisted of a hundred hides, or that the division was of a much older date, so that any original correspondence between the name and the assessment has been obliterated. Just how far the organization into hundreds altered pre-existing conditions it is difficult to say. There is evidence that the folk-moots met under the presidency of a king's reeve every four weeks long before any mention is made of the term hundred in this connexion. The hundreds themselves often bear names of an early form, and met at places whose names suggest that they have been places of assembly from early times, occasionally, as at Wye, Kent, which means 'sanctuary' or Thurstable, Essex, i.e. 'Thunor's pillar', even from heathen days. The later hundred seems to have taken over the meeting-place as well as the function of the earlier popular assembly. The tenth-century reorganization may mainly have aimed at securing regularity and uniformity over the country. The meetings took place in the open, often at some prominent landmark that gave its name to the hundred; barrows served this purpose at Babergh, Suffolk, Ploughley and *Cheneward'berge*, Oxfordshire; trees or stones at Appletree, Derbyshire, Staine, Cambridgeshire, Stone, Somerset and Buckinghamshire, Maidstone, Kent, etc. The activities of the courts are sometimes mirrored in the names, words meaning 'hill of assembly' as at Modbury, Dorset, or 'hill of speech' as at Spellow, Norfolk, Spelhoe, Northamptonshire, being fairly common.

Besides the hundred and the shire courts, references

occur from the tenth century onwards to a borough court which met three times a year. All these assemblies were held for other purposes besides the trial of suits. It was at them the king made known by messenger or writ his will to his people, and many transactions for which it was desirable, or legally essential, to have adequate witnesses were carried out there.

From early times kings were in the habit of granting to private landowners, lay or ecclesiastical, the profits of jurisdiction over their own lands or over their own men, and sometimes over wider areas. This is so already at the date of King Ine's laws. Such a grant came eventually to include the right to hold a private court in the area covered by this immunity. Sir Frank Stenton has pointed out that the existence of some sort of court of this kind is implicit in the terminology of certain ninth-century charters. It may underlie a regulation of King Athelstan (924–39), in which the statement of the penalties incurred by a reeve who takes bribes and allows them to influence his judgement is immediately followed by a chapter beginning: 'If it is a thane who does this.' Moreover, the judge, who according to the laws of Edgar (959–75) is to lose his 'thaneship' if he gives a false judgement is probably to be taken as the holder of a private court; for, if a royal official were all that was meant, one would have expected him to lose his office rather than his thaneship. Several serious offences, such as breach of the peace given by the king's own hand, the harbouring of outlaws, forcible entry into a house, violent obstruction of royal officials when discharging their duty, were almost always reserved for the king's courts when grants of private jurisdiction were made.

*

The procedure in law-suits was strictly formal, and any departure from the common form might cause the loss of a suit. The plaintiff summoned the defendant to appear to answer his charge, and if the defendant failed to appear, after a due number of lawfully given summonses, adequately witnessed, he lost his suit by default; if he, or his kindred for him, did not then pay the fines and compensations involved, he became an outlaw. Henceforward he bore 'a wolf's head', that is to say, anyone could kill him with impunity, and anyone who harboured him, or, worse still, took vengeance for his slaying, became liable to very heavy penalties. The outlaw could recover his rights only by the king's pardon.

If the defendant appeared in court to answer the charge, it was normal for the plaintiff to make a preliminary oath, to prove the honesty of his motives, that he was not acting out of 'hatred or malice or wrongful covetousness.' In most cases the defendant was then allowed to bring forward an oath to prove his innocence, for the law clung to the principle 'denial is always stronger than accusation.' He would do this with the aid of compurgators, or oath-helpers, whose number was conditioned by the nature and severity of the charge involved, and he was allowed a respite, often of thirty days, to get them together, after he had pledged himself to produce the oath. They were not required to supply information of the facts of the case at issue. The defendant swore: 'By the Lord, I am guiltless both of deed and instigation of the crime with which N charges me,' and the compurgators simply swore in support of this: 'By the Lord, the oath is pure and not false which M swore.' In early law, the number of compurgators required for a given charge is somewhat obscurely expressed as 'an oath of so many hides of land', which shows that something like a modern property qualification came into consideration. We are told that a king's 'companion', if a communicant, could swear for sixty hides, and there is evidence that suggests that a churl could swear for five. Sometimes, however, the size of the oath is expressed in terms of money, e.g. 'an oath of a pound in value' and it appears that a churl's oath was valued at five shillings. The size of the oath required was normally related to the amount of the fine involved if the defendant failed to clear himself; for example, a man might have to produce an oath of 120 hides or pay 120 shillings fine. In the later laws, it is more usual for the actual number of compurgators to be stated, as, indeed, had been done from early times in Kent; statements occur such as 'let him deny it with an oath of three twelves.'

If on the appointed day the defendant came to court and performed the oath in full, the suit was ended and he was clear. But there could be circumstances that cut the defendant off from the right to produce an oath. If he were a man of suspicious character who had been frequently accused, or if he had ever been convicted of perjury, he was no longer 'oath-worthy'; or he might have been taken in the act of committing his crime, or in suspicious circumstances, as, for example, in possession of stolen property for which he could not account. In such cases, the court awarded the right of bringing an oath to the plaintiff, who then brought forward his compurgators to swear to the defendant's guilt. Similarly, the plaintiff, instead of the defendant, was awarded the oath if he had witnesses of the crime, who would swear:

In the name of Almighty God, so I stand here by N in true witness, unbidden and unbought, as I saw with my eyes and heard with my ears that which I pronounce with him.

When the plaintiff had in this way produced his oath, or when the oath had been granted to the defendant and he had proved unable to give it, the defendant might then go to the ordeal, the judgement of God. The Church then took control of the proceedings. The ordeal was preceded by a three-days' fast and a mass in which the accused was charged to confess his guilt before receiving the sacrament. This part of the ceremony was in English, and in one version it runs:

I charge you by the Father and the Son and by the Holy Ghost, and by your Christianity which you have received, and by the holy cross on which God suffered, and by the holy gospel and the relics which are in this church, that you should not dare to partake of this sacrament nor to go to the altar if you did this of which you are accused, or know who did it.

In the ordeal of cold water, holy water was given to the accused to drink, and he was then thrown into the water, after the Deity had been adjured to accept the innocent into the water or cast out the guilty. If the accused floated, his guilt was taken to be established. The other forms of ordeal took place within the church itself, and while the preparations were going on each of the parties in the suit was represented by an equal number of members, to ensure that no trickery was attempted. In the ordeal of iron, the accused carried the glowing iron for nine feet, in the ordeal of hot water he plunged his hand into boiling water to take out a stone. The hand was then bound up, and if the wound had healed after three days without festering, the man was cleared of the charge. In serious charges, a man must clear himself by the threefold ordeal, that is to say, the weight of the iron was increased from one to three pounds in the ordeal of iron, the arm must be plunged to the elbow instead of the wrist in the ordeal of hot water. The accuser was allowed to decide between the ordeals of iron and of water.

If the accused were a member of the clergy, the ordeal used was that of the consecrated morsel, which the accused swallowed after pronouncing a prayer that it might choke him if he were speaking falsely. Elaborate rituals for use in ordeals of all kinds are contained in the ritual books of the Anglo-Saxon clergy.

If a man were convicted at the ordeal, he was condemned by the assembled court to the punishment laid down by the law for that particular crime. In one or two cases, this was more lenient than if he had been taken in the act, a circumstance that suggests some uncertainty as to the infallibility of the 'judgement of God'. Slaying by witchcraft is punished by death 'if the accused cannot deny it', i.e. if anyone is taken in circumstances considered so damning as to rob him of the right to an oath, but by prison and a fine if the accusation is proved by ordeal after the failure of his oath. A thief caught in the act 'shall die the death', but a man convicted of theft by the ordeal alone faces this extreme penalty only if he is a man frequently accused.

Some crimes – arson, house-breaking, open theft, obvious murder, treachery to one's lord – are called 'bootless' crimes, for which no compensation can be offered, but which are punishable by death and forfeiture of property. In some other cases, a criminal condemned to death can be redeemed at the price of his own wergild. The Church favoured the avoidance of the death-penalty, preferring even the substitution of mutilation, as this gave the malefactor an opportunity of expiating his crime in this world and thus saving his soul. This view is strongly expressed in the laws composed for Ethelred and Cnut by Archbishop Wulfstan:

> Christian men shall not be condemned to death for all too little; but one shall determine lenient punishments for the benefit of the people, and not destroy for a little matter God's own handiwork and his own purchase which he bought at a great price.

This attitude must have had some effect. Elsewhere,

Wulfstan shows that he includes mutilation among the 'lenient' punishments he advocates, and Abbot Ælfric begins the story of a miracle with the words 'A certain thane was mutilated for theft', whereas mutilation is not mentioned in the laws of his time as a punishment for theft. It occurs as the penalty for coining false money, but in general plays little part in the Anglo-Saxon legal system. In spite of Wulfstan's efforts, execution remained the normal fate of a thief; for example, a smith at Hatfield Broad Oak in Essex in the time of Edward the Confessor was put to death for theft and the thirty acres he had held were seized by the king's reeve.

Hanging was the commonest form of execution, and a poem known as *The Fates of Men* gives a gruesome picture of a thief's body left hanging on the gallows. These were often placed on the boundary between settlements, and hence phrases like 'to the gallow tree' or 'to the old place of execution' are not infrequent in lists of boundaries of estates. It is in agreement with native custom that the poet should cause St Juliana to be led out to execution 'near the land-boundary'. Other forms of execution are more rarely mentioned: beheading is one of them, and Ælfric expects his readers to be familiar with it when he says that God will have compassion on the criminal if he call on him 'before the sharp sword descend on his neck.' A woman convicted of encompassing death by witchcraft was drowned at London Bridge in the tenth century, while stoning might be the method of executing a thieving slave if male, burning if female, if we can trust a code of Athelstan which survives only in a later unreliable Latin version.

Some crimes were punished by slavery, and we find lords in possession of penal slaves long after the date of the last reference to this penalty in the laws, in the reign of Athelstan. It must often have resulted from the offender's inability to meet the fines and compensation which he had incurred. Occasionally imprisonment, at the king's estate, is mentioned. By far the commonest penalty was the payment of compensation and fines, the former to the injured party, the latter normally to the king, or to the holder of the private jurisdiction, if such had been granted. Some fines were divided between the king and the Church, such as that for perjury, as this involved the breaking of an oath sworn on sacred relics, or that for incest, as a breach of the marriage law of the Church. In a suit for homicide, compensation had to be paid to the kindred, and to the lord of the slain man, while a fine for fighting was due to the king, and if it took place in anyone's house, the owner was entitled to a compensation graduated in accordance with his rank, from the ealdorman who could claim sixty shillings, to the churl who received six. There were some other circumstances in which private persons other than the injured could claim a sum for breach of their protection. All fines and compensations were increased if the crime were committed in Lent, or certain other Church seasons, or inside a church or at court, or when the army had been called out, or against men going to or coming from an assembly, or in violation of the king's special peace. More than simple repayment of stolen goods had often to be made – the laws of Kent demand twelve-fold payment to the Church, nine-fold to the king. Finally, higher rank, while it entitled men to higher compensations, made them liable to pay bigger fines for their misdeeds. Both the fines and the compensations were fixed by the laws; there was quite a long tariff of the amounts due for bodily injuries of all kinds, while fines were mainly fixed at thirty, sixty, or a hundred and twenty shillings, though other sums occur sometimes. The amount to be paid for any offence was not left to the discretion of the court; it was for it to pronounce the sentence in accordance with the law-books.

*

Theft is the crime that occupies the biggest place in the codes, especially cattle-lifting. Many sections are filled with regulations that make it more difficult for the thief to dispose of stolen goods, and easier for the owner to track his property. All goods should be purchased before proper witnesses, so that the buyer can vouch the seller to warranty if the goods are later proved to have been stolen, and from time to time the conditions under which purchase can be made, and the procedure of vouching to warranty, are the subject of careful legislation. It was made incumbent on all men to help their neighbour to track his stolen cattle, and the laws are explicit on the formalities to be observed if the trail should lead into another area of jurisdiction. Athelstan's laws are particularly concerned with the suppression of cattle-stealing, and apparently were effective, for his successor, Edmund, is able to say proudly: 'I thank God and all of you who have supported me for the peace from thefts which we now have.' He was thus able to turn his attention to the limitation of blood-feuds which we considered in a previous chapter. In spite of his determination to suppress theft, Athelstan expressed horror at the execution of young thieves for petty theft, and allowed the death-penalty to be applied only if the thief were over fifteen years of age, instead of twelve years. The freedom from thefts of which King Edmund boasts was short-lived; his son, Edgar, issued elaborate measures in an attempt to make cattle-stealing difficult.

Ethelred the Unready issued at Wantage a code intended to suppress lawlessness and violence in the North. It imposes very heavy fines for a breach of the king's peace, and it employs a method of bringing malefactors to justice that is probably derived from Scandinavian law:

An assembly is to be held in each wapentake, and the twelve leading thanes and with them the reeve are to go out and swear on the relics which are placed in their hands that they will accuse no guiltless man nor conceal any guilty one. And they are to arrest the men frequently accused, who are at issue with the reeve.

Each of these men of ill repute is to pledge that he will stand trial, and to go to the threefold ordeal or pay four-fold payment. If convicted at the ordeal, he is to be beheaded.

These twelve leading thanes are to be compared with the 'lawmen' of whom we hear in later sources at Lincoln, York, Stamford, Chester, and Cambridge, and this measure of Ethelred's, which provides the first instance of a 'jury of presentment', seems called for to meet a situation in which the ordinary machinery of the law has proved inadequate to bring individuals to justice. The weakness of the executive in this reign can be illustrated from events in other parts of the country also, especially in the case of a certain Wulfbold in Kent, who committed many acts of violence and lived unmolested until his death, defying many sentences passed against him in the courts.

*

It may perhaps be of interest to examine one recorded lawsuit and see something of the law in the working. A man called Helmstan had been convicted of stealing a belt. A certain Æthelm then tried to obtain from him an estate by litigation, presumably seizing his opportunity because Helmstan's crime would make him less likely to be allowed to bring forward an oath in defence of his possession. He would normally have been allowed this oath since the law held that 'proof of possession is always

nearer to him who has than to him who claims.' Helmstan asked for help from the man who gives us the account of the case, probably Ealdorman Ordlaf, and because of his intercession King Alfred granted that Helmstan should be entitled to justice, and advised settlement
by arbitration. The arbitrators agreed that Helmstan
should be allowed to produce his title-deeds and make
good his right, the history of the estate was given, and all
thought that Helmstan 'was the nearer (of the parties)
to the oath'; but Æthelm would not accept their decision
without going to the king, who was in his chamber at
Wardour – 'he was washing his hands'. He upheld their
decision and named a day for the oath. Helmstan seems
to have doubted his power to get sufficient compurgators; at any rate, he applied to Ordlaf again, offering
him the estate if he would help him with the oath, and
Ordlaf replied that he would help him to obtain justice,
but not in any false practice, on condition that he granted
him the land. He pledged the estate and the oath was
duly performed.

Then we all said that that was a closed suit when the sentence was fulfilled. And, sire, when shall any suit be ended if
one cannot end it with compensation or with oath? Or if one
wishes to set aside every judgement which King Alfred established, when shall we have finished disputing?

Helmstan handed over his title-deeds to Ordlaf, who
permitted him to use the land while he lived, 'if he would
keep himself out of disgrace.' But a year and a half or
two years later, he stole some cattle and was tracked, and
in his flight he was scratched in the face by a bramble,
-and this was brought up against him when he wished to
deny the charge; it provided one of those suspicious circumstances which could cut off a defendant from the
right to bring an oath. The king's reeve seized all his
property because he was a thief and the king's man; but

he could not forfeit the estate which he had given to Ordlaf, for he was only holding it on lease. King Alfred was now dead, and King Edward declared Helmstan an outlaw. He then visited King Alfred's tomb and brought a 'seal' to Ordlaf, who gave it to the king at Chippenham, and he removed the sentence of outlawry. I am indebted to Sir Frank Stenton for the explanation that by 'seal' is probably meant a sealed document certifying that Helmstan had sworn some oath over King Alfred's tomb. Ordlaf exchanged the estate for another with the bishop of Winchester. The very existence of this long letter explaining the whole transaction to the king would seem to imply that it had not gone uncriticized. It contains many features of interest, and it is not the least of them that it brings us face to face with one of those 'often-accused' persons so much mentioned in the laws, and suggests that they were not always dealt with in accordance with the full rigour of the law.

*

Far less information is available on Anglo-Saxon family law. Much of the custom regulating matters like marriage and inheritance was handed on orally, and cannot all be recovered from the scattered references to these topics. It is in this province of the law that the acceptance of Christianity made most difference; the Church had to enforce its rules forbidding divorce and the marriage of persons within the prohibited degrees, and this was not done without a long struggle. Questions relating to marriage were referred to the decision of Pope Gregory by the earliest missionaries; Archbishop Theodore's penitential decrees show that various problems in this connexion were presented to him, and it was one of the subjects discussed at his synod at Hertford in 672; and after the settlement of the northern and eastern districts with heathen Danish immigrants in the ninth century the battle had to be fought afresh in these areas, and as far as Northumbria was concerned, it was fought with indifferent success.

Pope Gregory had been willing to admit marriage within the third and fourth degree of kinship, but the later Church forbade it within the sixth degree, and with the widows or widowers of kinsmen within the same degree, and between co-sponsors. Archbishop Wulfstan's fulminations against incest, rife in the eleventh century, may indicate nothing more than that these strict rules were being disregarded. A very early law-code, of Wihtred of Kent, prohibits illicit marriages, and excludes from the country foreigners who will not conform, and it was found necessary to revive this law well over four centuries later, in the reign of Cnut (1016–35), presumably to apply to the Scandinavians settled in England. One thing that caused grave scandal to the Church was the Germanic practice which allowed a man to marry his stepmother. King Eadbald of Kent did this on the death of his father Ethelbert in 616, but was brought to see the error of his ways by Archbishop Laurentius; his act was repeated in the ninth century, when Æthelbald, the son of the most pious King Æthelwulf, married the Frankish princess Judith, who had been married to Æthelwulf when she was a child; but the cases are not really parallel, for Æthelwulf's marriage had not been consummated.

The earliest Kentish laws suggest that divorce was originally as easy among the English as it was in heathen Scandinavia. They allow the wife who 'wishes to depart with her children' half the goods of the household; but if the husband wishes to keep the children, the wife is to have a share equal to that of a child. The same state of things was re-introduced into the north of England by the Danish settlers, and a Durham writer speaks quite

casually of an eleventh-century earl who divorced two
wives in succession in order to marry higher in the social
scale, and of the re-marriage and second divorce of his
first wife. We cannot wonder that Wulfstan, who was
archbishop of this northern province, should lament in
the pulpit the prevalence of breaches of the marriage
laws. One of his predecessors had taken action against a
flagrant outrage, and received an estate as payment of
a fine by two brothers who had shared one wife, but one
gets the impression that the Church had to tolerate
easy divorce in this part of the land. One may recall the
casual reference in Domesday Book to the separation of
Asa from her husband, mentioned in a previous chapter.

The wording of the Kentish laws suggests a crude view
of marriage, as the purchase of a wife, as in the injunction:

> If a freeman lie with the wife of a freeman, he shall pay his
> (or her?) wergeld, and get another wife with his own money
> and bring her to the other man's home.

There are similar implications in the laws of Ine, and in
the poem which says: 'A king shall buy a queen with
property, with goblets, and bracelets.' Yet the position of
women in Anglo-Saxon society was a high one (already
Tacitus had been struck by their influential position in
the Germanic races), and very soon the bride-price came
to be regarded as the property of the bride herself. It is
probably what is referred to later on as what the suitor
paid 'in order that she might accept his suit.' Before the
end of the period the law states categorically:

> No woman or maiden shall ever be forced to marry one
> whom she dislikes, nor be sold for money.

A widow was allowed to decide herself about a second
marriage. A woman had also undisputed control of her
'morning-gift', her husband's present to her the day after
the consummation of the marriage; if she died childless,

her own kinsmen inherited it; she retained it after her husband's death, unless she married again within a year. If she did, the gift became forfeit; Domesday Book tells us that Bishop Æthelmær of Elmham seized an estate at Plumstead, Norfolk, because a woman who held it married within a year of her previous husband's death. A woman had also a right to a proportion of the household goods; the fraction varied in different localities, but was often a third, though in a little legal text called *Concerning the marriage of a woman* the writer says that if it is formally agreed 'it is right that she be entitled to half the property – and all if they have a child together – unless she marry again.' Among the upper classes it would certainly appear that household furnishings were considered the wife's possessions, for it is only women who bequeath such things in their wills. A woman retained her due share of the goods if her husband were convicted of theft and forfeited his property. She was not responsible for stolen property found in her house, unless it were under her own lock and key, for 'she must obey her husband' and could not prevent him bringing what he wished into the house. Among the upper classes marriage agreements were often made about succession to land and goods on the death of either partner of the marriage. The freedom with which women could hold and dispose of land is in striking contrast to post-Conquest conditions.

There were two parts to a marriage: the 'wedding', that is, the pledging or betrothal, when the bride-price was paid and the terms were agreed on; and the 'gift', the bridal itself, when the bride was given to the bridegroom, with feasting and ceremony. Ecclesiastical blessing was not necessary to the legality of the marriage, though the Church advocated it. The Church discouraged second marriages and advised the priests to withhold their blessing from these.

The laws governing inheritance in Anglo-Saxon times are nowhere stated, and all that can be gathered is that it was normal for a man's sons to divide his land between them, and for females to inherit in the absence of male heirs of the same degree of kinship. There was, however, one type of land which the owner was free to bequeath as he liked, and this was known as 'bookland', from the circumstance that this type of holding was created by a title-deed called a 'book' in the vernacular. There can be little doubt that this method of holding land grew up in Christian times, and that the English, like other Germanic tribes, originally regarded land as something which could not easily or arbitrarily be alienated from the family. After the adoption of Christianity it would be necessary to find some means by which the Church could receive some permanent landed endowment. A system developed by which land was freed for religious purposes from the payment of royal dues, which would then go to the upkeep of the religious establishment, and also from the claims of the kindred; by the end of the seventh century, it had become customary to record this act of liberation in writing, and a great number of these 'books' have come down to us. They are an ecclesiastical importation, modelled on the late Roman private deed, and they show us that the consent of the king's council was obtained for the act of creating bookland. Sometimes they mention that money has been paid to the king, and no doubt his rights have been bought out in many cases where no reference to payment is made. They do not say that the consent of kinsmen is necessary, but instances occur where a religious house later had trouble with the donor's descendants, and probably a donor would be well advised to get the consent of his heirs to his gift. The title-deeds were introduced by a religious invocation, and usually by a proem either declaring

the advisability of having written record of acts of
piety, or advising the purchasing of eternal blessing, by
the gift of temporal possessions for pious uses; the dona-
tion was safeguarded from interference by an anathema
calling down the wrath of heaven on any who attempted
to set it aside. These religious sections of the deeds increase in length and elaboration as the period advances,
although before long it becomes common to make grants
of bookland to laymen without there being any intention of its being turned to pious use. The advantage to the
receiver of having land which he could alienate at will
and which was free from royal dues is obvious, and he
was willing to pay for it. Moreover, to the king who made
it, a grant of bookland may have afforded a means of
rewarding his thanes and others for services rendered, or
of raising ready money. The king always retained the
jurisdiction over those men who held bookland, which
meant that if any of them committed a deed which involved forfeiture, the land came into the king's hands.
Litigation about bookland is often brought before Church
synods in the eighth and ninth centuries, and later before
the king and his council. Land not so freed, land still
subject to the king's farm and other charges, and bound
by customary rules of descent, is probably what is meant
by the rare term 'folkland'. Disputes concerning this
were dealt with in the ordinary courts.

CHAPTER VIII

THE CHURCH

AFTER the coming of the English the British Church survived in Wales, Devon and Cornwall, Cumbria, and Strathclyde, and in the little British kingdom of Elmet in the West Riding until its conquest by the Northumbrians in the early seventh century. Bede blames the Britons for making no attempt to convert the hated invader, and regards their subsequent misfortunes as a sign of divine disfavour. Church dedications in Somerset suggest, however, that, unknown to Bede, a certain amount of missionary work was carried on by the Welsh across the Bristol Channel. When the mission sent from Rome by Pope Gregory under the leadership of Augustine arrived in Kent in 597, the king and his court were familiar with some of the outer forms of the Christian religion, for the queen was a Christian Frankish princess and had with her her own bishop to whom had been assigned a church, dedicated to St Martin, which had survived from the days of British Christianity. Men were aware that other buildings had once been Christian churches – Bede speaks of their restoration to this use by the missionaries. Some Englishmen had become acquainted with the new religion abroad; we hear of Saxons with St Columba at Iona a generation before Gregory's mission. Gregory wrote to the Frankish rulers that it had reached him that the English race wished to become Christian, but that the priests in their vicinity were not willing to undertake the task. But King Ethelbert certainly at first regarded the missionaries with suspicion, and there is no doubt that Christianity was a strange and foreign faith to the

vast majority of the English when it was preached to
them by the missionaries from Rome and Iona.

The process of conversion was a long one, in spite of
some early spectacular successes. Ethelbert, king of Kent
and overlord of all the lands south of the Humber, accepted the new faith and gave Augustine a see in Canterbury. Gregory wrote to Bishop Eulogius of Alexandria
that on Christmas Day, 597, more than ten thousand of
the English were reported to have been baptized.
Another band of missionaries was sent to join in the work
in 601, bearing letters of congratulation and instruction
to Augustine, and by this year the conversion had gone
far enough to justify the creation of a second bishop for
Kent, with his see at Rochester. The king of Essex, King
Ethelbert's nephew, had been persuaded to accept
Christianity, and one of the new arrivals from Rome,
Mellitus, was made bishop in his capital, London. The
laws issued by King Ethelbert put the Christian Church
in a highly favoured position. Yet it was not until nearly
fifty years after Augustine's landing that a Kentish king
dared to order the destruction of idols throughout his
land and to enforce the Lenten fast, while still another
fifty years later the laws of Wihtred of Kent found it
necessary to impose penalties for heathen worship.
Ethelbert's attempt to convert King Rædwald of East
Anglia came to nothing, and on Ethelbert's death in 616
there was a reaction in favour of paganism and for a time
the whole fate of Christianity in England hung in the
balance. Kent was saved, but not Essex, which remained
heathen for some forty years longer, when its permanent
conversion came from the North, not from the Kentish
Church.

It was not until ten years after Ethelbert's death that
the Church made any recorded progress outside the
borders of Kent. The marriage of a Kentish princess to

King Edwin of Northumbria caused that king, after some hesitation and a consultation with his council which Bede has graphically described, to be baptized. As in Kent, the spread of the Christian faith appeared to be rapid; all the nobility of Northumbria and many persons of lower rank are said to have been converted in the same year as the king, and we read of baptisms of people in great numbers, in the river Swale near Catterick, and in the Glen near Yeavering; Edwin persuaded Eorpwald, king of East Anglia, to embrace the faith, and it was also accepted in the province of Lindsey, where an old man who lived until Bede's time saw as a boy Paulinus baptizing people in great numbers in the Trent at Littleborough. Churches were built at York, *Campodonum*, and Lincoln, and Pope Honorius sent to Paulinus an archiepiscopal pallium in 634, for Gregory had laid down that Britain should be divided into two provinces, with archbishop's sees at London and York, and it seemed time to put the latter part of the plan into effect. But the pope's information was out of date: more than eighteen months before he took this action King Edwin had been killed in battle, Paulinus had escorted the queen back to Kent, the church at *Campodonum* had been burnt by the pagans, the building of the stone church at York given up, and there had been a widespread relapse into heathenism. The results of Paulinus's work were perhaps not entirely eradicated; his deacon, James, stayed on after the catastrophe, and Christianity was restored a year later, but it was mainly from another source, unconnected with the Kentish Church, that this restoration came about. In East Anglia, too, Christianity was for the time being short-lived, for Eorpwald was killed by a heathen successor very soon after his conversion. Three years later, however, the permanent conversion of this kingdom was brought about, for a king ascended the throne who had become a Christian while an exile in Gaul, and a Burgundian bishop called Felix, who came, intent on missionary work, to Canterbury, was sent by Archbishop Honorius to work in this province.

Gregory had intended that the bishops of Wales and the other territories in British hands should be under Augustine's authority, but the latter's attempt to establish relations with them failed completely. According to the story that reached Bede, this was largely because of his arrogant behaviour, but it was not to be expected that they would welcome subjection to the head of the Church of their hated invaders. Moreover, this invasion had cut them off from intercourse with the rest of the Church, with the result that they were observing an antiquated method of calculating Easter, and had also their own customs in some other matters; they were unwilling to give these up at Augustine's orders, nor did they do so till a long time later. The same peculiarities were shared by the Irish Church, which was an offshoot from British Christianity, but differed from it in the fervour of its missionary zeal in the sixth and seventh centuries. Irish missionaries were active on the Continent towards the end of the sixth century, when one called Columbanus founded the monastery of Luxeuil, preached among the Burgundians and Franks, and eventually crossed into Italy and founded Bobbio. Meanwhile St Columba had crossed from Ireland to the Irish colony in western Scotland, and there he founded the famous monastery of Iona. It was from this centre that most of the remaining districts of England were won to the Christian faith after the breakdown of Edwin's Christian kingdom in 632. The sons of Edwin's predecessor and rival had taken refuge in Iona during his reign and had been converted there, and it was therefore natural that King Oswald should apply to Iona for a missionary bishop once he was established on the Northumbrian throne; and, as Oswald and his successor Oswiu became overlords of southern England also, the Church of Northumbria brought about the conversion of all the Midlands and of Essex. Wessex, however, received a missionary direct from Rome, a certain Birinus, who appears to have had no connexion with the Church at Canterbury. Though he must have taught the Roman, not the Celtic usages, Oswald took no objection to him; as overlord, he joined with the West Saxon king in giving him an endowment for his see at Dorchester-on-Thames. For a time, the English Church was divided, East Anglia and Kent following the practices of Rome, under the authority of the archbishop of Canterbury, Wessex also Roman in usage, but apparently in a position of isolation, and all the rest of the country owing allegiance to the mother church of Iona, except for Sussex and the Isle of Wight, which remained heathen until after the Church had become united under Rome. Yet this picture is over-simplified: in both East Anglia and Wessex Irish ecclesiastics had settled and helped with the work of conversion, Fursey and his brothers at Burgh Castle in Suffolk, Maildubh at Maimesbury, while a band of Irish monks were living at Bosham, Sussex, before this kingdom was converted; on the other hand, James the Deacon continued to teach the practices of the Roman Church in Northumbria for a generation after the arrival of the missionaries from Iona. Roman influence in this kingdom was reinforced when Oswiu married Edwin's daughter, for she had been brought up in Kent and brought her chaplain, Romanus, with her. Oswiu's son, the underking of Deira, learnt to adopt the Roman forms under the influence of his friend King Cenwealh of Wessex, and attracted to him young men who had studied on the Continent or been to Rome, of whom the most important was St Wilfrid, founder of

Ripon and later bishop of Northumbria. The southern Irish had accepted the Roman Easter already in 643 and most of the Irish on the Continent had conformed, including one called Ronan who came to Northumbria. Here, in the autumn of 664, a synod was held in which the Roman party, reinforced by a foreign guest, Agilbert, bishop of Paris, who had formerly held the see of the West Saxons, gained their point. They appealed to the authority of St Peter, and King Oswiu, who had probably decided his line of action beforehand, judged in their favour 'lest, when I come to the gates of the kingdom of heaven, there should be none to open them, he being my adversary who is known to possess the keys.' The extremists of the Irish party returned to Ireland, and founded a monastery on the island of Inishbofin off the coast of Mayo. Because of dissensions, the Englishmen among them were moved to another site, leaving their Irish brethren on the island. English bishops of Mayo are mentioned occasionally in English sources of eighth-century history.

Most of the English clergy who had been reared in the Irish usages remained and conformed on points of observance. They handed on much of the spirit of the Irish Church, its love of simplicity, poverty, and humility, its often exaggerated asceticism, its stress on pilgrimage and voluntary exile for the love of God, its burning missionary zeal. Though the period in which more than half of the English Church looked to Iona for guidance lasted only thirty years, it left permanent results on the ritual, the scholarship, and the penitential system of the English Church. Nor was there any complete cleavage with Iona after the synod of Whitby. One of its later abbots, Adamnan, was a friend of King Aldfrith of Northumbria, and recounts two visits to his court, in 686 and 688, and in the middle of the next century Abbot Slebhine visited

Ripon, where he obtained some information about an historical date he was interested in. Intercourse would become easier after the Englishman Egbert, who lived as a voluntary exile in Ireland, finally prevailed on the monks of Iona to accept the Roman Easter in 716.

*

Much more was involved in the decision at Whitby than the question of usage that was discussed there. The two Churches differed fundamentally in their organization. The Irish Church was purely monastic; a monastery might include among its members or in its daughter houses a number of men in bishop's orders, who were nevertheless under the authority of the abbot. They had no fixed dioceses, but were free to exercise their office wherever they were required. They made long journeys, preaching, baptizing, and confirming wherever they came, and eventually returning to their monastery. They had no personal possessions and they made no attempt to set up permanently-served, non-monastic churches. It was a system well suited to missionary work in a new field; it produced men devoid of all personal ambition, free from any duties of organization that might restrict their preaching work; men who attracted people to the faith by their warm sincerity, their austerity of life, and utter unworldliness. But it was not a system to supply the permanent religious needs of the population when the first stage of the conversion was over, being too haphazard, too dependent on the fervour of the individual preacher. The diocesan system of the Roman Church supplied the necessary stability, and some of the men who opposed the Irish Church realized this.

Some of them had been to Rome, and had been impressed by its magnificence. They came back laden with treasures, books, pictures, and sacred vessels. They imported masons to build churches such as they had seen abroad. They did not admire the poverty of the Irish church buildings, but desired beautiful buildings, services as impressive as gorgeous altar-furnishings, gold and silver plate, and skilful chanting could make them. They wished that bishops should live with dignity, with a retinue befitting their high office. But above all they were alive to the advantage of union with the universal Church, the one society with the experience of government to enable it to supply the organization the English Church so badly needed.

The acceptance of Roman usage now made it possible for the English Church to be organized as a single body, and this was emphasized in 667 when Egbert of Kent and Oswiu of Northumbria together chose an archbishop to succeed Deusdedit at Canterbury 'with the consent of the English people.' Their nominee died in Rome, and Pope Vitalian filled the vacancy by consecrating a Greek monk, a scholar with a great reputation, sending with him another man of learning, Hadrian, an African by origin, who was abbot of a monastery near Naples. As we shall see in a later chapter, these men brought a priceless gift of learning and culture. To Theodore fell the task of organizing the recently united English Church, a task all the more pressing because the great plague of 664 had carried off many of the clergy, and in some areas had caused men to revert to their heathen gods for help.

He made a visitation of the whole country, teaching 'the right rule of life and the canonical rite of celebrating Easter', encouraging ecclesiastical learning, and the Roman method of chanting, consecrating bishops to vacant sees and investigating the validity of previous consecrations. He held at Hertford in 672 the first synod of the whole English Church, in which, among other things, he established the principle of annual synods, passed measures directed against the Irish habit by which bishops did not confine their activities to a fixed diocese, and dealt with questions of Christian marriage. The synod admitted that more bishops ought to be made, but decided to postpone this matter for the present.

Pope Gregory, who may have thought more easily of Britain as a lost Roman province than as a group of distinct kingdoms, had planned its organization as a single Church, divided into two archbishoprics with sees at London and York, each archbishop to have twelve suffragan bishops under him, and, after the death of Augustine, precedence between the archbishops to depend on seniority of appointment. But at the time of the mission, a Kentish king was supreme in southern England and established Augustine in his chief city, Canterbury; before Essex (in which London was situated) was permanently won for Christianity, usage had sanctified the position of Canterbury as the archiepiscopal see. Paulinus had fled from York before he received his pallium, and the North did not receive an archbishop of its own for another hundred years. When it did, he had only three suffragans. Gregory's figure was probably based on the assumption that some sees in the non-English parts of Britain would be under his control, and at a later date York claimed supremacy over the bishops of Scotland, and on occasions consecrated bishops for these sees. South of the Humber at the time of Theodore's arrival there were only five sees besides Canterbury and all were vacant except London. Theodore took every opportunity to divide these great bishoprics, which – except for Rochester – had been conterminous with the kingdoms in which they stood, but he met with much opposition, especially from Wilfrid, bishop of the Northumbrians, whose appeal to Rome on the matter is the first appeal of an English ecclesiastic to Rome. By the time of his death, Theodore had divided East Anglia into the sees of Dunwich and Elmham, Mercia and its dependencies into those of Lichfield, Worcester, and Hereford, Northumbria into the sees of York, Lindisfarne, Hexham, and Abercorn (though this last soon ceased to exist because the Northumbrians lost control of this territory to the Picts), and had also appointed a separate bishop for Lindsey, at that time under Northumbrian control, but soon to be reconquered by the Mercians. The Mercian dependency of Middle Anglia also had bishops of its own in Theodore's time, though the see was not permanently established until 737, Leicester becoming its bishop's seat. After Theodore's death, Wessex was divided, the diocese of Sherborne being carved out of that of Winchester in 705, and the last of the English kingdoms to be converted, Sussex, was given a see of its own, at Selsey, in the time of Theodore's successor. This brought the number of suffragan sees south of the Humber to twelve, for Essex was left undivided, with its see at London, and no changes were made in Kent. A new Northumbrian see was formed at Whithorn in Galloway about 731. The grant of an archiepiscopal pallium to Egbert of York in 735, and the temporary elevation of Lichfield into an archiepiscopal see from 788 to 803, are the only major alterations in this state of things until the disruption caused by the Viking invasions.

*

In Italy dioceses were usually small and could be administered from the episcopal see, where the bishop had his church, his household of clergy, and a school for the training of priests. In England, even after the subdivision effected by Theodore, the dioceses covered far too extensive an area for central administration to be sufficient.

The growth of the parochial system is obscure at many points of its history. Paulinus seems to have worked from royal estates, especially places of Roman origin, as at York, Lincoln, Catterick, and Littleborough; we read of three churches built or commenced in his time. The mission from Iona built many churches, perhaps mainly at royal estates, and Bede speaks more than once of noblemen who had churches built on their estates. In one of his commentaries he says:

> When perchance we enter any village or town or any other place in which there is a house of prayer dedicated to God, let us first turn aside to this.

It is not clear, however, that these places normally received an endowment to support a permanent priest, and Bede's words to Archbishop Egbert in 734 show that there was at that time nothing like an organized parochial system in existence. He points out that the archbishop could not visit all the places in his diocese in a whole year, and therefore advises him to appoint others to help him 'by ordaining priests and instituting teachers, who may devote themselves to preaching the word of God in the individual villages, and to celebrating the celestial mysteries, and especially to performing the sacred rites of baptism.'

Some of the injunctions of the Synod of *Clofesho* of 746 relate to the institution of priests to local churches by bishops, and throughout the Anglo-Saxon period churches continued to be built in the villages, but there remained many districts of some size which were served by 'minsters', that is, small communities of priests supplying the needs of the surrounding countryside from large churches, some of which still survive. It was necessary to safeguard the financial interests of these minsters as the habit spread of landowners building churches on their estates, and so a law of King Edgar (959–75) orders that all tithes and church-scot are to be paid to the old minister to which obedience is due, though it allows a thane to pay one-third of his own tithe to a church on his own land, provided it has a burial-place; if it has not, he must pay his tithe in full to the old church, and endow his private church out of the rest of his income. Soul-scot, that is, burial fee, is always to be paid to the minster that has the right to it, no matter where the body is buried. Ethelred's laws in 1014 graduate churches as regards their right to obtain compensation for the violation of their sanctuary, on the following scale: five pounds is to be paid in English districts to a 'head' minster, 120 shillings to a smaller minster, 60 shillings to one smaller still, where there is nevertheless a burial-place, and 30 shillings to a 'field' church.

The churches had received landed endowment of varying extent, but their main income was drawn from the dues paid to them. By the tenth century these consist of plough-alms, a penny for every working plough-team, to be paid fifteen days after Easter; tithe of young stock, payable at Whitsuntide; tithe of the fruits of the earth, to be rendered by All Saints' Day; Peter's Pence due by St Peter's Day; church-scot, due at Martinmas. By the early eleventh century a payment for lights, due three times a year, was added. Then there was also the burial fee, which was 'best paid at the open grave'. The oldest of these dues, apart from the burial fee, was the church-scot, non-payment of which was punishable by a heavy fine and twelve-fold payment already in Ine's laws about 700, and very similar regulations were in force in Worcestershire at the time of the Domesday Survey. This states, for example:

From every hide of land . . . the bishop ought to have on St Martin's day one load of grain, of the best that is grown there.

But if that day should pass without the grain being rendered, he who has kept it back shall render the grain and shall pay elevenfold; and the bishop moreover shall receive such penalty as he ought to have from his land.

The same amount, one load of grain, had to be paid to the church of Aylesbury, Buckinghamshire, by every 'sokeman' possessing one hide of land or more in any of the surrounding eight hundreds.

Tithe is mentioned as a voluntary payment in Theodore's time, to be devoted to the poor, to pilgrims, and to churches. In the tenth century, however, its payment was enforced by heavy penalties: the king's reeve, the bishop's reeve, and the priest are to go and take one-tenth of the produce of the defaulter, the lord and the bishop are to share eight-tenths, leaving the defaulter only one-tenth of the whole. The same law insists that he who fails to pay Peter's Pence in time must take it himself to Rome and in addition pay a heavy fine to the king. Continued contumacy occasioned still heavier loss. Whether laws of such exaggerated stringency could have been enforced seems doubtful. At any rate an eleventh-century code applying to an area of Danish settlement imposes only reasonable penalties, varying with the rank of the defaulter. About the same time, Archbishop Wulfstan declares that tithe should be divided into three portions, one for the repair of churches, one for the servants of God, one for God's poor, and poor slaves, and that the income that the Church derived from fines should be expended on the provision of prayers, the relief of poor men, the repair of churches, education, the clothing and feeding of those who serve God, books, bells, and church-vestments, and never on vain worldly pomp.

Although the law insisted on the payment of church-scot, soul-scot, and tithe to the old church that originally had the right to them, the churches founded by landowners still might receive enough income for them to be regarded as profitable, and the descendants of the founders treated them as their own property, sometimes in a way that shocked ecclesiastical opinion. Thus Ælfric writes at the end of the tenth century:

Some men let out churches for hire, just like common mills. The glorious house of God was devoted to the worship of God. . . . It is not fitting that God's house be treated like a mill for wretched toll, and whoever does so, he sins very deeply.

Testators sometimes make arrangements about their churches in their wills – 'my church is to be free and Wulfmær my priest is to sing thereat, he and his issue, as long as they are in holy orders' – and the private ownership of churches, or even of fractions of churches, is frequently recorded in Domesday Book. It is more than a right of patronage that is implied, for the owner could take to his own use a portion of the income, according to whatever bargain he made with the priest he appointed. A striking example of trafficking with a church occurs in the Domesday account of Huntingdon, for the jurors describe how the church of St Mary and the land belonging to it were given by the abbot of Thorney in pledge to the burgesses, and then King Edward gave it to Vitalis and Bernard, his priests, who sold it to King Edward's chamberlain, Hugh, who in his turn sold it to two priests of Huntingdon. At the time of the survey, these priests had been dispossessed, although they had King Edward's sealed writ, and Eustace was holding the church without any evidence of lawful possession, neither livery, writ, nor seisin. But, as Sir Frank Stenton has pointed out, it is the speed with which transaction follows transaction that makes this case remarkable, not the nature of the transactions themselves.

*

The first age of Christianity in England was one of very great monastic fervour. Augustine, himself a monk, began the monastery of St Peter and St Paul, outside the walls of Canterbury, where he and the early archbishops of Canterbury were buried. Seventh-century Kentish monasteries were founded at Reculver and Dover, and nunneries at Folkestone, Lyminge, and Minster in Thanet. To assist in their foundation, at least one continental house, the nunnery at Chelles, had been asked to send disciples. Already before this, Kentish women had entered the religious life at the continental houses such as Chelles and Burgundofara. In the North the first monasteries were of the Celtic type, in which the monks lived in separate cells built close together, with a common church, and the abbot's cell some distance away, the whole surrounded by a wall. The earliest was Lindisfarne, founded by the first missionary, Aidan, himself; it was soon followed by others at Gilling, Melrose, Tynemouth, Gateshead, and Lastingham, and by communities for both sexes at Hartlepool, Whitby, and Coldingham. Many Northumbrians went to Irish monasteries, to add the merit of exile from their native land to their renunciation of the world's pleasures. Some men were searching for a broader, more humane type of monastic life; Wilfrid had spent some time at Lindisfarne in his youth, but after his sojourn in Rome, it was a different form of monasticism that he introduced into Northumbria at his foundations of Ripon and Hexham, based on the Benedictine rule, which he claimed to have first introduced into northern England; Ceolfrith entered the monastery of Gilling, but left it, first going to Ripon and then, in search of an ideal form of monastic life, to study the usages at the abbey of St Peter and St Paul at Canterbury and at the East Anglian monastery of *Icanho*, founded by St Botolph. He finally joined company with

Benedict Biscop. This was a Northumbrian who made several visits to Rome, spent two years at the abbey of Lerins off the south coast of France, escorted Theodore to England on his appointment as archbishop, was for two years abbot of the abbey of St Peter and St Paul, Canterbury, and finally, after another visit to Rome, returned to Northumbria and founded the twin monasteries of St Peter at Monkwearmouth (674) and St Paul at Jarrow (682). In the latter, over which Ceolfrith became abbot, Bede spent most of his life.

Owing to Wilfred's influence, the Benedictine rule was introduced into Mercia, where many small monasteries were placed under his authority. Moreover, the great abbey of Peterborough was founded soon after the middle of the seventh century, and soon had daughter houses in places as widely scattered as Breedon, Leicestershire; Bermondsey and Woking, Surrey; and Hoo, Kent, thus affording a striking illustration of the way in which ecclesiastical arrangements overrode tribal boundaries. Early West Saxon monasteries existed at Nursling and Tisbury, at Glastonbury, and at Malmesbury, originally an Irish foundation, but ruled in the late seventh century by the English scholar Aldhelm, who had studied in Canterbury; in the Thames valley were Abingdon and Chertsey, East Anglia had *Beadricesworth* (later Bury St Edmunds) and *Icanho*, Lindsey had Barrow and Partney, all before the seventh century came to an end. In addition, there were a number of early foundations of whose existence we know from a chance reference here and there, in a charter, a saint's life, or a letter.

The double monasteries of Northumbria have been mentioned above, but this kind of house was not peculiar to that kingdom. Of the same type were the great fenland abbey of Ely, founded by the queen of Ecgfrith of Northumbria, Repton in Mercia, where St Guthlac entered

religion, Barking in Essex, to whose nuns Aldhelm
dedicated his treatise on chastity, Much Wenlock in the
ancient province of the *Magonsæte*, Bardney in Lincolnshire, Minster in Thanet, and Wimborne in Dorset. This
type of foundation was primarily a house for nuns, but
had alongside it a house of monks, who saw to the external administration and provided the priests to serve
the community of women. The whole was under an
abbess, often of royal birth, and many of these double
monasteries rose to distinction as places of learning and
education. Whitby supplied several bishops to the
church. Leofgyth, Boniface's chief woman helper in his
mission to the Germans, was educated first at Minster,
then at Wimborne. Her biographer tells us that at the
latter place there were separate monasteries for the
monks and the nuns, and the segregation seems to have
been more complete than it was, as far as our evidence
goes, at other places, for even the abbess spoke to the
monks only through a window. Boniface and his fellow-
missionaries founded similar establishments in the lands
which they converted. After the middle of the eighth
century there is no clear reference to them in England,
but our evidence is rather scanty, and it would be unsafe
to assume that they ceased to exist about this time.
Most of the places mentioned above were destroyed in
the Danish invasions, and were not refounded as double
monasteries.

Like the churches, monasteries were considered the
property of the family which had founded them. Alcuin
tells us that a small monastery on Spurn Point had
descended to him by inheritance, as he was of the
kindred of the founder, St Willibrord's father. Such
monasteries are mentioned in documents as changing
hands by gift, exchange, sale, and bequest. Synods had to
interfere to insist that the laity should not be appointed

as abbots and abbesses of these houses and that the diocesan bishop must see that proper religious observances were maintained. Bede wrote in 734 complaining that many such foundations were of fraudulent origin, a mere pretext on the part of landowners to get their lands exempted from payment of royal dues as being set apart for religious purposes, with the result that by such frauds the royal resources, which should be available for rewarding the king's followers, were being diminished. He advised Archbishop Egbert to investigate such cases and suppress unworthy houses. The archbishop evidently acted on this advice and it produced papal remonstrance, for Pope Paul I complained to the archbishop's brother, King Eadberht, about the removal of three monasteries from an abbot to give them to one of his nobles. Such suppression of spurious houses did not, however, affect the principle that monasteries were the property of the family that founded and endowed them.

No institution remains for ever in its first fervour, and it is not only in relation to fraudulent foundations that complaints are made of lax behaviour. Bede himself tells how discipline had been relaxed at Coldingham, and Alcuin's letters are full of exhortations to monks to live up to their vows, to avoid luxury in dress, to study the scriptures, and not go fox-hunting, to listen to the voice of the lector in the refectory rather than to the songs of the heathen. The author of a poem on St Guthlac went out of his way to create an opportunity to rail at the slackness in monasteries in respect of vigils and prayers. A calamity such as the sack of Lindisfarne in 793 could not, in contemporary eyes, have occurred unless God were displeased with the monastery. We need not take such admonitions as evidence that corruption was rife in religious houses at this time; but there is Alfred's testimony that, before the destruction of monasteries by the Viking raids, divine studies and Latin scholarship had greatly decayed. When he tried to revive interest in the monastic ideal, he met with little success, and it was not until the middle of the next century that a great and effective monastic revival was carried through.

*

There is no need to doubt the sincerity of the majority of the founders of houses of religion or of the men and women who renounced the world to enter them. These included people of all ranks; kings like Sigeberht of East Anglia, Ethelred of Mercia, Ceolwulf of Northumbria, and that Eadberht whom Pope Paul rebuked for suppressing monasteries, all gave up their thrones to enter monasteries. Royal princesses chose to enter religion, or in some cases were devoted to the service of God from infancy, Oswiu's infant daughter, Ælflæd, whom he devoted to God with a large gift of land in thanksgiving for his victory over Penda in 654, being the most famous instance. Queens often entered nunneries in their widowhood. Other kings gave up their rank to retire to Rome and end their days near the tombs of the Apostles. Cenred of Mercia, Offa of Essex, Ceadwalla and Ine of Wessex all took this course, as at a later date did Burgred of Mercia when the Danes conquered his kingdom. People of other ranks were not behind their rulers in piety. They entered monasteries in great numbers, or became hermits, or chose voluntary exile from their land in Ireland, the Frankish kingdom, or Rome, quoting the example of Abraham and relying on the promise of Matthew xix. 29: 'And every one that hath forsaken houses, or brethren, or sisters, or father, or mother, or wife, or children, or lands, for my name's sake, shall receive an hundredfold, and shall inherit everlasting life.'

The desire for such exile was so strong in some families that the kindred that remained at home was sadly weakened. An abbess writes dolefully to St Boniface of her unprotected condition arising partly from this cause, and the father of the missionaries Willibald and Wynnebald was reluctant to accompany his sons, declaring stoutly that it was shameful to leave one's womenfolk without protection. He gave way in the end, perhaps realizing that he was a dying man. He did not live to reach Rome.

Besides those who went on permanent exile were others who made pilgrimages to pray at foreign shrines. The express statements of contemporaries, and the survival of documents arranging the sale of estates to provide money for the journey, or disposing of property in case of death on the way, and the need to make arrangements for the reception of pilgrims en route and at Rome itself, are all evidence for the prevalence of pilgrimage, especially to Rome. Bede speaks in one place as if he thought that its spiritual benefits could be exaggerated: referring to Bishop Oftfor's resolve to make a journey to Rome, he says: 'which in those days was considered to be of great virtue.' Boniface writes with concern of the moral dangers involved when women pilgrims got stranded; he suggests to Archbishop Cuthbert that it would be a good thing if they were forbidden by a synod to go: 'because for the most part they are lost, few remaining pure. There are indeed few cities in Lombardy, or in France, or in Gaul, in which there is not an adulteress or harlot of the English race.' In the tenth century a Breton pilgrim, living as an anchorite in England, finds it necessary to defend the practice of pilgrimage against those sceptical of its value: 'where the battle is harder, the crown is more glorious.'

His opinion represented the view of the majority, and

pilgrimages remain common throughout the period. The protection of pilgrims was a subject of correspondence between Offa of Mercia and Charles the Great in 796; King Alfred's father journeyed to Rome in 855 taking the child Alfred with him, and Cnut went in 1027, and used the opportunity to secure that English travellers should not be so heavily mulcted in future; it may have been on a pilgrimage to Rome that Bishop Theodred of London (about 926-51) bought at Pavia two chasubles, a white and a yellow, that he valued enough to bequeath them specifically in his will; a Kentish reeve and his wife made the pilgrimage, and so did various West Saxon thanes, and an Anglo-Dane called Ketel with his step-daughter, and Earl Tostig and his wife Judith. The appeal was felt by men of violent temperament like Earl Aldred and Carl, Thurbrand's son, who planned to go to Rome when they had settled their family feud, but were hindered by a storm, with disastrous results. The members of an eleventh-century gild were bound to contribute to the expenses of one of their number going to Rome. In this city there was a quarter known as 'the School of the English', with a church dedicated to St Mary and a hostelry for pilgrims, and hostelries existed at many points on the main routes. There survives an itinerary of Archbishop Siric on his return journey from fetching his pallium in 990, which gives the names of seventy-nine stages from Rome to the Somme.

The journey was no pleasure trip. It was sometimes imposed on men as penance for heavy sins, and those who defended against critics its value as mortification could have listed a number of dangers that beset travellers, whether pilgrims, ecclesiastics, and messengers to the papal curia, or merchants. The first abbot of the monastery of St Peter and St Paul, Canterbury, was drowned crossing the Channel, and St Wilfrid suffered shipwreck on one of his crossings; an English priest sent by the pope to King Eardwulf of Northumbria in 809 was captured by pirates on his return; more than one band of pilgrims was slaughtered by Saracens in the ninth century; in the mid tenth century an archbishop of Canterbury was frozen to death crossing the Alps; in the eleventh century Archbishop Ealdred of York was robbed by brigands and had to return to the pope for financial assistance to continue. We know of these incidents when they affected personages of importance; they were not likely to have been isolated events. The travellers were often subjected to exactions on their way, and it is unlikely that it was only the unhappy women mentioned by Boniface who found their money giving out before their safe return; and some people failed to support the physical hardships of the journey and died on the way, from Abbot Ceolfrith of Jarrow who died at Langres in 716 to the son of the eleventh-century Earl Ælfgar of Mercia, whose body was buried by the clergy of Reims, an act which procured for them the grant of two estates in Staffordshire from the grateful father. It was clearly a wise precaution for pilgrims to make arrangements before they went for the disposal of their possessions 'if death befall us on the way to Rome.'

Yet even the hardships of the journey to Rome did not content some pilgrims; a few went to Jerusalem. There survives the life of an eighth-century pilgrim to Syria written by an Anglo-Saxon nun at the German monastery at Heidenheim from the account received from his own lips. In the eleventh century the pilgrimage to Jerusalem is mentioned several times. Earl Godwine's unruly son Swein undertook it. He had the treacherous and brutal murder of his cousin on his conscience; but there is no hint that other persons mentioned are expiating heavy sins. Leofgifu, a London woman, died on the road to Jerusalem in about 1060, and a Lincolnshire thane called Ulf set out for this city with his wife just after the Norman Conquest, making testamentary arrangements before he left 'if I do not come home'. He was a friend of Archbishop Ealdred, who had himself been to Jerusalem in 1058. If Ulf did come home, it would be to find his lands possessed by Norman lords, and we hear nothing more of him.

*

The voluntary embracing of exile, 'to live as a stranger for our Lord in order the more easily to enter into the heavenly kingdom', combined with the desire to spread the Christian faith among their Germanic kinsmen on the Continent, sent numbers of English men and women as missionaries across the sea. The work was begun by Wilfrid, in 677, three years before he began to convert the South Saxons, when he delayed on his first journey of appeal to Rome to convert the Frisians. But his success was only temporary. The permanent mission to the Frisians was inspired by an Englishman called Egbert living as a voluntary exile in Ireland, who wished to go himself to bring to the faith the nations from which his people derived their origin. He was prevented by what he believed to be an expression of the divine will, but it was at his instigation that Willibrord, the Apostle to the Frisians, set out in 690, after the failure of a mission sent two years earlier, and it was from Ireland, too, that two English priests made an abortive attempt to convert the Old Saxons, which ended in their martyrdom. Space does not allow a detailed account of Willibrord's work, which ended in the conversion of Frankish Frisia and the creation of the see of Utrecht; nor of that of his even greater colleague, the West Saxon Wynfrith, who took the name of Boniface, and who was appointed papal legate and archbishop to the Germans. He preached for a time in Frisia, but his main missionary work was in Thuringia and Hesse; his other achievements include the introduction of the diocesan organization in Bavaria, and the persuasion of the kings of the Franks to undertake the reform of their church. Both he and Willibrord possessed the veneration for the Papacy that was a mark of the gratitude felt by the English Church for its conversion from Rome. They acted all along in close cooperation with it. The far-reaching effect of this on the relations of the Papacy with the Frankish empire, and on the subsequent history of Western Europe, lies outside the subject of this volume. It is more important for our purpose to stress the great numbers of English helpers that went out to Willibrord and Boniface, whose great achievements would have been impossible without such aid. Englishmen were placed as bishops of newly created sees, and monasteries were founded with English abbots and abbesses at their head. Willibrord consecrated bishops of English race whose names are unknown, but we know more about Boniface's helpers because of the survival of his correspondence. Seven continental prelates of English birth joined with him about 746 in writing to Æthelbald of Mercia, including one archbishop, Abel of Reims. Abbots include Wigbert of Fritzlar, Beornred of Echternach, who became archbishop of Sens (died 797), and Wynnebald of Heidenheim, a double monastery like those they were accustomed to at home, in which he was succeeded by his sister Waldburg. Boniface's chief woman-helper was Leofgyth, abbess of Tauberbischofsheim, mentioned above. Other positions of importance were held by continental pupils of Willibrord and Boniface, for neither neglected to train native clergy from the first.

The work was followed with great interest at home,

for the missionaries wrote home frequently, and received letters from kings, nobles, bishops, abbots, abbesses, and priests – letters of encouragement and of request for their prayers, accompanied by gifts, the most precious being copies of the Scriptures and of theological works. The men abroad did not lose interest in the affairs of their native land, but sent home advice, encouragement, and if need be admonition. Boniface sent to Archbishop Cuthbert the statutes of reform adopted at a Frankish synod, and many of them were accepted in a synod of the English Church. He and his fellow bishops, of English birth, sent a long letter to King Æthelbald of Mercia, urging him to reform his behaviour. In 738, when there seemed a likelihood that the conversion of the Old Saxons might be undertaken, Boniface addressed a letter asking for the support and prayers of all the English nation. When he was martyred at Dokkum in 754, the words that Archbishop Cuthbert wrote to his successor Lul were uttered in the name of the English people; he thanks God that the race of the English 'has deserved to send out from itself before the eyes of all to spiritual agonies and, by the grace of Almighty God, for the safety of many souls, so famous an investigator of divine books and so noble a soldier of Christ, along with many well-trained and excellently instructed disciples.'

English missionary enterprise did not come to an end with the death of Boniface, nor did the interest of people in England flag. A particularly close concern was felt by the Northumbrians in the continuance of the conversion of the Frisians. Young Frisians from the abbey of Utrecht were sent by their abbot, a Frankish pupil of Boniface, to study at York, and one of them, called Liudger, was later called to play a part in the conversion of the Old Saxons, when at last their conquest by Charles the Great made their conversion possible. Meanwhile an

Englishman, Aluberht, was consecrated as bishop for the Old Saxons at York in 767, and somewhere about the same time a Northumbrian synod, under King Alhred, sent out to North Frisia a Northumbrian priest called Willehad, who operated for a time from Dokkum, but was later called by Charles the Great to lead the mission to the Old Saxons. After various set-backs, he was consecrated as the bishop of this people in 787, and he fixed his see at Bremen. There were other Anglo-Saxon missionaries working at this time, along with men of Frankish and Frisian birth from the monasteries founded by the earlier generation of English missionaries, and English influence left a long-lasting effect on the German Church. But in the ninth century the Viking raids depleted the Church in England, and after the Danish settlement Englishmen must have found enough to absorb their missionary zeal at home.

*

Lindisfarne was sacked by the Danes in 793 and Jarrow in the following year, but religious life was resumed after the raiders had gone, and it was not until the large-scale invasions in the second half of the next century, which aimed at the conquest of the country, that churches and monasteries were destroyed in great number and left deserted. The kingdoms of Northumbria and East Anglia, and Mercia north-east of the Watling Street, received a large immigration of heathen Danish settlers, and all the church organization was dislocated for a time. The remaining monks of Lindisfarne took up St Cuthbert's body and their other most treasured relics and wandered for some years before the see was established at Chester-le-Street, to be removed to Durham in 995; the see of Hexham ceased to exist, the fate of Whithorn is obscure; only at York does the continuity seem to have been un-

broken, except for a gap of a year when the archbishop
fled to Mercia. In the Midlands the see of Leicester was
moved for safety to Dorchester-on-Thames and at some
uncertain date joined to that of Lindsey. After the
Norman Conquest, the combined see was moved from
Dorchester to Lincoln. The East Anglian sees of Dunwich and Elmham were both destroyed, and there was
no bishop for this area until about 956, when Elmham
was restored as the see of the whole province. All this area
had been full of important religious houses, but now they
came to an end. One result of this was that little of what
took place in these districts for the next two generations
found anyone to record it, and we know nothing of the
means used to convert the settlers to the Christian religion.

In the eastern counties heathenism seems to have been
fairly quickly eradicated. The Danish king of East
Anglia had agreed to be baptized as part of the terms
he made with King Alfred in 878. Before the end of the
century the cult of St Edmund, the king slain by the
Danes in 869, was well-established, and by 918 the district had been reconquered by the English. Up to the
middle of the century it appears to have been under the
authority of the bishop of London, Theodred 'the Good',
probably a native of the area, and its control in secular
affairs was entrusted to a religiously-minded ealdorman
of West Saxon origin, who was succeeded by equally
pious sons when he retired to end his life in the monastery
of Glastonbury. We cannot tell whether the native
priesthood which had survived the Danish invasion was
adequate to the task of converting the newcomers, or
whether help was forthcoming from the parts of England
outside Danish control. This is probable on general
grounds, for there is evidence that Edward the Elder
encouraged his thanes to settle among 'the pagans'

before he won back the Danelaw, and he may well have
directed priests to the area also. It is perhaps worth
noting that Bishop Theodred makes bequests in his will
to clergy with German names, which makes one wonder
whether the continental Churches established by English
missionaries sent contingents to their mother-church
when it required more clergy to convert the Danes than it
could supply, depleted as it was by the Viking ravages.
This can only be conjecture. What is clear is that from
the middle of the century there are references to small
religious communities in the eastern Danelaw, and the
foundation of the great fenland abbeys from 970 onwards
made this area as advanced as any part of the country in
ecclesiastical matters.

It is probable that the Danes of North-East Mercia
were converted not much later. They are certainly considered Christians in 942. In 956 and 958 large estates in
Nottinghamshire were granted by the king to the archbishop of York, on one of which, Southwell, an important
minster, was subsequently founded. Soon after the middle
of the tenth century the see of Lindsey seems to have been
temporarily revived, but possibly only as a subordinate
see to that of Dorchester, with which it merged again
later. In Northumbria there was a Christian Danish king
reigning some years before the close of the ninth century,
and there was hardly a break in continuity at the see of
York. But Northumbria was conquered in the early tenth
century by a fresh heathen invasion, that of the Irish
Norsemen from Dublin, and it is probably on this account
that more is heard of heathen worship here. The name
Othenesberg, 'Othin's hill', was given to Roseberry Top-
ping and a tenth-century encroacher on the lands of St
Cuthbert swore by Thor and Othin. The Scandinavians
took oath to suppress paganism at their treaty with King
Athelstan in 927, but the English chronicler regards the

Norsemen of York as heathen in 942. Northumbria passed permanently under the English crown in 954. We hear no more of heathen gods; but heathen customs were not so easily eradicated, and they are still being preached against and legislated against in the early eleventh century. As we have seen, the laws of the Church relating to marriage and divorce were often ignored. The monasteries destroyed by the invaders were not restored in the North. Yet Northumbria was not cut off from the ecclesiastical movements of the South. Even before the last Scandinavian king was driven out in 954, it had been ruled by the English kings for several periods of some years, and during these the archbishop of York normally attended the meetings of the English council, sometimes in Athelstan's reign accompanied by the bishop of Chester-le-Street (to which place the see of Lindisfarne had been removed) and by at least one other suffragan, of some unknown see. From 956 the archbishops of York were not chosen from the Northumbrian clergy, perhaps because the last holder of the see under the Scandinavian kings had been suspected of favouring these kings rather than the West Saxon royal house. Men of southern education were appointed, and usually men from the eastern counties, who would be familiar with the Anglo-Scandinavian speech and customs; and, because the northern province had been impoverished by the Danish invasions, it became customary to allow the see of York to be held in plurality with that of Worcester. The benefits of this arrangement would not be material only, for Worcester had an ancient tradition of learning and belonged to the one part of England that had escaped serious ravaging. It meant, however, that the archbishops might spend much of their time outside their northern diocese, but for all we know the kings may have considered that they thus kept a closer control over the

primates of a part of the kingdom whose loyalty to the
West Saxon rulers was suspect.

*

The long drawn-out Viking wars had brought about a
decline in the Church also in the parts of England that
were not ceded to the Danes. Only the Severn valley had
suffered little from the raiding armies, and even its
churches had not escaped impoverishment caused by the
general dislocation of affairs and the taxation imposed
to pay tribute to the Danes. King Alfred's labours
brought about some degree of recovery in Wessex, with
outside aid from Mercia, Wales, and the Continent, and
his successor subdivided the great diocese of western
Wessex by creating three new sees, Ramsbury, Wells, and
Crediton, which must have resulted in more effective
episcopal control. Alfred also founded a monastery at
Athelney and a nunnery at Shaftesbury, and his son
completed the church of Newminster, Winchester,
which his father had planned. But there was little
monastic zeal in the country at that time; many places
that had once been monasteries were possessed by bodies
of secular clerks, often married, and though many of
them may have been sincere and religious men – for we
need not accept all that their enemies and supplanters
tell us at a later date – before the middle of the tenth
century there was a widespread feeling that the situation
was unsatisfactory and that reform was desirable.

Meanwhile there had been a great Benedictine revival
on the Continent and it profoundly influenced the reform
in England. Of the main English movers in this matter,
Dunstan had spent two years at the reformed house of
Blandinium in Ghent, and he continued to keep up a
correspondence with his hosts after he returned to England, where he was made archbishop of Canterbury in

960; one of his predecessors, Oda, a Dane by birth and an effective reforming prelate, sent his nephew Oswald to study the new monasticism at the great abbey of Fleury-sur-Loire, and this Oswald became bishop of Worcester and archbishop of York. He placed a fellow student from Fleury over his foundation at Winchcombe, and when later he founded at the request of the East Anglian ealdorman a large monastery at Ramsey in Huntingdonshire he invited from Fleury a distinguished continental scholar, Abbo, to instruct his novices. The most energetic of all the reformers, Athelwold, abbot of Abingdon and later bishop of Winchester, had wished to go to Fleury; when prevented, he sent a monk from Abingdon to learn the practice of the rule there. The reform was strongly supported by King Edgar, who earned the epithet 'father of the monks'; the secular clerics were replaced by monks in many existing houses and new houses were founded, especially at places where former abbeys had been destroyed by the Danes, the most important being the fenland abbeys of Peterborough, Ely, and Thorney, which Athelwold restored. A common form of usage was drawn up, and monks from Ghent and Fleury came over to assist in its preparation.

The influence of this movement on art, learning, and literature will be considered in a later chapter. A reaction, on the death of Edgar in 975, especially in Mercia, had only a temporary success; the monks were supported by most of the great nobles, and the founding of Benedictine houses continued. A great West Saxon family, Ælfric's patrons, founded Cerne Abbas, Dorset, and Eynsham, Oxfordshire, and, more important, a very wealthy and influential Mercian thane, Wulfric Spott, endowed in the North-East Midlands, an area otherwise lacking such houses, the great abbey of Burton-on-Trent. The movement made no headway in the North, though most archbishops there were men trained in houses founded by it. It probably proved impossible to interest sufficient Anglo-Danish nobles in the endowment of monasteries.

Great effort was made in the late tenth and early eleventh centuries to improve the quality of the parish clergy. Abbot Ælfric produced a pastoral letter for Bishop Wulfsige of Sherborne to circulate to his clergy, setting out what the canons demanded of men in their office, and Archbishop Wulfstan, himself a man very learned in the ecclesiastical canons, obtained from Ælfric two such letters for the clergy of his own diocese. He had himself composed an address of exhortation to 'all the thanes, lay and ecclesiastical, entrusted to his direction in spiritual concerns' and a set of ecclesiastical injunctions known as *The Canons of Edgar*. Ælfric's books of homilies for the whole Christian year were aimed at improving the preaching of the clergy, and Byrhtferth of Ramsey wrote in 1011 a treatise on computation to help priests 'to relax their dice-playing and obtain a knowledge of this art.' Secular canons are enjoined to live a communal life and two of the best-known Frankish works regulating this manner of life, the rule of Chrodegang of Metz and that of Amalarius of Metz, were translated into Old English. Complaints of the shortcomings of the clergy are not lacking; some men seek orders because of the greater dignity of station; bishops should examine carefully the qualifications of candidates for ordination; tirades against ignorance, neglect of duty, and drunkenness occur. Many village priests were supporting existence in a position little better than a poor peasant, and it would be too mucn to expect high standards of scholarship everywhere. But the episcopate cannot be accused of neglecting their duty of supervision. All these pastoral letters try to impress on the clergy the principle of celibacy, but in this they failed. Frequently references to married priests occur; a testator can leave a church to a priest and his issue, and it is not uncommon for a son to follow his father in his clerical office. It is definitely accepted in the eleventh-century law issued for the priests of the diocese of York that they are likely to be married.

Reform in the Church seems to have gone on steadily in spite of the resumption of Danish invasions in the reign of Ethelred the Unready, but churchmen must have had an anxious time when the kingdom passed to Cnut at the end of 1016. However, the young king came under the influence of the English bishops, especially the veteran Archbishop Wulfstan of York, who drew up his laws for him and may well have been instrumental in inspiring him with the ambition to reign like his Christian predecessors. The agreement reached between English and Danes at Oxford in 1018 decided: 'that above all other things they would ever honour one God and steadfastly hold one Christian faith.' Cnut showed himself a defender of the rights of the Church, and a generous donor to religious houses. His laws include statutes against heathen practices. During the rest of the Anglo-Saxon period most sees were occupied by men of learning and integrity, and as Professor Darlington has shown, the English Church was neither decadent nor corrupt when the Normans came.

Moreover, it had the vitality in the tenth and eleventh centuries to be active again in missionary work. If only we had as good evidence, the story of the English missions to Scandinavia might be little less interesting than that of the conversion of Germany. But no correspondence relating to it has survived. There are references to English priests working for Hakon the Good and Olaf Tryggvason in tenth-century Norway, to an English bishop who was given an estate in Skåne in the reign of Swein Forkbeard, which he used as a base for work in Sweden and Norway, and to bishops and priests from England in attendance on St Olaf in the eleventh century. In general, however, the part played by the English Church has to be surmised from the undoubted influence it had on the organization and ritual of the Churches of Scandinavia, especially that of Norway.

CHAPTER IX

EDUCATION AND LATIN
SCHOLARSHIP

SINCE under the Roman system a bishop was bound to have at his see a school for educating suitable persons for the ministry, Augustine at Canterbury and his suffragan at Rochester would establish such schools. Afterwards, when East Anglia was converted, King Sigeberht, who had been converted in Gaul and 'was eager to imitate the things which he saw well ordered there', set up a school in his own land, 'Bishop Felix helping him and furnishing him with masters and teachers according to the custom of the people of Kent.' These early schools probably attracted pupils from beyond the frontiers of the kingdom in which they were situated; already before the middle of the seventh century men of Anglo-Saxon race were equipped to become bishops, and two of them, Deusdedit the West Saxon who was made archbishop in 654, and Damian the South Saxon who became a bishop in the next year, were from areas where no education was obtainable at that early date. Similarly, the Irish missionaries at once commenced the education of a native clergy. Aidan was given twelve boys to train for this purpose, and one of them, Eata, was abbot of Melrose by 651. About the middle of the century, education could also be acquired from the Irish community settled at Malmesbury, and it was here that Aldhelm was introduced to learning.

In these early schools attention was first concentrated on the knowledge essential for the priestly office – the Latin language, the Scriptures, the computation of the

Church seasons, the music necessary for the services. How far beyond this studies went before the days of Theodore and Hadrian is uncertain, but Ogilvy has drawn attention to the citation of Rufinus's Latin translation of the Greek *Ecclesiastical History* of Eusebius at the synod of Whitby in 664, and to the familiarity with Latin authors revealed by Aldhelm very early in his literary career.

Northumbrians flocked to the monasteries of Ireland in the second half of the seventh century. Aldfrith, later king of Northumbria, went 'to acquire celestial wisdom', and Cynefrith, brother of Abbot Ceolfrith, 'to study the Scriptures'. Theology held first place in the curriculum, but as the Irish schools had lain far from the path of the barbarian invasions, they had not shared in the general decline, and continued to study grammar and rhetoric, which included some attention to secular Latin literature. By the end of the century Aldhelm is claiming that as good an education is obtainable in England, though many unnecessarily go to Ireland. We have already seen that before this several young Northumbrians looked towards Canterbury and the Continent, even as far as Rome, and a new era set in for scholarship in England with the arrival of Archbishop Theodore, whom Bede calls 'a man deep in all secular and ecclesiastical learning, whether Greek or Latin', and Abbot Hadrian, a man of similar attainments. Benedict Biscop stayed two years with them in Canterbury, and his foundations of Monkwearmouth and Jarrow doubtless benefited by their teaching.

Bede, who spent his life in these foundations, and his older contemporary Aldhelm, who was educated at Malmesbury and then at Canterbury and who became bishop of Sherborne in 705, were both men of great erudition and must have had access to libraries well equipped with the works of Latin authors. They were, of course, familiar with the Bible and the writings of the Christian Fathers, and with the Christian poets, Juvencus, Prudentius, Sedulius, Prosper, Fortunatus, Lactantius, and Arator. Bede makes use of a number of historical writings, of Josephus, Eusebius (in Latin translation from the Greek), Orosius, Cassiodorus, Gregory of Tours, etc., and of saints' lives such as Paulinus's *Life of Ambrose*, Possidius's *Life of Augustine*, Constantius's *Life of Germanus*. Of classical authors, both Bede and Aldhelm knew Virgil and Pliny at first hand, and Aldhelm used Lucan, Ovid, Cicero, and Sallust. Citations of other authors occur, but could have been taken from the works of Isidore of Seville, or from the Latin grammarians, of whom a really remarkable number were available in England already in the seventh century. Some very rare works had already found their way to England, and one, the grammar of Julian of Toledo, owes its preservation to this circumstance, for all surviving manuscripts go back to an English copy. The apocryphal literature of the early Church also was known in England, and works like *The Gospel of Nicodemus*, *The Vision of St Paul*, various legends of the Apostles, and rarer works like *The Pseudo-gospel of St Matthew*, and the legend of Jamnes and Mambres, influenced both Anglo-Latin and vernacular literature.

Books must have been imported in great numbers soon after the conversion for such learning to have been possible. King Alfred believed that Augustine's equipment included Pope Gregory's *Pastoral Care*, which is probable enough. Theodore and Hadrian may have come provided with some Greek books as well as Latin works, for Bede testifies to the proficiency of their disciples in the Greek language, but it is difficult to discover direct influence of Greek writings in Anglo-Saxon authors, though some Greek influence on liturgical manuscripts can be demonstrated. We read also of the book-collecting activities of Benedict Biscop, Acca, and Bishop Cuthwine of Dunwich (716–31), who collected illuminated manuscripts, and of the dispatch to England of many books from a monastery in Gaul in the seventh century. William of Malmesbury has preserved a tradition of Aldhelm looking among the merchandise landed at Dover for valuable books, and it is likely enough that traders were quick to realize that there was a market for books in England.

The books that were introduced were not left to lie fallow. They were industriously copied in the scriptoria of English monasteries. Already by 678 Wilfrid ordered for his church of Ripon the four gospels 'in letters of purest gold on purpled parchment and illuminated'; the first abbot of Jarrow, Ceolfrith, ordered three whole bibles, of the 'new' translation by Jerome, to be transcribed in his monastery. One which he had meant to present to the Pope, if death had not overtaken him on his way to Rome, still survives to witness to the skill of this recently founded house, and fragments of another are in the British Museum and Durham. The famous Lindisfarne Gospels were produced about this time. Other biblical manuscripts and copies of other works were produced in England in considerable number in the eighth century. The missionaries on the Continent frequently write home to ask for books to be written, both elaborate, impressive copies of the Scriptures for ceremonial use, and also plainer texts, and it is of interest to note that women practised this art, not men alone. Boniface asked the Abbess Eadburh to copy the Epistles of St Peter in gold. Meanwhile the import of books from abroad did not cease and by the time of Alcuin York had an excellent library, of which he gives some account in his poem on the saints of York, and for which he sighed after he left England in 782 to help Charles the Great in his educational schemes. As late as the mid ninth century, an abbot of Ferrières applies to it for the loan of some rare books. Well could Alfred say in about 890: 'I remembered how I saw, before everything was ravaged and burnt, that the churches throughout all England were filled with treasures and books.'

*

It was not very long after the conversion to Christianity that the English were producing original works themselves, in the Latin language. Aldhelm's major works, his poem and prose treatise on virginity, are alien to modern taste both in subject and style, but the number of surviving manuscripts witnesses to their great popularity in the Middle Ages. His style was ornate and artificial, fond of rare words and elaborate similes, and full of alliteration. It was admired in his own day, and imitated by many later writers, though fortunately others preferred the simple straightforward style of Bede. Aldhelm's letters and shorter poems have more interest for us; he describes in detail a contemporary church, and tells us something of Theodore's teaching at Canterbury; a long letter addressed to King Aldfrith of Northumbria includes a hundred metrical riddles, the first examples in this country of a type of intellectual activity that proved popular among men of scholarship in their lighter moments. It had classical authority in the work of the fifth-century poet Symphosius, and the example was followed by Hwætberht, abbot of Monkwearmouth in succession to Ceolfrith, and by Tatwine, archbishop of Canterbury from 731 to 734. Boniface and his fellows also amused themselves with riddles and acrostics, and the metrical riddle was adopted by vernacular poets. While the riddles vary greatly in literary quality, they often show the authors' acute observation of the things around them, and are of assistance to the historian who desires a picture of everyday things. As far as we know, Aldhelm was the first Englishman to compose Latin verse.

Meanwhile Northumbria was producing a crop of biographies. Prior to the work of Bede are anonymous lives of St Cuthbert and of Ceolfrith, abbot of Jarrow, the life of St Gregory by an anonymous monk of Whitby, and Eddius's interesting life of St Wilfrid. These were all known and used by Bede, who also had access to a lost life of St Æthelburh of Barking, the nunnery for which Aldhelm wrote his prose work on virginity; the writing of saints' lives was therefore not confined to Northumbria. Bede was in communication with learned men from all over the country. It was Albinus, abbot of the monastery of St Peter and St Paul at Canterbury, who encouraged him to write his *Ecclesiastical History*, and supplied him with material from Kent, and Nothhelm, a priest of London, searched the papal archives in Rome to find for Bede the letters relating to the English mission. Bishop Daniel of Winchester, the writer later on of shrewd advice to Boniface on the conversion of the heathen, corresponded with Bede about the history of the conversion of Wessex and Sussex, and an East Anglian abbot Esius and Cyneberht, bishop of Lindsey, were consulted on matters in their provinces. We have seen that Aldhelm was in correspondence with the learned king, Aldfrith of Northumbria, and Bede speaks with appreciation of Tobias, bishop of Rochester, and Tatwine, who was a Mercian. It is clear that political boundaries formed no obstacle to scholarly intercourse. Aldhelm was also in correspondence with a continental abbot, Cellan of Péronne.

Bede was not, first and foremost, a historian in contemporary eyes, and his most famous work, his *Ecclesiastical History of the English Nation*, belongs to the end of his literary career, which began with the writing of textbooks, on metrics, orthography, science, and chronology. In connexion with the latter subject, he included a short chronicle of world history, and his verse *Life of St Cuthbert* was written early in his career, but between these works and his major historical works must be placed volume after volume of commentaries on various books of the Bible, and it was as a theologian rather than a historian that the Middle Ages honoured him most. In 721 he wrote his prose *Life of St Cuthbert*, followed a few years later by his *Lives of the Abbots*. His longer chronicle can be dated 725, and he finished his *Ecclesiastical History* in 731. Between this and his death in 735 can be placed a commentary on the Acts, and a long letter on Church organization addressed to his pupil Egbert, archbishop of York, and there survive also a number of theological treatises, homilies, hymns, etc., whose date is uncertain. In contrast to the writings of Aldhelm, there has never been a period in which Bede's work was entirely neglected; manuscripts were multiplied throughout the Middle Ages, and it has always formed the basis of modern historical studies of the early Saxon period. One cannot sum up better the reason for this than to quote Sir Frank Stenton's words: 'But the quality which makes his work great is not his scholarship, nor the faculty of narrative which he shared with many contemporaries, but his astonishing power of co-ordinating the fragments of information which came to him through tradition, the relation of friends, or documentary evidence. In an age when little was attempted beyond the registration of fact, he had reached the conception of history.'

During Bede's lifetime a work of a different kind was

compiled by a man who called himself 'a disciple of the Humbrians'. It consists of a collection of the answers and decisions given by Archbishop Theodore on matters of penance and canon law, and goes under the name of *Theodore's Penitential*. Bede's pupil Cuthbert wrote an account of the last days of his master, and to the pen of another pupil, Archbishop Egbert, there is ascribed a penitential and a dialogue concerning ecclesiastical government. This last work illustrates the system of teaching used in the school of York, a school which under Egbert and his kinsman Ethelbert became one of the most famous centres of learning in Europe. It was here that Alcuin was educated, and he speaks with great reverence of his master Ethelbert, the founder of the great library there, and Egbert's successor in the see. From the work of Alcuin and his biographer we find that pupils were instructed both by exposition and by disputation, and the purpose of the dialogue was to give practice in discourse in the Latin tongue, and at the same time impart necessary information on an important subject. Alcuin carried the method with him to the Continent, and some of his own work is couched in dialogue form. He had himself succeeded Ethelbert as master of the school of York, and acquired a reputation that brought foreigners to study there, before he was invited to take charge of Charles the Great's palace school, and left Northumbria in 782 to spend most of the rest of his life abroad, assisting the revival of learning in the Carolingian empire. Latin poems, sent to him by his students at York, on the miracles of St Ninian, are extant, and much work from his own pen, treatises, letters, poems, etc. He saw himself divinely called to the Continent to combat the Adoptionist heresy, and much of his writing is on religious polemic. Of greater general interest are his poem on York, and his life of the Anglo-

Saxon missionary St Willibrord. He was not an original
scholar, but his work was influential out of all proportion
to its literary merits, and Dr Levison has pointed out that
his methods opened the way for later thinkers of greater
independence. His work as a liturgical and biblical
scholar had very far-reaching results, and he left behind a
number of men, some of them of English nationality, to
carry on his work in the ninth-century Frankish empire.
He lived to see and be overwhelmed with grief by the
first of the Viking raids, the sack of Lindisfarne in 793,
but not to know that this was but the beginning of a
catastrophe destined within a century totally to destroy
Northumbrian scholarship. It was on the Continent, not
at home, that his work had permanent results.

From the lands south of the Humber few original
works have been preserved, though the letters of St Boniface reveal a powerful intellect that might have been
productive of distinguished literary work if the writer's
energies had not been so completely occupied in other
affairs. As it is, there are only these letters and a grammar
from his pen. There were many men and women throughout England of adequate education to write good Latin
letters to him and his successor Lul, and an English nun
at Heidenheim, one of the monasteries founded in
Germany by the missionaries, by name Hygeburh, has
left us a most interesting work, the *Lives of St Willibald
and St Wynnebald*, in the third quarter of the eighth century. It includes a fascinating account of a pilgrimage
undertaken by Willibald to the Holy Land, written from
his recollections. From the Midlands a generation earlier
comes Felix's *Life of St Guthlac of Crowland*, a work which
throws some welcome light on a period and locality for
which evidence is hard to come by. In spite of scanty
evidence, one gets the impression that in almost all parts
of England during the eighth century there were centres

where a liberal education could be obtained, and it was not confined to the male sex. Aldhelm's writings for the nuns of Barking and Rudolf's *Life of St Leofgyth*, Boniface's helper in his missionary work, who was educated at Minster and at Wimborne, show that women, like men, studied the scriptures and their fourfold interpretation, the works of the Fathers, chronography, grammar, and metrics.

*

Already Bede's *Ecclesiastical History* includes several examples of a type of literature that attained a great vogue, the accounts of visions of heaven and hell revealed to various individuals to whom it is permitted to return to earth to relate what they have seen for the benefit of others. The visions of the Irish hermit Fursey and of the Northumbrian Dryhthelm became particularly renowned, and often survive as separate extracts in our manuscripts. One of Boniface's letters describes at length a similar vision seen by a man at the abbey of Wenlock, in which he saw prophetically King Ceolred of Mercia among the damned, and this letter was later translated into English. The terror of the Danish invasions in the ninth century caused men to see more visions, and in 839 envoys sent by King Æthelwulf of Wessex to the Emperor Louis warned him of the vision revealed to a certain religious priest, which threatened famine and pagan attack if men did not amend their ways and, in particular, keep religiously the proper observance of Sunday. This seems like a reference to the work of a priest Pehtred, who wrote in the province of York (though not in that diocese or that of Lindisfarne) before 837 a book which has been lost, but whose contents are known in part from the horror its heresy roused in the breasts of the archbishop and of his suffragan at Lindisfarne. It told of a deacon Nial who came to life after being dead for seven weeks, and never partook of food afterwards; of a letter of gold written by the hand of God, dealing with the due observance of Sunday, and found on St Peter's altar in the days of Pope Florentius. This tale had been condemned by a Frankish capitulary already in the eighth century, and the bishop of Lindisfarne is urgent that effective steps be taken to suppress this heresy. With a historical sense proper to a countryman of Bede he had consulted lists of popes and failed to find any trace of a Pope Florentius. Yet the fact that no fewer than six vernacular homilies are to be found in tenth- and eleventh-century manuscripts which accept the authenticity of this letter from heaven indicates how unsuccessful were the efforts of the saner element of the population to prevent the spread of such wild tales.

However, Northumbria was not only producing heresy in the ninth century. A certain Æthilwulf wrote a long Latin poem on the abbots of an unidentified Northumbrian monastery, as well as a work on the English saints which has not survived; and the monks of Lindisfarne wrote in letters of silver and gold their 'Book of Life', containing the names of those for whom they were bound to pray. York was still in touch with at least one continental monastery. Wessex, too, had its continental connexions: King Æthelwulf at one time employed a Frankish secretary, and was a benefactor to continental houses. The knowledge shown of the lives of Frankish saints in the ninth-century Old English *Martyrology* is further evidence of intercourse across the Channel. Book-production had not entirely ceased. Yet already Alcuin had complained of a decline in the zeal for study in England, and this can only have been hastened by the constant threat of Viking raids. King Alfred's impression was that before the monasteries were destroyed by these raids

the monks in them did not know Latin and could make
no use of their richly equipped libraries.

*

Alfred's educational reforms, which he found time to put
into force during the latter part of his reign, aimed at
spreading the ability to read English and at supplying
suitable books in English – a subject which belongs to the
next chapter. Men destined for the Church are, however,
to study Latin, and it is clear that Alfred regrets that the
decay of Latin scholarship should have made translation
necessary. The half-century following his death is not
prolific in signs of intellectual activity, and it may well be
that men's energies were largely absorbed in the re-
conquest and re-conversion of the areas ceded to the
Danes; yet it was not as utterly devoid of such signs as
the mid tenth-century reformers and their pupils were
ready to believe. Oda, who became archbishop of Canterbury in 942, and who is the author of a short series of
Latin canons, had been able to obtain an education in a
thane's household. King Athelstan was generous in gifts
of books to religious houses, obtaining some from abroad.
The copy of Bede's *Life of St Cuthbert*, in prose and verse,
which he gave to the church of that saint at Chester-le-
Street, was however an English production, probably
from Glastonbury; and there survive manuscripts of
works of Bede and Aldhelm which are assigned to this
period. The influence of Aldhelm's style is visible in the
highly flamboyant Latinity of the charters of this period.
There is evidence of the production in England of a
version of the *History of the Britons* of Nennius during the
reign of King Edmund (939–46), and a Latin poem on
the life of St Wilfrid by a certain Frithegod was dedicated
to Archbishop Oda. Parts of a Latin verse panegyric on

King Athelstan are quoted by William of Malmesbury. Manuscripts of vernacular prose were being copied. Nevertheless the best minds of the time thought that in scholarship as in monastic usage England was behind the Continent, and the reform movement drew its inspiration from abroad.

The monastic reformers devoted great care to the teaching of Latin in their monasteries. Works meant solely for use there are in Latin. Athelwold translated the Benedictine Rule into English, but there is a possibility that he did so for the use of communities of women. At any rate, it was at the special request of the king and queen that he undertook this task, receiving an estate in recompense. His own compilation for securing uniformity of observance in the monasteries of England, the *Regularis Concordia*, he wrote in Latin, and similarly his pupil Ælfric, master of Old English prose though he was, used Latin for his letter to his monks at Eynsham which is based on this *Concordia*, and for the Life of St Athelwold which he meant for monastic reading. This life contains a brief comment on Athelwold as a teacher:

It was always a pleasure to him to teach young men and boys, and to explain books to them in English, and with kindly exhortations to encourage them to better things.

Archbishop Oswald brought over from Fleury a distinguished continental scholar, Abbo, to teach his monks at Ramsey, and Abbo wrote a grammar for their use and a Latin *Life of St Edmund*. It was a monk of Ramsey who wrote a Latin biography of St Oswald. When Ælfric and Byrhtferth of Ramsey write works in English, they are thinking of a wider public than those trained in monasteries. Byrhtferth shows his belief that the education of the average priest would be below that obtainable in the cloister, when he says:

But because we know that these things seem complex enough to clerks and rustic priests, we will now address our words to the young monks who have occupied their childhood with scientific books. I mention a few such, out of many; they have investigated Sergius and Priscian, and gone slowly through the *Distichs* of the bald fellow Cato, and the narratives of Bede, the venerable scholar.

To assist in the teaching of Latin, Ælfric wrote a Latin grammar, a Latin-English glossary, and a colloquy to exercise his pupils in Latin conversation. The characters are a master, a novice, and representatives of the various crafts. This work has been drawn on in previous chapters for the evidence it affords of contemporary conditions.

It is clear both from extant manuscripts and also from the knowledge revealed by writers of the period, chiefly by Ælfric and Wulfstan, that the monastic revival led to the introduction into England of many Latin works of the Carolingian revival and later, especially canonistic writings, some of which were translated into English. Scholars of this age knew, in addition to the works of the Fathers and classical writers, those of the more recent authors Alcuin, Hrabanus Maurus, Amalarius of Metz, Atto of Vercelli, Smaragdus, Haymo of Halberstadt, and so on. And Abbo was not the only foreigner to write in England; one of the earliest lives of St Dunstan was the work of a foreigner, and an account of the miracles of St Swithin was written at Winchester by someone whom Ælfric calls 'Landferth, the man from across the sea.' Winchester possessed also a writer of Latin verse, an Englishman called Wulfstan the precentor, whose poem on St Swithin is extant, and to whom William of Malmesbury attributes a life of St Athelwold.

One Latin work is written by a layman, Ealdorman Æthelweard, a patron of Ælfric. He was a descendant of King Alfred's elder brother, and he wrote, for the benefit of his kinswoman, Matilda, abbess of Essen, a descendant of Alfred, a Latin chronicle, based in general on the Anglo-Saxon Chronicle, of which he seems to have possessed a manuscript better in some respects than any that have survived. If the printed text of his work, which, except for a few badly scorched and illegible fragments of the burnt manuscript, is all that we possess, fairly represents him, he wrote a strange and at times incomprehensible Latin; but it is remarkable that a layman should attempt such a task at all.

Another result of the revival was an enormous activity in manuscript production, which continued for the rest of the Saxon period. There poured out elaborate illuminated manuscripts and plainer utilitarian ones; manuscripts in Latin and in English; gospels, psalters, service books of all kinds; works of earlier Latin writers, including the English scholars Aldhelm and Bede, Felix's Life of St Guthlac, and the Life of King Alfred by the Welshman Asser; collections of canons; books of extracts from various sources; calendars, almanacs, etc. Before 1066 the libraries must have again become as full as ever they were in the days before the Viking ravages.

CHAPTER X

VERNACULAR LITERATURE

FAR back in heathen days the Germanic races had their songs. Tacitus speaks of these as the only type of memorial and chronicle they possessed, mentioning specifically that the former leader Arminius was celebrated in song; and the historians of the individual Germanic nations, Jordanes who wrote of the Goths, Paul, the historian of the Lombards, the anonymous Frank who wrote of the acts of Charlemagne, could draw information from poems which have not survived. The English tribes brought over with them traditions in verse form, relating to the heroes of their homeland, and naturally they would continue to compose such poems in their new settlements. Some of the statements in Bede's works and in the Anglo-Saxon Chronicle are probably derived from such sources. Though historical writers, from Tacitus onwards, are mainly interested in poems celebrating the heroes of the past, it is probable that poems of other kinds existed from early times – dirges for the dead, hymns in honour of heathen gods, and mnemonic poems, by which the wisdom of the past could be handed on in easily remembered form; but in England pre-Christian poems had little chance of being written down, and only a few fragments survive, embedded in the work of later Christian writers. Thus a poem of Christian date, *Widsith*, which purports to be a minstrel's account of the races and courts he has visited, includes catalogues of kings and peoples which express the point of view of the age of national migration rather than that of England in Christian times; and the gnomic poetry, which seems to be a collection of the more memorable utterances of wise men, added to from age to age, includes a passage accepting cremation as the normal burial-rite –

The holly shall be kindled; the inheritance of the dead man divided; fame is best –

side by side with passages of Christian date, such as:

Feud first came to mankind when the earth swallowed Abel's blood. That was no enmity of a single day, from which sprang for men, for many peoples far and wide, bloodshed from strife, great crime, pernicious hatred.

The poet of *Beowulf*, who was undoubtedly a Christian, knows that his audience will be familiar with tales of family feuds among the races who were neighbours of the English on the Continent, and it is probable that he drew his descriptions of long-discontinued funeral rites from poems with their roots in a distant past. In the charms one even gets an occasional remembrance of a heathen deity as a protective power.

The survival into Christian times of the older poetry was aided by the interest which the Anglo-Saxon royal and noble families took in the traditions of the deeds of their ancestors. Bede sent his *Ecclesiastical History* to King Ceolwulf of Northumbria for his criticism because he was well versed in the ancient traditions of his race, and it may be that heroic verse was included among the Saxon songs which King Alfred made his children learn. Aldhelm, bishop of Sherborne from 705 to 709, sang and composed vernacular songs, and his contemporary St Guthlac was in his youth inspired to the profession of arms by remembering the deeds of the heroes of old; both these men were related to royal houses. So also was St Dunstan, whom we know to have been interested in native poetry, while the chronicler Æthelweard, who betrays in his work a knowledge of the old traditions, was descended from King Alfred's elder brother. Men such as these could see to it that what they were interested in should be written down, and it is to them or others like them that we owe the preservation of works that are without ecclesiastical interest; but we need not assume that their tastes were not shared by the lesser folk who could not employ the services of scribes. It was not by the scribe, but by the minstrel, whether professional or amateur, whether king's thane or humble singer in taverns, that this poetry was normally transmitted, and the bulk of it has not come down to us.

*

According to Bede, it was a man of the peasant class who first had the inspiration to employ the diction and metre of native verse for Christian themes; it was while he was taking his turn at guarding the cattle of the abbey of Whitby that Cædmon saw one night in a vision a man who told him to sing of the Creation. The lines which he composed in his sleep and repeated next morning constitute the earliest datable English poetry, for they survive in a manuscript written two or three years after Bede's death. It may therefore be of interest to quote them in the original as well as in translation. They are as follows:

> Nu scylun hergan hefænricaes uard,
> metudæs maecti end his modgidanc,
> uerc uuldurfadur, sue he uundra gihuaes,
> eci dryctin, or astelidæ;
> he ærist scop aelda barnum
> heben til hrofe, haleg scepen.
> Tha middungeard moncynnæs uard,
> eci dryctin, æfter tiadæ
> firum foldu, frea allmectig.

(Now we must praise the guardian of the heavenly kingdom, the powers of the Creator and his thoughts, the works of the Father of glory, as he, the eternal Lord, appointed the beginning of every wondrous thing; he, the holy Lord, the Guardian of mankind, first created for the children of men the heaven as a roof. Then the eternal Lord, Ruler Almighty, afterwards adorned the world, the earth, for men.)

The metre of Old English verse is sufficiently akin to that of Old Norse, Old Saxon, and Old High German to prove that it descends from the same Germanic verse-form. Rhyme is rarely used, and then only as an additional ornament; it is alliteration that binds together the two halves of the line, which is divided into more or less equal parts by a caesura; either one or two strongly stressed syllables of the first half-line alliterate with the first stress of the second half-line (any vowel being able to alliterate with any other). Each half-line belongs to one of a limited number of rhythmical types, the most widely acknowledged system of scansion recognizing five main types with various subdivisions; the number of syllables is not fixed, and it is generally held that the normal half-line consisted of two stressed portions, known as lifts, and a varying number of unstressed syllables. This is not the place to go into technical detail – nor, in fact, is there complete agreement on the subject; but it should be noted that rhythm and alliteration follow the natural logical emphasis of the lines, and that the sentences are often long and may be stopped at the caesura as well as at the end of the line. The length of the sentence arises not so much from elaborate periodic structure as from 'parallelism', the restatement in fresh words of significant elements in the sentence – as for example the expressions for God in Cædmon's hymn – or even of whole clauses. In the best Old English poetry this is not empty repetition; the concept is given a fresh significance by each new reference to it: Hrothgar's 'hall-troop' becomes his 'war-band', the vague 'land' is particularized as 'steep hills' and 'broad sea-headlands' in the succeeding lines, 'famine' is personified as a 'pale guest at table'.

What was carried over into the service of the Christian religion was far more than the metre. Poetry had its own diction. The requirements of alliteration had already brought into being a large vocabulary of synonyms, many of which are not found in prose. To some extent this is a question of date: some words had become archaic when we begin to get vernacular prose, but others may have been poetic from the beginning. This applies especially to the poetic compounds and kennings (brief descriptive expressions used instead of the name of the thing itself, such as 'gannet's bath' for the sea, 'candle of the heavens' for the sun, etc.), which made it possible for an Old English poet to pack into a few words great richness of description and association. By the time of Cædmon many stereotyped expressions were in use and were taken over by the religious poetry; words such as 'battlemen', 'warriors', brave leaders', were applied to the disciples, and the Christian God was spoken of in the various terms used of the chieftains of heroic poetry. How far this terminology retained its original martial connotation is a moot point, but it came easy to the Anglo-Saxon to conceive the relationship between God and his angels, or Christ and his disciples, in terms of the Teutonic code of loyalty between man and lord, and it required little modification to turn pre-Christian lines advocating liberality into praises of the Christian virtue of almsgiving, or to give a Christian emphasis to the Germanic insistence on the acquisition of a good reputation. The mnemonic poetry could enlarge its compass to include the Christian account of the origin of all things, as one poet puts it (in W. S. Mackie's translation):

It is, thinking man, an obvious example to every one who can by wisdom comprehend in his mind all the world, that long ago men, well-advised people, could often utter and say the truth in the art of song, by means of lays, so that most of mankind, by always asking and repeating and remembering, gained knowledge of the web of mysteries. So let him who is zealous, the studious man, inquire about the secrets of Creation, inscribe in his understanding the art of narrating them, fix his mind on them, ponder over them well. An earnest man must not become weary of wisely completing his knowledge of the world.

And thus we have poems that illustrate the workings of divine providence in the distribution of gifts and fortunes to men by a series of cameo-like descriptions of men's various occupations – minstrelsy, seamanship, the goldsmith's craft, hunting and hawking – and of the ways by which men meet their end; and poems of practical mnemonics, on the festivals of the Church and the fasting seasons. There are also poems of direct religious and moral exhortation, such as *An Admonition to Christian Living* and *The Advice of a Father to his Son*. An address of a sinful soul to the body it has just left is one of the few poems to survive in more than one version, and there are poems that deal dramatically with the Last Judgement.

Of the many poems on religious themes which Bede tells us Cædmon composed, nothing has come down that can with certainty be ascribed to him except the few lines quoted above. He had many, in Bede's opinion inferior, imitators before 731, and some surviving poems may date from this time. During the eighth century the English missionaries to the Continent probably spread the habit of composing biblical paraphrases in alliterative verse, for the extant Old Saxon poetry betrays English influence. The extant Anglo-Saxon religious verse is varied in range and style. Besides the works already mentioned, it includes close paraphrases of the Old Testament, as in *Genesis* and *Daniel;* a heroic poem on how Moses led the

Israelites across the Red Sea; poems on Christ's descent into Hell and his Second Coming; and saints' lives, of Andrew, Helena, Juliana, Guthlac, all based on Latin originals and none earlier than the second half of the eighth century. Two of these are the work of a poet called Cynewulf, of the late eighth or the ninth century, whose work is distinguished by a graceful mastery of technique and by a logical clarity and smoothness of syntax that owes something to his classical scholarship. Two other poems, one on the Ascension, and one a brief summary of the deaths of the Apostles, are known to be his. Of learned origin also are some fragments of a *Physiologus*, and a poem on the Phoenix based on the Latin poem ascribed to Lactantius, and Latin inspiration lies behind the verse riddles. Much more original is the well-known poem called *The Dream of the Rood*, of which some lines were carved in runes on the stone cross at Ruthwell; in this a poet with deep religious feeling, imaginative insight and an amazing restraint and economy of expression, allows the cross to tell its own story of the crucifixion and of its metamorphosis from forest tree to instrument of death and then to a glorious and venerated symbol of redemption.

It is not true, as is sometimes maintained, that all Anglo-Saxon poetry is gloomy. Another type of religious poetry deals poignantly with the transitory nature of all earthly joy, but it is only for those who dismiss as mere empty convention the final conclusion of *The Wanderer*: 'Well will it be with him who seeks mercy and consolation from the Father in heaven, where for us all that security stands', or the claim of *The Seafarer*: 'for my heart warms more to the joys of the Lord than to this dead life', that these poems sound a despairing note. Moreover, these poems would move us little if their authors were less conscious of the beauty of the world around them and of the human relationships that will not last for ever. Anglo-Saxon poets excel at painting nature in its stormy and forbidding moods, but they did not see it exclusively like this; it was the Christian's duty to esteem the works of the Creator, and any impression of the poetry is one-sided that leaves out of count passages such as the following:

Full often, O King of Glory, thou sendest through the air the soft morning rain for the benefit of men. Many a plant shall then awaken, and the groves of the forest teem with branches.

or again:

Groves begin to blossom, the courts become fair, the plains grow beautiful, the world quickens.

The poet of the longest extant poem, *Beowulf*, is similarly alive to the beauty of nature and of some of the works of men's hands; of shining headlands, of the sailing ship driven by the wind 'most like a bird', of the flash of the sun on the gold-adorned helmets of a marching band of men. Like most Old English poetry, this poem cannot be dated exactly. Most scholars place it between 650 and 750; to me the extent of Christian education it assumes in its audience suggests a date late in this period, or even during the following half-century. It tells how a strong and valiant hero, trusting in the help of God, saves first the Danish royal hall, and later his own people, from the ravages of evil monsters, the descendants of the first murderer, Cain. By subtle reminders to an audience steeped in stories of the past, the poet supplies a realistic background to this theme, and a foil to it, putting it in a setting of human strife, of civil or foreign warfare; and he seems to point a moral that there are intangible and permanent values that remain untouched by the vicissitudes of fortunes in this life, where all is transitory. Both the races the hero delivers have a tragic history ahead of them, and the hero slays the dragon only at the cost of his own life; but, dying, he is not afraid to face 'the Ruler of men', and the poem closes with the building of a barrow to his memory, that it may, as he wished:

tower high on *Hronesnæs*, so that in after days seafarers, who urge their tall ships from afar over the mists of the ocean, may call it Beowulf's barrow.

Another poet, using the stories of old heroes to impart a moral, has left us the little lyric *Deor*, which purports to be the utterance of a minstrel who has been supplanted by a rival, and who comforts himself in a series of strophes each referring to the sorrows of a character of heroic legend, and concluding with the refrain: 'That was surmounted, so can this be.' In other so-called lyrics the speaker is anonymous. In one, a woman laments her unhappy situation, due to the machinations of her husband's kinsfolk and his alienation from her; some would connect with this poem another in which a man who has gone into exile across the sea sends for his wife to join him in his new-found prosperity. It is probable that such poems are concerned with the sentiments of people in typical situations, not with personages of specific story. Neither conveys any religious message, whereas a poem known as *The Wanderer* poignantly describes the desolation of a lordless man and of a ruined city in order to contrast it with the security of trust in the eternal Lord, and another, known as *The Seafarer*, shows how a man's yearning for 'the joys of the Lord' impels him to undertake afresh a journey across the sea in spite of his sufferings, most graphically recounted, on former voyages. Both poems, and also a fragment called *The Ruin*, contain laments for the splendour of earlier and greater civilizations. Only fragments remain of direct heroic narrative, two of a poem on Waldere, the Walter of continental story, and one of a highly dramatic account of a fight at Finn's hall, which was also the theme of a lay sung by a minstrel in *Beowulf*.

*

The vast bulk of Old English poetry has come down to us in four codices compiled towards the end of the tenth century or early in the eleventh; it is mostly of much earlier date than these manuscripts, which must owe their existence to a desire to preserve the work of the past. Little survives from the second half of the ninth century or later, but it would be unsafe to assume that this means that little was being produced, for the chances of survival, at any rate for secular verse, were not high. Somewhat prosaic verse renderings of the *Metra* of Boethius and of the Psalms have been preserved, and the latter part of a vigorous poem on *Judith*. A manuscript containing a long Old Saxon poetic paraphrase of parts of the Bible reached England some time towards the end of the ninth century or in the first half of the tenth, and the English were sufficiently interested in the productions of a daughter church on the Continent to make an illuminated manuscript of one of these poems, the *Héliand*, and a translation of part, at least, of the other, the *Genesis*. Several hundred lines of this were inserted into the Old English poems on this subject. It stands out from this not only by differences in language and metre, but also by its spirit, for it is a vigorous, dramatic, and unorthodox treatment of the story of the Fall of the Angels and the Fall of Man. Some historical poems are entered into the Anglo-Saxon Chronicle of the tenth and eleventh centuries, and show that the conventional expressions of the old heroic poetry were still in use. By far the best poem of the later Saxon period, that on the battle of

Maldon fought in 991, has been preserved by the accidental circumstance that the leader in this battle was also a great benefactor of monasteries. There may have been many poems of a like nature which were never entered in manuscripts at all. *The Battle of Maldon* employs very few of the clichés of the older poems, but it inherits their spirit, dealing as it does with men whose loyalty forbids them to return from a fight in which their lord has fallen. As in *Beowulf* it is not success that matters, but a living up to a code of honour even when it leads to certain death.

*

Vernacular prose for utilitarian purposes began early. Laws were from the first written in English, beginning with those of Ethelbert of Kent, and interlinear glosses in the vernacular were written in Latin texts in the seventh century, and had begun to be collected into glossaries by the end of the century. Bede was engaged in translating into consecutive prose the Gospel of St John when he died. This has not survived, and except for laws and a few charters, the history of English prose has to begin with the reign of Alfred. It is probably accident that this is so; as we know that pre-Alfredian manuscripts of verse existed and have been lost, the same may have happened with prose works. Alfred declares that many in his day could read what was written in English, which may suggest that there were things for them to read which have not survived. It is likely that there were homilies in the vernacular, for preaching was done in the native tongue, and it is improbable that every preacher composed his own sermons. The spread of the heretical matter from Pehtred's book, mentioned above, would presumably be among the less learned, since it was frowned on by the higher clergy, and it may well have been facilitated by English versions. Some of the materials available to the compiler of the Anglo-Saxon Chronicle in Alfred's day may have been in English. An Old English martyrology, of which fragments survive in manuscripts of Alfred's reign, may date from before the Alfredian revival. The works of Bede, Aldhelm, Adamnan, Eddius, Felix, as well as of older Latin writers like Gregory and Jerome, were used for this compilation, and also lives of Frankish saints and apocryphal matter such as the *Passions of the Apostles*.

King Alfred grew up in a court with Frankish affinities. He was almost certainly aware of what Charles the Great had done to improve the standard of learning among his people, and the measures he employed in his distress at the decline occasioned by the Danish invasions may owe something to this example. Like Charles, he invited learned men from abroad; he asked assistance from Fulk, archbishop of Reims, who sent him a Frankish scholar called Grimbald, and he invited Asser from Wales and John from the Old Saxons. Other helpers, Plegmund, later archbishop of Canterbury, and Werferth, bishop of Worcester, and two priests came from Mercia. Probably in, or soon after, 890, Alfred sent to each of his bishops a letter accompanying a gift of his translation of *The Pastoral Care* of Gregory the Great, and in it he outlined his plan by which all free-born youths of adequate means were to be taught to read English, and the books 'which are most necessary for all men to know' translated into English. The books chosen were *The Pastoral Care*, which had always been a book much used by the English clergy; the *Dialogues* of the same author; two history books, the *Universal History against the Pagans* of Orosius and Bede's *Ecclesiastical History of the English Nation;* Boethius' *On the Consolation of Philosophy*, the book which handed down to the Middle Ages some of the ideas of the Greek philosophers; and part of St Augustine's *Soliloquies*, to which was added material from other writers on similar topics, the heavenly wisdom and the relation to God of the human soul. Gregory's *Dialogues*, which treat of the lives of the early saints of Italy, and Bede's *Ecclesiastical History* were translated by Mercian scholars, and there is great doubt whether Alfred himself translated Orosius; but the other works are his own, with the help of his assistants. As translations, they do not rank very high; at times the rendering is clumsy and the meaning, especially in the philosophical works, misrepresented. Yet it is these works which have the greatest interest, for in them Alfred, who had no slavish attitude of literal fidelity to the texts, often adds passages from other sources and from his own experience and ponderings on such matters; sometimes he gives a concrete simile to make clear the abstract reasoning of his author, as when he compares God's foreknowledge to the steersman's anticipation of a great wind at sea before it comes, and occasionally he inserts a whole chapter, like that on the art of government quoted in Chapter IV above. The *Orosius* also has additions to the source, including an account of the geography of Northern Europe with two seamen's accounts of voyages in these regions. In such passages one has a chance to judge what Old English prose could be when unshackled by the need to render Latin, and though the balance and smoothness of an Ælfric is lacking, it is a workmanlike medium enough. Early post-Conquest authors attributed to Alfred a translation of the Psalms, part of which may well be preserved in the *Paris Psalter*, and even of the whole Bible, but it is natural that the thought of a king translating for his people's good should fire men's imaginations and cause works not his to be attributed to him. We see something of the impression his work made already in his lifetime, in a Latin acrostic on him in a Cornish (or perhaps Welsh) manuscript, which ends (in W. M. Lindsay's translation):

Rightly do you teach, hastening from the false sweetness of the world. Behold you are ever fit to turn shining talents to profit. Learnedly run through the fields of foreign lore.

The author is much hampered by his need to begin and end his lines with the letters of Alfred's name, but through his stilted language we glimpse genuine admiration of a king who turns from temporal pleasures to the discipline of scholarship.

There is manuscript evidence that the Old English *Orosius*, *Bede*, *Boethius*, and *The Pastoral Care* were being copied in, or soon after, the first half of the tenth century, and so was the *Martyrology*. Copies of all the Alfredian works survive from the time after the monastic revival, and we have Ælfric's evidence that they were obtainable in his day a century after they were composed. Moreover Æthelweard about the same period speaks of his translations with admiration, especially the *Boethius*, and his words imply that this work was read aloud to those unskilled in reading. Alfred's labours had more than a temporary effect.

*

Modern, like medieval, scholars have been ready to attribute works to Alfred. There is no clear evidence that he was responsible for the compilation of the Anglo-Saxon Chronicle, though it is possible that the rather rapid multiplication of manuscripts of this work owes something to royal encouragement. The Chronicle was based on older records, on Bede and regnal lists, on some epitome of world history, and on various sets of brief early annals, in Latin and perhaps sometimes in English; these materials were put together in Alfred's reign, the annals becoming much fuller as the period within living memory was reached. Round about 890 copies began to be disseminated. The oldest extant copy is written up to 891 in a single handwriting, and it is already two stages removed from the original work; this version was at Winchester in the tenth century and may have been originally copied for this house. All other surviving manuscripts are later, and represent copies of versions kept at different religious establishments. Three of the manuscripts go back to a text which had been at some northern centre, probably York, and had there had dove-tailed into it a large amount of northern material, from Bede and from some sets of local annals, and one of these manuscripts reached Peterborough by the early twelfth century, where it was kept up until the early days of 1155, all the other versions having come to a close at various earlier dates. Each version contains passages peculiar to it, usually of local interest, but over long stretches several versions – and sometimes all – are in agreement. The problems of relationship and transmission of the various versions are too complicated to be dealt with in a para-graph. More independence is shown from the reign of the Confessor on. The extent to which the Chronicle is kept up varies at different periods; the later campaigns of Alfred, and the re-conquest of the Danelaw by his son, are recorded in minute detail, though the latter account reached only one of our extant manuscripts. There is a full and excellently written record of the reign of Ethelred the Unready, possibly written at Abingdon, which achieved wide circulation. In the intervening period the Chronicle was neglected, and the gap filled later with scrappy entries, poems, and notices of events of mere domestic interest. But unequal though it is, the Chronicle is a remarkable achievement, a historical source of the first importance over centuries, which allows us to study the development of prose writing, not based on Latin originals, over a long period. From a brief record of outstanding events it develops at times into a moving and vivid narrative, letting us see the contemporary attitude to events as well as the events themselves.

*

Our materials suggest that the period of more than half a century between Alfred's death and the revival due to the Benedictine reform of the mid tenth century was somewhat barren of literature. It was prolific in lawcodes, following Alfred's example, for he had issued a long code, moved by the example of the early Kentish kings, his predecessor Ine, and Offa of Mercia, whose laws are lost. The Chronicle was kept up fully until the end of his son's reign, and a short set of annals known as the *Mercian Register* was written in Mercia. The works of Alfred's reign continued to be copied, and the period was not altogether devoid of Latin culture, but we cannot assign with certainty much original work to this age. It is possible that some of the homilies collected in the Blickling and Vercelli manuscripts may belong to the first half of the tenth century; they are little touched by the standards of the post-revival writers. There may have been writings that have perished, for Ælfric complains in 990–1 of the currency of many English books that contained error, and works frowned on as unorthodox by the monastic party would have small chance of survival. We know of conditions in the religious houses prior to the revival only from the writings of the reformers themselves, and the picture given of the sloth and ignorance of their predecessors may well be overdrawn.

The first vernacular work to result from the tenth-century monastic revival was Bishop Athelwold's translation of the *Benedictine Rule*, about 960, but the real harvest of post-revival literature begins with the generation of students taught by the first reformers. The homilist Ælfric, a pupil of Athelwold, issues his first work about 990, Wulfstan's datable work begins in the next decade, while Abbo's pupil, Byrhtferth of Ramsey, wrote his scientific manual in 1011. Works of about the same period have come down from many writers whose names we do not know. The range is varied. There are direct translations of continental canonistic and penitential books, of Chrodegang and Amalarius of Metz, Theodulf of Orleans, Halitgar of Cambrai, and Benedict of Aniane; Ælfric and Byrhtferth both wrote works on scientific matters, based largely on Bede, but using later work, like that of Hrabanus Maurus, as well; the Gospels and a part of the book of Genesis were translated by anonymous writers, while Ælfric is responsible for renderings of parts of the Hexateuch, of Judges, Job, Esther, and Judith, and he wrote a treatise on the Old and New Testaments. All these translators show a competence above that of the Alfredian writers, and an ability to write a smooth and often a distinguished prose style. The more exacting standards of this age in the matter of style can be seen by comparing the revision made at this time of Werferth's translation of the *Dialogues* of Gregory with Werferth's own work. Ælfric prefers to translate afresh passages from Bede instead of using the existing English version.

Great variety exists in the subject matter of the very extensive homiletic literature of this date. There are sermons of plain moral instruction, perhaps diversified with *exempla*, and of straightforward teaching on the outlines of the Christian faith; there are impassioned denunciations of society and appeals for repentance, and semi-poetical descriptions of the Last Judgement and the torments of the damned; there are homilies of exegesis, explaining the symbolism of the gospel for the day, and numbers of saints' lives and apocryphal legends. These are mostly of a length suitable for preaching, for it was the aim of writers like Ælfric to raise the level of morality by providing the priesthood with material for sermons, but Felix's *Life of St Guthlac* is translated in full. There are great differences in style as in theme. Ælfric holds the first place in this, as he does also by the sheer bulk of his work; he developed, under the influence of his classical training, a restrained and balanced style which carries his argument to its conclusion so inevitably that the reader is almost unaware of the artistry by which this marvellous lucidity has been obtained – of the carefully chosen rhythms, accentuated by alliteration, of the use of antithesis, rhetorical question, and other devices. We know that much of his work is based on Latin originals, on the Latin Fathers, historians, and canonistic writers, but we should not have guessed this from his style. The stilted translation prose is a thing of the past.

But Ælfric is not the only stylist of distinction. Equally remarkable is the fiery eloquence of Archbishop Wulfstan, who like him wrote a deliberately rhythmical prose, but with a vehemence and intensity as suited to his denunciatory sermons as Ælfric's calm reasonableness is to his logical expositions. One is surprised to find that Wulfstan's utterances are often translated from Latin canonists, most carefully selected and translated with attention to a felicitous and forcible rendering. And there are anonymous homilists capable of writing a highly rhetorical prose, heightened by poetic diction, simile, and metaphor; and at the other end of the scale, there is the stylist who added to the Chronicle the account of the reign of Ethelred, in comparatively straightforward narrative, with an economy of artistic device, which he can yet use effectively to convey his emotions at what he has to relate – exasperation, contempt, and occasionally pride. He is a master of ironic understatement. The general high level of English writing is truly remarkable, and Chambers has demonstrated that its influence never died out, but was handed on to modern times through a line of Middle English authors.

Apart from the Chronicle and legal documents, the amount of extant prose that was written for non-religious ends is small; naturally so, for such is less likely to survive. Yet we have a few small pieces to indicate a taste in the literature of the marvellous, which descends ultimately from Greek texts of the early Christian era. Of this genre are the two texts immediately preceding *Beowulf* in our only manuscript, the so-called *Letter of Alexander to Aristotle* and the *Marvels of the East*, which survives in another manuscript as well. Both deal with the strange creatures men were willing to believe lived in remote lands, such, for example, as the men with such enormous ears that they could sleep on one and cover themselves up with the other. Here, surely, we have the prose of entertainment rather than instruction, and so also one must regard the fragment of a Greek romance *Apollonius of Tyre*. More didactic in purpose are dialogues in prose and verse such as that of *Salomon and Saturn*, a collection of strange lore from many sources, especially the Orient, and finally must be mentioned manuscripts with collections of medical recipes of various origin, presumably for practical use – though one hopes that some were left untested –, and lunar almanacs, which Förster has shown hand on, practically unchanged, material that ultimately goes back to ancient Babylon.

CHAPTER XI

ANGLO-SAXON ART

THE artistic ability of the Anglo-Saxons can be studied to some extent in the actual remains which date from this period, in the churches and parts of churches, in the stone crosses and tombstones, in the jewellery and weapons, the church-plate and ivories, the coins, and the illuminated manuscripts. All such things give us some insight into the taste, the technical skill, and the various influences to which the art of our forefathers was exposed. Nevertheless, information so gathered is incomplete. Objects of secular use have rarely survived except from the heathen period, when they were buried with the dead; some types of work, such as wood-carving and embroidery, are little represented because of the perishable nature of the material; while few of the more valuable objects, of gold, silver, and gems, escaped the rapacity of later generations. The larger church ornaments, great crosses covered with gold and silver, crucifixion scenes, with figures of St Mary and St John, which were given by various donors to churches in the late tenth and eleventh centuries, were carried off by plunderers or sold to pay the debts of the church. The cathedrals and greater monastic churches have been replaced by later buildings. It is necessary in considering Anglo-Saxon art to make use of documentary evidence as well as that of surviving works; thus, while the St Cuthbert stole and the Bayeux tapestry let us understand why English needle-work was so prized on the Continent, it is the constant reference to precious objects – a cloak of remarkable purple, interwoven throughout with gold in the manner

of a corselet, which was turned into a chasuble; robes of
silk interwoven with precious work of gold and gems; a
beautiful chasuble that shone like gold when worn in the
house of the Lord; a chalice of gold flashing with gems
'as the heavens glow with blazing stars'; great can-
delabra, all of gold; images of the saints, covered with
gold and silver and precious stones; and countless other
treasures – vestments, altar-cloths, tapestries, dorsals,
shrines, croziers, bells, etc. – which explains the great
impression made on the Norman conquerors by the richness of the equipment of the English churches. We should
never have guessed this without the aid of literary records.

*

Poetry shows that the Anglo-Saxons were alive to the
beauty of metal-work and to the impressive splendour of
the warrior in his grey steel mail with its glittering ap-
pliqués, his sword-hilt adorned with gold plates or filigree,
his boar-crested helmet and polished spear-tip glancing
in the sun. Remains show that skilled weapon-smiths and
jewellers existed even in the heathen age, and some of
their products, such as their garnet-inlaid brooches and
buckles, their drinking-horns mounted with chased gold
bands, arouse general admiration. Many of the objects of
this time, however, are covered all over with vigorous
design, full of vitality and energy, which is unrestrained
and often misdirected. The commonest decoration is the
Germanic zoomorphic style, which, long before the
Anglo-Saxons used it, had lost all naturalistic intention
and become a mere pattern formed by distorted animal
or bird forms, or even by detached parts of such forms,
heads or limbs arranged as mere elements in a design.
This motif is sometimes combined with another, the interlace, and a space may be adorned with a pattern of
beasts or birds with intertwined necks or legs. Other

types of decoration go to make up the advanced decorative art of the Anglo-Saxon period, seen at its best in manuscript illumination of the late seventh and early eighth centuries; there is a purely abstract, curvilinear style derived eventually from late Celtic art, transmitted to the Saxon invaders by some obscure, or at least disputed, means; and geometric patterns of a simple nature are used also.

To these motifs others of Mediterranean origin were added in Christian times. This was to be expected. Our sources refer frequently to the introduction from the Continent both of objects of art and foreign workmen. Augustine probably introduced Italian masons, whereas Benedict Biscop brought his from Gaul, and there is a corresponding difference in style between the southern group of early churches, with their wide nave, their eastern apse, almost as wide as the nave, from which it was separated by a triple arch, their several porticos, and the narrower northern type of church with very high walls and a small rectangular chancel. Wilfrid brought masons from Rome for his ambitious buildings at Ripon and Hexham. From descriptions we know that these churches had side-aisles and columns, spiral staircases and passages – but nothing is left but the crypts. From Gaul Benedict Biscop brought glaziers, and they taught their art to the English; perhaps not all branches of it, however, for in 764 a later abbot of his monastery asked the missionary Lul to send him from Germany a man who could make vessels of glass well. Wilfrid had the windows of the church of York glazed, and he also brought across from the Continent 'artisans of every kind'.

Mention has been made in a previous chapter of the great influx of books from abroad. Some of them were illuminated. Pictures also were brought from Rome, so that in Bede's day the church at Monkwearmouth had its walls surrounded with paintings of the Virgin and the twelve Apostles, of scenes from the Gospels and the Book of Revelation, while the church of Jarrow had pictures to illustrate the connexion between the Old and the New Testaments, and the Lady Chapel a series depicting the life of our Lord. Pictures of the Virgin were brought back from Rome by three unnamed pilgrims, along with books and with silk vestments of brilliant colours. Two cloaks, all of silk and of incomparable workmanship, which Benedict Biscop brought back, were considered so valuable that King Aldfrith gave him an estate of three hides in exchange for them.

Men such as Benedict, Wilfrid, and Aldhelm spared nothing that would make the worship of the Christian God impressive and beautiful, and a contrast to the sacrifices to heathen deities. Wilfrid had a case of the purest gold set with most precious gems made for his magnificent gospel-book, and the altar at Ripon was vested in purple woven with gold; Aldhelm describes a church with an altar-frontal of gold filament, and a chalice of gold and paten of wrought silver; it had twelve lesser altars dedicated to the twelve apostles, and its windows were glazed; Acca filled Hexham with ornaments of gold, silver, and precious stones. We are not told that all these things were imported, and it is likely that native craftsmen, skilled in metal work as we know them to have been, learnt to turn their talents to the service of the Church, and to copy the treasures from abroad. It is easy to see how foreign styles and motifs could be introduced into native art.

The most important of the new decorative motifs is the vine scroll, whether with birds and animals in the volutions of the scroll or not. Its closest parallels seem to be with the eastern Mediterranean, and its appearance in England must be attributed to foreign craftsmen or objects. But foreign influence was not confined to the importation of new patterns; it introduced the English to a representational art, to pictures of human beings and the scenes of biblical and other narrative, and it taught them to restrain the over-exuberance of their decoration and to impose some feeling for order over the whole. A combination of native and foreign influences is seen in the manuscript illumination; Italian representations of figures are imitated in the pictures of the Evangelists, or of David, while the pages of ornament are filled with the motifs of the earlier native art, greatly advanced in grandeur and sumptuousness, and, in the best examples, such as the famous Lindisfarne Gospels of about 700, arranged in panels so that the rich and elaborate detail is subordinated to a clear and dignified main theme. The use of bright contrasting colours adds to the general effect of magnificence. More and more, however, the native love of decoration triumphed over the classical art of natural representation, and even the figures of the Evangelists were not immune from a decorative treatment; they become less realistic, and are schematized as if they are merely part of a pattern. Manuscripts illuminated in this style, though with less restraint, are also produced in Ireland, and hence the style is known as Hiberno-Saxon, but scholars are not agreed as to which country originated this manner of illumination.

Remarkable though it is to get so soon after the conversion to Christianity the production in England of a decorative art of the high standard of the illuminated manuscripts, a still more striking phenomenon is the appearance about the same time of a school of Christian sculptors which has no parallel anywhere in Europe at that date. The excellence of some of the figure sculptures on the great Anglian crosses at Bewcastle in Cumberland and Ruthwell in Dumfriesshire led some scholars to believe that they could not be earlier than the twelfth century, but the art-motifs, the form of the inscribed runes, and the language of the inscriptions show that they belong to the earlier period of Northumbrian art. It has been suggested that it was the sculptured remains of the Romano-British period that gave the Anglo-Saxons the idea of erecting large monuments in stone, into which medium they could translate figures, scenes, and decorative motifs introduced into England on small objects such as ivories. The belief that the Bewcastle cross bears the names of Alhfrith, sub-king of southern Northumbria until soon after 664, and his wife Cyneburh, which would suggest a date when he was still remembered, has been strongly questioned.

There is also literary evidence for the existence of such crosses, and one reference is of particular interest in showing that they were not confined to Northumbria, and in indicating the purpose for which they might be raised. We are told in the *Life of St Willibald*, a West Saxon who left England in 720 and later became bishop of Eichstadt, that he was taken as a child in the hope that he might be cured of an illness to the cross of the Saviour, it being the custom of the Saxon people to erect a cross for the daily service of prayer on the estates of noble and good men, where there was no church. Such a purpose would be well served by the Bewcastle and Ruthwell crosses, for, as it has been recently emphasized, the subjects sculptured on them were chosen to 'convey to the faithful the essential ideas of Christianity.' Both crosses give central place to the majestic figure of Christ as judge, trampling on the beasts; the Bewcastle has above this a representation of St John the Baptist, below it one of St John the Evangelist, and the other three sides of the cross have decorative motifs only, vine scrolls, plaits, and chequer patterns. At Ruthwell two faces have figures sub-

jects, the Magdalen at the feet of Christ, the healing of
the blind man, the Visitation, the Annunciation, the
Flight into Egypt, St John the Baptist, the hermits Paul
and Anthony in the desert, breaking bread, an allusion
to the Mass. The cross-head is mutilated, but probably
originally had the symbols of the four Evangelists; the
narrower faces of the shaft have ornamental scrolls. All
over the north of England crosses or cross fragments are
common, though few can have attained the grandeur and
dignity of these two; but we have seen that in Wessex
also it was apparently a common thing for a cross to be
erected, and this is supported by William of Malmesbury,
who describes two stone pyramids with sculptured figures
which he saw at Glastonbury, one of which bore names
of persons living at the end of the seventh century and
the very beginning of the eighth. It seems likely, in view
of the rarity of remains from the south of England,
that the elaborately sculptured stone cross never had the
vogue there which it had in Northumbria, where it continued, with modifications in style by natural development and by Scandinavian influence, into the eleventh
century. From Northumbria it spread into Mercia in the
ninth century. Crosses in wood were set up also, as for
example that raised at Oundle over the place where St
Wilfrid's body was washed, but naturally these have not
survived.

Some surviving crosses have inscriptions that say they
were set up in memory of a particular person or persons.
This would not prevent them from serving the purpose
mentioned above, but sometimes they were simply
funeral monuments, set up in the graveyard of a church.
Æthelwold, who was bishop of Lindisfarne from 724 to 740,
had a stone cross made of skilful workmanship, and inscribed with his name in memory of him. It can hardly
have been on a large scale, for the monks of Lindisfarne

carried it with them when they wandered with St Cuthbert's body. It was eventually erected in the cemetery of Durham and was there in Symeon's day. The grave of Bishop Acca of Hexham, we are told, had two carved crosses, one at its head and the other at its foot, and it is generally assumed that the remains of a beautiful cross now restored to the church of Hexham are from one of these. They have no figure subjects, but are ornamented solely by vine scrolls, without any bird or animal figures in the scrolls. The purpose of another cross mentioned in our records is uncertain. A Northumbrian nobleman founded a monastery at an unidentified place in the early eighth century, and later the fifth abbot of the house was buried by the high cross which the 'prince' set up. Perhaps the founder set it up as a memorial to himself, or as a place from which the Gospel could be preached. At a much later date Bishop Oswald of Worcester (961–92) was in the habit of preaching by a cross set up as a sepulchral monument when his congregation was greater than his church could hold.

*

Throughout the eighth century sculpture and illuminated manuscripts continued to be produced in the same style in Northumbria. The name of an early eighth-century illuminator has come down to us, an inmate of the unnamed monastery just mentioned, called Ultan. He was a priest of Irish race, and a ninth-century writer considered that his work surpassed anything which his own age could produce. Contact with the Continent was maintained, and in fact probably increased, during this period. Pilgrimages and visits to Rome continued, and gifts and letters were exchanged with the English missionaries in Frisia and Germany. Foreign works of art reached the North. We are not told what the royal gifts sent by Pippin, king of the Franks, to King Eadberht (737–58) consisted of. Archbishop Lul sent to Jarrow a robe all of silk for the relics of Bede, and a multicoloured coverlet to protect Abbot Cuthberht from the cold; this must have been considered too good for such a use, for the abbot gave it to clothe the altar in the church of St Paul. Alcuin also sent home to Northumbria silk robes, and Charles the Great sent dalmatics and palls to all the episcopal sees in Northumbria and Mercia. When Alcuin was at home, his demands on his continental friends are for simpler things, garments and hoods of goat-hair and wool, and linen; his most interesting request is for pigments of colours good for painting. But the Northumbrians could give as well as receive; their illuminated manuscripts went abroad and were much copied in continental scriptoria, and Abbot Cuthberht sent to Lul in return for his gifts 'two palls of subtle workmanship, one white, the other coloured', along with books which had been asked for.

As a result of the intercourse with the Frankish kingdom, the effects of the Carolingian revival reached Northumbria. The vine-scroll becomes more natural, with recognizable leaves and delicate tendrils as in Carolingian ivories, and there is a return to a more realistic representation of figures. The Easby and Rothbury crosses have crowded figure scenes which in general arrangement and in some of their detail resemble those of Carolingian illuminations and ivory carvings. Dr Kendrick thinks that the North would have developed further in a classical direction if the Danish settlement in the latter part of the ninth century had not taken place.

*

It is now necessary to turn back to consider what was going on meanwhile in the South and Midlands. From the days of the first missionaries onwards these areas received art treasures from abroad, just as Northumbria did. An illuminated copy of the Gospels, now at Corpus Christi College, Cambridge, may well have been brought to Canterbury by Augustine himself, and churches in Wessex could be richly equipped already in Aldhem's time. The letters of St Boniface show that elaborately illuminated manuscripts were being produced at southern monasteries in the early eighth century. The earliest surviving Christian works of art from the lands south of the Humber seem to be the Golden Gospels, now in Stockholm, and the Vespasian Psalter, which probably were produced at Canterbury about 750, or a little later, though they have been claimed for Lichfield. There now seems to be some doubt whether a carved column at Reculver, which used to be assigned to the seventh century, belongs to anything like so early a date. In these manuscripts the decoration is mainly of the Hiberno-Saxon type, but, as might be expected from the close contact with the lands across the Channel, foreign influence is visible also, in the use of the acanthus leaf and the rosette in the decorative portions, and in the greater naturalness and solidity of the figure subjects.

Though one cannot with certainty assign manuscripts to East Anglia or the Midlands during this period, it must not be supposed that the monasteries and churches in this area were necessarily unproductive. Among the many Anglo-Saxon illuminated manuscripts which were taken to the Continent by the missionaries, one was a copy of an Italian manuscript of Sedulius's *Carmen Paschale* which had been owned by Cuthwine, bishop of Dunwich; while it was from Worcester that Lul tried to obtain the work of Porphyrius on metre. Some of the manuscripts of mixed continental and Hiberno-Saxon styles may have been executed in Mercia. The most spacious and impressive of surviving pre-Viking Age churches is a Mercian one, Brixworth in Northamptonshire, an aisled basilica which, like the early Kentish churches, had originally a triple arcade at the east end, opening into a square presbytery with an apse beyond it. Towards the end of the eighth century and during the early part of the ninth, stone carving was being produced in Mercia. In Derbyshire there are crosses imitating Northumbrian work, but the best Mercian work is on friezes and other architectural ornaments, as at Breedon-on-the-Hill, Leicestershire, and Fletton, Huntingdonshire, and shows some influence from Frankish art, having features which occur in Merovingian illumination. In the early ninth century there is evidence for book-production at Lichfield, and one of its results is the *Book of Cerne*; some of its contents – it is a book of prayers – are of Northumbrian origin, and Dr Kendrick considers some features of its illumination to be closer to contemporary work in the North than that in the South. Some of the manuscripts of the late eighth century, and early ninth, which art historians designate vaguely 'southern' may come from West Saxon scriptoria; but we cannot be certain. There are also a few pieces of sculpture and minor objects of metal from early ninth-century Wessex which reveal Frankish influence.

*

The Viking Age was naturally not a period of great productiveness in the arts, though King Alfred encouraged them, as he did literature. Asser tells us of his building of halls and chambers wondrously constructed in wood or stone. He even speaks of buildings in gold and silver, which cannot be dismissed altogether as empty rhetoric, for the *Beowulf* poet conceives a royal hall as 'gold-adorned', 'treasure-adorned', 'adorned with (gold-)

plating'. Alfred invited craftsmen from all nations, in great numbers. The description of the church of his foundation at Athelney shows that he followed Carolingian models. It has been suggested that the angel-panel at Deerhurst dates from Alfred's reign, and as a representative of minor works there remains the famous Alfred Jewel. Each of the copies of the *Pastoral Care* which the king gave to his bishops' sees was to be accompanied by a precious object, perhaps a pointer, of fifty mancuses, i.e. about 3,500 grains, of gold.

In the reigns of Alfred's immediate successors one reads of the continued exchange of gifts with foreign royalties, by which foreign works of art reached this country, and King Athelstan gave to Christ Church, Canterbury, a gospel-book which contains the names of Otto the Great and his mother, and which was probably a gift from this German prince. Athelstan gave to other religious houses illuminated manuscripts which had been produced in France, and one from Ireland. One of the books which he gave to St Cuthbert's was, however, an illuminated copy of Bede's *Life of St Cuthbert*, of southern English origin, perhaps made at Glastonbury, and English illuminations were added to a psalter obtained from France. The beautiful stole, woven with figures of saints and prophets, which was found in St Cuthbert's coffin, is English work of the second decade of the tenth century. It is not, however, until after the monastic revival of the mid tenth century, and as a result of it, that the second 'golden age' of English art begins. The centre of this is as definitely in the south of England as that of the earlier 'golden age' had been in the north, and it is often, for convenience, called the 'Winchester School'. This place took an important part in the revival of art and learning, and some works of art can be located there; but the name is used to cover works in the new style, many of which

were not from Winchester, but from all over the area
where the monastic revival was effective.

The monastic revival owed much of its inspiration to
the Frankish Empire, and it is from there that the art
styles come also. To some extent it was the repayment of
a debt, for the art of the Carolingian revival, which
exercised such a strong influence in England at this time,
was in itself partly based on the earlier Anglo-Saxon
manuscripts taken over in the eighth century by the
English missionaries. It drew from this source its fond-
ness for covering whole pages with ornament, and the
arrangement of this in panels filled with minute patterns.
The interlace survives, but the commonest decorative
pattern is not one derived from insular art, but the
acanthus of classical art. Far more important than any
new decorative motif, however, was the return to a
representational art. The Caroligian schools of il-
luminators went back to late antique models of the fifth
and sixth centuries and produced illustrated psalters,
bibles, sacramentaries, etc., and these in their turn were
imitated in England. There are numbers of such manuscripts, for this is the period of tremendous activity in
many English scriptoria. Early in the series is the *Benedictional of St Athelwold*, written about 980 by Godemann,
later abbot of Thorney, a beautiful manuscript of
gorgeous colours and rich in gold, with the figure paintings in architectural settings and heavily framed in
borders of acanthus. Later examples in this style show
greater mastery and grace in figure drawing. Outline
drawing is also common on the manuscripts of this
period, and it is often both dignified and expressive. All
manner of subjects are represented, and the artists are
skilful in suggesting swift action and deep emotion.
There is a breakaway from the older, static representation; the figures are clothed in fluttering draperies, which

give a restless quality. This is especially present in manuscripts affected by the mannerisms of a continental school of outline-drawing best known from the Utrecht Psalter, a work of the early ninth century, from near Reims, which was much copied. The figures have shrugging shoulders, necks poked forward, exaggerated fluttering garments; yet the drawings are full of vitality and vigour, they depict crowded scenes and other difficult subjects, and are drawn with swift clear strokes. They attempt both architectural and landscape backgrounds to the figure scenes. Illumination in these styles continued throughout the rest of the Saxon period, and before very long English manuscripts were being taken across the Channel, and some still survive in French libraries. A benedictional from Fleury, now in Paris, may be the one given to that house by the abbey of Ramsey between 1004 and 1029, and another was given by Queen Emma to Archbishop Robert of Rouen, and remains in the library there. Judith, wife of Earl Tostig, gave to Weingarten an illuminated gospel-book, which is now in the Pierpont Morgan Library in New York.

The artistic revival produced also a 'Winchester' school of sculptors, who carved naturalistic figures in low relief, such as the angels at Bradford-on-Avon and Winterborne Steepleton, the Harrowing of Hell in Bristol Cathedral, the Virgin and Child at Inglesham. It is disputed whether the Romsey Rood and the Chichester panels, depicting Christ coming to Mary's house and the raising of Lazarus, are of this period or poet-Conquest. As there are no examples of stone sculpture on the Continent at this time, it is probable that the figures were copied from ivories.

*

Only little of the 'Winchester' art reached the North, as far as we can judge. Some illuminated manuscripts reached Durham, and some of the treasures given by the archbishops of York, who were all men from south of the Humber, may have been of southern or continental provenance. Aldred's great pulpit and crucifix at Beverley was 'of German work'. But it has not survived, nor has the shrine of gold and silver and precious stones 'of incomparable workmanship', made at Beverley in the time of his predecessor. When the Normans burnt the church of York, its ornaments and books perished. Earl Tostig and his wife gave to Durham a great crucifix flanked by images of St Mary and St John, such as we hear of in southern churches, and it is possible that the equipment of the major churches of the North did not represent a very different taste from that in vogue elsewhere; but the unhappy years after the Norman Conquest were not favourable to the survival of works of art. The North did not share in the great activity in book production, for this was mainly carried on in monasteries, and there were none north of the Humber.

The very beautiful, though mutilated, carved stone slab of the Virgin and Child in York Minster is sometimes claimed as pre-Conquest work, though some would date it twelfth-century. It is in any case exceptional; the stone carving of the North is abundant, but is influenced by Scandinavian, not continental, taste. Stone crosses and grave-slabs in the Hiberno-Saxon style continue to be set up, with its animal-ornament influenced more or less by what Dr Kendrick has called 'a Scandinavian wildness and evenly distributed heaviness.' The main type of decoration goes by the name of Jellinge, after a seat of the Danish kings in Jutland where work in this style is found, and it is a barbaric interpretation of the Anglian beast motif of the Northumbrian crosses. Vine-scrolls are retained but in a flattened and stylized form. There are also some crosses put up by the Irish-Norse settlers, with

Celtic designs, and subjects from Scandinavian legend take their place beside Christian themes on some monuments. The most spectacular is the cross at Gosforth, Cumberland, with tiny figure subjects more like those on Manx crosses than the monumental figures of earlier Anglian crosses. This is a round shafted cross, and there is a group of these mainly in Derbyshire and Staffordshire and in that area of South Yorkshire which from documentary evidence we know was being penetrated by Mercian thanes in the tenth century. It is probable therefore that the round-shafted cross represents Mercian taste, and it appears to be a survival of pre-Viking art represented by remains at Dewsbury and Collingham. Remnants of Hiberno-Saxon art, untouched by Viking devices, are also to be found on grave slabs in East Anglia, Lincolnshire, and Cambridgeshire.

When the Danish invasions culminated in the conquest of England by Cnut, another form of Scandinavian art became influential in England. This, known as the Ringerike style, is a development in Scandinavian hands of the acanthus pattern of English illumination and ivories, etc., and it is found, not in the areas of Scandinavian settlement, but in the south of England. It presumably indicates a vogue for Scandinavian motifs during the reigns of the Danish kings. As one might expect, various types of art met in London; several examples of Viking art occur, whereas recent fragments discovered at All-Hallows-by-the-Tower are in the style of the Anglian panelled crosses, although apparently of eleventh-century date.

*

Most of our surviving Saxon churches date from the tenth or eleventh centuries, and in the sources for this late period, such as the *Life of St Wulfstan*, one not infrequently reads of the bishop being called to dedicate a new church. Churches of this later Saxon period are often easy to distinguish; they have 'long and short work', that is stones set alternately upright and horizontal, at the quoins, walls decorated by pilaster strips and rounded or triangular arcading, double-splayed windows and mid-wall shafts, west-end towers sometimes divided into stages by horizontal strips. Doorways are occasionally triangular-headed, but arches always rounded. The greater number of Saxon churches still standing, whether in part or complete, are small, but there are a few of impressive size, such as Bosham in Sussex and Great Paxton in Huntingdonshire, which were 'minsters', that is churches served by a body of priests and acting as the mother-church of a considerable area. This style of architecture seems to have drawn its inspiration from the Rhineland, and it is in the Carolingian empire also that one gets parallels to the great cathedral and monastic churches. None of these survives, but enough can be gathered from literary sources and uncovered foundations to show the influence of the Carolingian buildings. Like these, many English buildings had altars at both ends of the church, the western one being placed either in a gallery, or a western transept, or a western apse. They had towers at the west end and over the central crossing, as well as minor circular towers containing spiral staircases. The major towers were sometimes a series of receding stages of open arcading, built in timber. The churches built by Bishop Athelwold for his cathedral at Winchester and his foundations of Ely, Peterborough, and Thorney, and Archbishop Oswald's church at Ramsey all had some of these features, but Athelwold's earliest building, the church of Abingdon, was a round church. Sporadic examples of centrally-planned churches occurred elsewhere, in the eighth century in Hexham, in the ninth at Athelney, in the tenth at Bury St Edmunds, and in the eleventh at St Augustine's, Canterbury, where, however, the great rotunda begun by Abbot Wulfric was never finished. Extensive building was going on in the later Anglo-Saxon period; St Oswald built a new church at his see of Worcester, St Dunstan extended Glastonbury, Bishop Aldhun built a cathedral at Durham 995–9, the last three Saxon archbishops of York made great additions to Beverley, Exeter was restored in the time of Cnut, and all the time new religious houses were being built. We cannot judge Anglo-Saxon architecture from its minor monuments, which are all that are left. Sir Alfred Clapham has well summed up the position: 'In the major art of architecture it is not unreasonable to suppose that, left to themselves, the Saxons would have travelled along the same road as their Rhineland kinsmen and, given peace and prosperity, would have produced an architecture not unlike the Carolingian Romanesque of the great cathedrals and abbey churches of that province. . . . As it was, the greater Saxon churches of the tenth and eleventh centuries, though lacking the scale of their continental contemporaries, were probably not unworthy to survive, and in every other direction were quite up to the standards of the age.'

CHAPTER XII

CONCLUSION

A MILLENNIUM and a half separates us from 'the Coming of the English' and close on nine hundred years from the last persons mentioned in these chapters. We still call most of our towns and villages by the names the Anglo-Saxons gave them, often after the man or woman who settled there in this distant past. Sometimes we know a little about the persons who thus left their names: about Pega, St Guthlac's saintly sister, whose name survives in Peakirk; Wulfrun, a noble Mercian lady, who possessed Wolverhampton; or Esgar, an official of Edward the Confessor, the name of whose 'town' has been corrupted to East Garston; or Tola, of Tolpuddle, a Danish lady who was a benefactor of Abbotsbury. More often they were lesser folk whose doings history does not record.

Tangible remains of Anglo-Saxon civilization are not lacking. It is true that the great Saxon churches have vanished, superseded by the grander buildings of a later age. Only the crypts survive of Wilfrid's buildings which contemporaries thought to be unsurpassed on this side of the Alps. But many smaller churches – whole or in part – have continued in use until to-day, and several of them, Brixworth, Great Paxton, Deerhurst, Earls Barton, are not unimpressive, nor to be venerated on grounds of antiquity alone. Beautiful carved crosses have come down to us, some still *in situ*, others preserved inside churches and museums. The latter are full of specimens of Anglo-Saxon handicrafts, the garnet inlays of Kent and Sutton Hoo, the elaborate gold filigree work, the ivory caskets and diptychs, and other objects, including some, like the Alfred Jewel and the St Cuthbert stole, which add to

their intrinsic interest the more sentimental appeal of
their connexion with historic figures.

Our older libraries are full of their manuscripts, many
with a beauty of script and illumination that has never
been surpassed. Some bring us very near to the people
of whom we read. Among the treasures of the Bodleian
Library are the Italian copy of the Acts of the Apostles
which Bede used when writing his commentary; the copy
of King Alfred's translation of Gregory's *Pastorai Care*
which the king himself sent as a gift to his friend and
helper Bishop Werferth of Worcester; and a book of
tropes and sequences, with musical notation, in which
the litany prays: 'that thou wilt deign to preserve King
Ethelred and the army of the English.' The Lindisfarne
Gospels, now in the British Museum, accompanied St
Cuthbert's body as its guardians bore it from place to
place in search of safety in the chaotic years that followed
the Danish invasion. The medieval monks of Canterbury
were very ready to claim that books in their possession had
been brought over by St Augustine, and they were usually
wrong, but a Canterbury book of Gospels at Corpus
Christi College, Cambridge, is old enough to have been
brought by the first missionaries, as the monks of St
Augustine's Abbey, to whom it once belonged, believed.
Continental libraries have numbers of manuscripts produced in England in pre-Conquest times. Among the
most interesting are the great bible codex at Florence,
which Abbot Ceolfrith of Jarrow, with pardonable pride,
intended to present to the pope in 716, as a specimen of
what was being produced in this northern outpost of
Christendom; and the calendar at Paris which belonged
to St Willibrord, the missionary to the Frisians, in
which the saint has entered in his own hand his consecra-
tion by Pope Sergius in 695, adding the words 'although
unworthy'.

And in the books and documents that survive are many passages that bring us nearer still to these remote ancestors of ours. One reads the tactful remark with which King Alfred disarmed criticism as he sent to his bishops an English version of a Latin work: 'It is uncertain how long there may be such learned bishops as now, by the grace of God, are almost everywhere'; or the angry reply of a litigant, whose brother will pay a fine for him if he will relinquish an estate, that 'he would rather that fire or flood had it'; or the noble letter of condolence written by the archbishop of Canterbury to Boniface's followers after his martyrdom; and as one reads, the Anglo-Saxons come alive as individuals whose mental processes we can follow and whose aspirations and sorrows rouse our sympathy.

Subsequent volumes in this series will doubtless show how the society here depicted changed gradually by natural growth or more violently by external influence. The time is past when historians regarded the Norman Conquest as a complete break in the continuity of our history. Quite apart, however, from any question of what they handed on to us, the people who in the eighth century led the scholarship of Western Europe, who were mainly responsible for the conversion to Christianity of the German and Scandinavian peoples, and who, alone of the Germanic races, have left behind from so early a date a noble literature in verse and prose, are worthy of respect and study for their own sake.

SELECT BIBLIOGRAPHY

The following list of suggestions is confined to works written in English. It only exceptionally includes articles in periodicals and journals. The reader who wishes to pursue any subject more deeply should consult the bibliographies given below, and also W. Bonser, *An Anglo-Saxon and Celtic Bibliography* (Blackwell, Oxford, 1957) and the new periodical, *Anglo-Saxon England* (Cambridge, 1972–), which deals with all aspects of the period. Valuable articles on many topics are in *England before the Conquest: Studies in primary sources presented to Dorothy Whitelock*, ed. P. Clemoes and K. Hughes (Cambridge, 1971).

A. *General and Political History*

F. M. Stenton's *Anglo-Saxon England* (Oxford History of England, II, 3rd edn, 1971) has largely superseded previous general histories. It has an excellent bibliography. His collected papers are published as *Preparatory to Anglo-Saxon England* (ed. D. M. Stenton, Oxford, 1970). See also P. Hunter Blair, *An Introduction to Anglo-Saxon England* (Cambridge, 1956); H. R. Loyn, *Anglo-Saxon England and the Norman Conquest* (2nd edn, London, 1968). For special periods, see R. G. Collingwood and J. N. L. Myres, *Roman Britain and the English Settlements* (Oxford History of England, I, 2nd edn, 1937); P. Hunter Blair, *Roman Britain and Early England 55 B.C.–A.D. 871* (Edinburgh, 1963); R. H. Hodgkin, *A History of the Anglo-Saxons* (3rd edn, Oxford, 1952); E. S. Duckett, *Alfred the Great and his England* (London, 1957); H. R. Loyn, *Alfred the Great* (The Clarendon Biographies, O.U.P., 1967); L. M. Larson, *Canute the Great* (New York, 1912); F. Barlow, *Edward the Confessor* (London, 1970); D. C. Douglas, *William the Conqueror: The Norman Impact upon England* (London, 1964); R. R. Darlington, *The Norman Conquest* (The Creighton Lecture in History, London, 1963); H. R. Loyn, *The Norman Conquest* (Hutchinson University Library, London, 1965); and D. Whitelock and others, *The Norman Conquest: Its Setting and Impact* (ed. C. T. Chevallier, London, 1966). Many books on the Vikings include T. D. Kendrick, *A History of the Vikings* (London, 1930); J. Brøndsted, *The Vikings* (Pelican Books, 1960); Gwyn Jones, *A History of the Vikings* (London, 1968); D. M. Wilson, *The Vikings and their Origins* (London, 1970); and P. H. Sawyer, *The Age of the Vikings* (2nd edn, London, 1971).

B. *Institutions, Social and Economic History*

For early Germanic society, see H. M. Chadwick, *The Heroic Age* (Cambridge, 1912). For Anglo-Saxon society, see R. I. Page, *Life in Anglo-Saxon England* (London, 1970). On agrarian matters, see C. S. and C. S. Orwin, *The Open Fields* (3rd edn, Oxford, 1967); and H. P. R. Finberg, *The Agrarian History of England and Wales, I, Part II, A.D. 43–1042* (Cambridge, 1972). F. M. Stenton, *The Latin Charters of the Anglo-Saxon Period* (Oxford, 1955) is important for land tenure and other matters. For geographical factors, see S. W. Woodbridge and E. Ekwall, in *A Historical Geography of England before A.D. 1800* (Cambridge, 1936). On towns, see J. Tait, *The Medieval English Borough* (Manchester, 1936) and J. W. Benton, *Town Origins: the Evidence for Medieval England* (Boston, 1968). Principles of law are dealt with in F. Pollock and F. W. Maitland, *The History of English Law* (2nd edn, Cambridge, 1898) and T. F. T. Plucknett, *A Concise History of the Common Law* (London, 5th edn, 1956).

C. *Ecclesiastical History*

General accounts are given by W. Hunt, *History of the English Church* (ed. W. W. Stephens and W. Hunt, London, 1907), Vol. I; and J. Godfrey, *The Church in Anglo-Saxon England* (Cambridge, 1962). For the early period see P. Hunter Blair, *The World of Bede* (London, 1970); S. J. Crawford, *Anglo-Saxon Influence on Western Christendom* (Oxford, 1933); and W. Levison, *England and the Continent in the Eighth Century* (Oxford, 1946). For the later period see J. Armitage Robinson, *The Times of St Dunstan* (Oxford, 1923); Dom David Knowles, *The Monastic Order in England* (2nd edn, Cambridge, 1961); R. R. Darlington, 'Ecclesiastical Reform in the Late Old English Period' (*English Historical Review*, li, 1936); F. Barlow, *The English Church, 1000–1066: A Constitutional History* (London, 1963).

D. *Literature and Learning*

On Anglo-Latin scholarship, see M. L. W. Laistner, *Thought and Letters in Western Europe* (revised edn, London, 1957) and J. D. A. Ogilvy, *Books known to the English, 597–1066* (Cambridge, Mass., 1967). On vernacular literature, see S. B. Greenfield, *A Critical History of Old English Literature* (New York, 1965); *Continuations and Beginnings* (ed. E. G. Stanley, London and Edinburgh, 1966), which contains seven studies by experts on important authors or aspects; and K. Sisam, *Studies in the History of Old English Literature* (Oxford, 1953). The following works on *Beowulf* are most illuminating to the general reader: C. W. Kennedy, *The Earliest English Poetry* (O.U.P., 1943); W. W. Lawrence, *Beowulf and Epic Tradition* (Cambridge, Mass., 1928); K. Sisam, *The Structure of Beowulf* (Oxford, 1965); and D. Whitelock, *The Audience of Beowulf* (Oxford, 1951). On Wulfstan see the introductions to D. Bethurum, *The Homilies of Wulfstan* (Oxford, 1957) and D. Whitelock, *Sermo Lupi ad Anglos* (3rd edn, London, 1963). For further bibliography see *The Cambridge Bibliography of English Literature* (Vol. I, ed. F. W. Bateson, 1940, Supplement, ed. G. Watson, 1957) and the annual issues of the *Year's Work in English Studies* (English Association, from 1921) and of the periodical *Anglo-Saxon England*.

E. *Art and Archaeology*

Only a small selection of works on these subjects can be mentioned. General works: G. Baldwin Brown, *The Arts in Early England* (London, 1903–37); T. D. Kendrick, *Anglo-Saxon Art to A.D. 900* (London,

1938) and *Late Saxon and Viking Art* (London, 1948); *Dark Age Britain: Studies presented to E. T. Leeds* (ed. D. B. Harden, London, 1956); and D. M. Wilson, *The Anglo-Saxons* (London, 1960). The periodical, *Medieval Archaeology*, begun in 1957, is valuable. For evidence relating to the Saxon settlements, see works cited in A above, and also J. N. L. Myres, *Anglo-Saxon Pottery and the Settlement of England* (Oxford, 1969). Rupert Bruce-Mitford, *The Sutton-Hoo Ship Burial: A Handbook* (British Museum, 2nd edn, 1972), largely supersedes earlier works on this subject, and has a good bibliography. Sir Cyril Fox, *Offa's Dyke* (London, 1955) is a definitive study. On Viking antiquities, see works cited under A above, and also H. Shetelig and H. Falk, *Scandinavian Archaeology* (English translation by E. V. Gordon, Oxford, 1937). On architecture, see A. W. Clapham, *English Romanesque Architecture before the Norman Conquest* (Oxford, 1930) and H. M. Taylor and Joan Taylor, *Anglo-Saxon Architecture* (2 vols, Cambridge, 1965). On illumination, see O. E. Saunders, *English Illumination* (I, Florence and Paris, 1928); E. G. Millar, *English Illuminated Manuscripts from Xth to XII Century* (Paris and Brussels, 1926); W. Oakeshott, *The Sequence of English Medieval Art* (London, 1950); F. Wormald, *English Drawings of the Tenth and Eleventh Centuries* (London, 1952); and R. L. S. Bruce Mitford, *The Art of Codex Amiatinus* (Jarrow Lecture, 1967). Expensive facsimiles of illuminated manuscripts can be consulted in our major libraries, e.g. those published by the Palaeographical Society (1873–94) and the New Palaeographical Society (1903–30); the British Museum publication, *Schools of Illumination*, Part I: *Hiberno-Saxon and Early English Schools, 700–1000* (1914); Sir E. M. Thompson, *English Illuminated Manuscripts* (London, 1895); E. T. De-Wald, *The Utrecht Psalter* (Princeton, 1933); *The Cædmon Manuscript of Anglo-Saxon Biblical Poetry*, with introduction by Sir Israel Gollancz (O.U.P., 1927); *Evangeliorum quattuor Codex Lindisfarnensis* (ed. T. D. Kendrick and others, Oltun and Lausanne, 1956–60); and F. Wormald, *The Benedictional of St Ethelwold* (London, 1959). Other specialist studies include W. G. Collingwood, *Northumbrian Crosses* (London, 1927); M. H. Longhurst, *English Ivories* (London, 1926); R. Jessop, *Anglo-Saxon Jewellery* (London, 1950); D. M. Wilson, *Anglo-Saxon Ornamental Metal Work 700–1100 in the British Museum* (Catalogue of Antiquities of the Late Saxon Period, vol. I, 1964); *The Relics of St Cuthbert* (ed. C. F. Battiscombe, O.U.P., 1956); and *The Bayeux Tapestry* (ed. Sir Frank Stenton, London, 1957).

F. *Main sources available in Modern English Translation*

A large selection, with studies and bibliographies, is contained in *English Historical Documents* (general editor D. C. Douglas), Vol. I, *c.* 500–1042 (ed. D. Whitelock, 1955), Vol. II, 1042–1189 (ed. D. C. Douglas and G. W. Greenaway, 1953). Latin sources: Bede, *Ecclesiastical History*, translated by L. Sherley-Price (Penguin Classics,

revised edn by R. E. Latham, 1968) and in the edition by B. Colgrave
and R. A. B. Mynors (Oxford, 1969); B. Colgrave, *The Life of Bishop
Wilfrid by Eddius Stephanus* (Cambridge, 1927), *Two Lives of St
Cuthbert* (Cambridge, 1940), *Felix's Life of Saint Guthlac* (Cambridge,
1956), and *The Earliest Life of Gregory the Great* (University of Kansas
Press, 1968); E. Kylie, *The English Correspondence of St Boniface* (London,
1911); C. H. Talbot, *The Anglo-Saxon Missionaries in Germany* (London
and New York, 1954); L. C. Jane, *Asser's Life of King Alfred* (London,
1926); A. Campbell, *Æthelwulf, De Abbatibus* (Oxford, 1967) and
The Chronicle of Æthelweard (Nelson's Medieval Texts, 1962); Dom
Thomas Symons, *The Regularis Concordia: The Monastic Agreement*
(ibid., 1953); A. Campbell, *Encomium Emmae Reginae* (Camden 3rd
Series, lxxii, 1949); and F. Barlow, *The Life of King Edward the Confessor* (Nelson's Medieval Texts, 1962). Of Anglo-Norman historians
who used lost pre-Conquest sources, William of Malmesbury and
Florence of Worcester are translated in *Bohn's Antiquarian Library*,
and Symeon of Durham in *The Church Historians of England*, Vol. III,
Part II. Domesday Book for most counties is translated in the *Victoria
County Histories*; see also C. W. Foster and T. Longley, *The Lincolnshire Domesday and the Lindsey Survey* (Lincoln Record Society, 1924)
and J. Tait, *The Domesday Survey of Cheshire* (Chetham Society,
Manchester, 1916).

Vernacular sources: *The Anglo-Saxon Chronicle* is translated by
G. N. Garmonsway for Everyman's Library (revised edn, 1960) and
by D. Whitelock, with D. C. Douglas and S. I. Tucker (London,
corrected impression, 1965); the laws by F. L. Attenborough, *The
Laws of the Earliest English Kings* (Cambridge, 1922) and by A. J.
Robertson, *The Laws of the Kings of England from Edmund to Henry I*
(Cambridge, 1925); the charters by F. E. Harmer, *Select English
Historical Documents of the Ninth and Tenth Centuries* (Cambridge, 1914)
and *Anglo-Saxon Writs* (Manchester, 1953), by D. Whitelock, *Anglo-
Saxon Wills* (Cambridge, 1930), and by A. J. Robertson, *Anglo-Saxon
Charters* (2nd edn, Cambridge, 1956). The best prose translation of
Beowulf is by E. Talbot Donaldson (New York, 1966) and among
verse renderings may be mentioned those by A. T. Strong (London,
1925) and C. W. Kennedy (O.U.P., 1940). For other poems, see
R. K. Gordon, *Anglo-Saxon Poetry* (Everyman's Library, revised edn,
1956); C. W. Kennedy, *The Cædmon Poems* (London, 1916), *The Poems
of Cynewulf* (London, 1910) and *Early English Christian Poetry* (London,
1952); *The Exeter Book* (E.E.T.S., Part I, ed. Sir Israel Gollancz,
1895, Part II, ed. W. S. Mackie, 1934); A. Campbell, *The Battle of
Brunnanburh* (London, 1938). Standard editions of prose works with
translations are *King Alfred's West Saxon Version of Gregory's Pastoral
Care* (ed. H. Sweet, E.E.T.S., 1871), *The Homilies of Ælfric* (ed. B.
Thorpe, London, 1844–6), *Ælfric's Lives of Saints* (ed. W. W. Skeat,
E.E.T.S., 1881–1900) and *Byrhtferth's Manual* (ed. S. J. Crawford,

E.E.T.S., 1929). Alfred's version of *The Soliloquies of St Augustine* is translated by H. L. Hargrove (Yale Studies in English, 22, New York, 1904) and Alfred's *Boethius* by W. J. Sedgfield (Oxford, 1900).

G. *Ancilliary Sources*

Place-names should be studied in the publications of the English Place-Name Society and in E. Ekwall, *The Concise Oxford Dictionary of English Place-Names* (4th edn, 1960). For general accounts, see P. H. Reaney, *The Origin of English Place-Names* (London, 1961) and K. Cameron, *English Place-Names* (London, 1961). Very important is F. M. Stenton, 'The Historical Bearing of Place-Name Studies', delivered to the Royal Historical Society, 1939–43, now reprinted in his collected papers (see A above), pp. 253–324.

Collections of Anglo-Saxon coins are being published in *Sylloge of Coins of the British Isles*; twenty vols. (O.U.P., 1958–73) have appeared. See also Michael Dolley, *Anglo-Saxon Pennies* (British Museum, 1964); C. E. Blunt, 'The Anglo-Saxon Coinage and the Historian' (*Medieval Archaeology*, iv, 1960); and *Anglo-Saxon Coins: Studies presented to F. M. Stenton* (ed. R. H. M. Dolley, London, 1961).

An important contribution to Anglo-Saxon studies is the *Map of Britain in the Dark Ages* (Ordnance Survey, 2nd edn, 1966.

SELECT INDEX

Abbo of Fleury, 185, 201 f., 220

Abercorn, 164

Abingdon, 61, 67, 126, 135, 170, 185, 218, 239

Acca, Bishop, 192, 226; cross of, 230

Adamnan, 62, 160, 215

Ælfgar, Earl, 176

Ælfheah, Archbishop 69

Ælfhere, Ealdorman, 137

Ælfric the Homilist, 23, 27, 51, *et passim*

Æthelbald, King of Mercia, 31, 33, 49, 115, 121, 178 f.

Æthelbald, King of Wessex, 150

Æthelflœd, Lady of the Mercians, 76

Æthelweard, Ealdorman, 78, 93, 202, 205, 217; Chronicle of, 93, 102

Æthelwulf, King of Wessex, 58, 60, 150, 198

Æthilwulf, Northumbrian poet, 199

Agilbert, Bishop, 160

agriculture, 14, 18, 98–104

Aidan, St, 169, 189

Alcuin, 37, 43, 171 f., 192 f., 196 f., 199, 202, 231

Aldfrith, King of Northumbria, 62, 160, 190, 193 f., 226

Aldhelm, St, 12, 31, 91, 107, 170 f., 189–95, 198, 200, 205, 215, 226, 232

Aldred, Earl, 44 f., 175

Aldwulf, King of East Anglia, 24

Alfred, King of Wessex, 7, 12, *et passim;* Cornish poem on, 216 f., laws of, 38, 40, 43, 81, 109, 137; life of, *see* Asser; tomb of, 149; works of, 59, 66, 215–17, 234

Alfred Jewel, 234, 241

Alhred, King of Northumbria, 53, 179

amusements, 90–2, 107 f.

Angles, 11 f., 13, 19, 48

Anglo-Saxon Chronicle, 16, 32, 72, 74, 81, 88, 202, 204, 213 f., 217–22

apocryphal literature, 191, 215, 220

archaeological remains, 17, 49, 108, 118 f., 223 f.

architecture; domestic, 88 f., 108, 131 f., 233 f.; church, 161, 225, 233 f., 239 f.

army, 64, 66, 72–5, 145; desertion from, 30, 72, 74

art motifs, 224–38

Asser, 55, 60, 66 f., 70, 76, 88, 105, 127, 203, 215, 253

assessment, 68, 76, 137 f.

Athelstan, King, 46 f., 55, etc.; laws of, 55, 74 f., 76, 110, 139, 144, 146; panegyric on, 200

Athelstan, Half-King, Ealdorman 78

Athelwold, St, 185, 201, 219, 239; benedictional of, 235; lives of, 201 f.

Augustine, St, of Canterbury, 155 f., 158, etc.

Bath, 17, 50, 53, 62, 81, 89, 113

Bayeux tapestry, 88 f., 223

bear-baiting, 66

Bede, 11–16, 21, *et passim;* translation of, 215

Bedwyn, Wilts, 46, 98, 113, 126

Benedict Biscop, 36, 170, 190, 192, 225 f.

Benedictine Rule, 169 f., 201, 219

Beorhtric, King of Wessex, 120

Beorhtwulf, King of Mercia, 77

Beowulf, 21, 25, 27, 29–31, 39–42, 59, 89, 91 f., 94, 205, 211–13, 222, 233

Berhtwald, Archbishop, 111

Bewcastle cross, 227 f.

Bible, translation of, 215, 220

Birinus, St, 159

blood-feud, *see* vengeance

boar-emblem, 21

Boethius, translation of, 66, 213, 215, 217

Boniface, St, 12, 171, 173–9, 192–8, 232, 242

bookland, 153 f.

books: export of, 179, 192 f., 231; import of, 161, 191 f., 200, 225 f.; production of, 192, 199 f., 203, 232 f., 235–7
bootless crimes, 143
borough-moot, 133, 139
boroughs, 58, 75 f., 79 f., 126–33
Bretwalda, 48
bridge-repair, 64 f., 76 f., 85
Brihtnoth, Ealdorman, 34 f., 87, 89–91
Bristol, 112, 120, 129, 236
British Church, 155, 158, 163
Britons 15, 17 f., 111, 155
bull-baiting, 107
Burghal Hidage, 76, 127
Burgred, King of Mercia, 173
Burton-on-Trent, Staffs, 86, 185
Byrtferth of Ramsey, 89, 93, 186, 201, 219 f.

Cædmon, 107, 206–9
Cambridge, 15, 46, 117, 125, 147
Canterbury, 24, 31, *et passim*; archbishops of, Ælfheah, Augustine, Berhtwald, Cuthbert, Deusdedit, Dunstan, Honorius, Laurentius, Oda, Plegmund, Siric, Tatwine, Theodore; St Augustine's at, 113, 128, 169 f., 175, 194, 240, 242, *see also* Abbots, Benedict Biscop, Hadrian; St Martin's at, 155; St Pancras at, 24
Carolingian influence, 231, 234, 238–40
Carolingian revival, 196, 202, 215, 231, 235
cattle-stealing, 47, 92, 108, 146, 148
Ceadwalla, King of Wessex, 173
Celtic art, 225, 238
Cenred, King of Mercia, 173
Cenwealh, King of Wessex, 159
Ceolfrith, Abbot, 169, 176, 190, 192, 242; life of, 193
Ceolred, King of Mercia, 198
Ceolwulf, King of Northumbria, 173, 205
Ceolwulf II, King of Mercia, 121
chancery, 58

Charles the Great, 31, 33, 37, 60 f., 95, 119, 123, 175, 179 f., 193, 196, 204, 215
charms, 21–3, 25 f.
Cheddar, 88
Chelsea, council of, 112
Chester, 60, 70, 76, 119, 122, 129 f., 131, 147
Chester-le-Street, Durham, 56, 60, 180, 183, 200, 234
children, upbringing of, 45, 94
Christianity: conversion to, 7, 16, 24 f., 55, 58, 119, 155–64, 194; influence of, 19, 22 f., *et passim*
church, 155–88; income of, 153 f., 165–7; legal position of, 134, 137, 142 f., 145, 166; private ownership of, 165–8
churl, 73, 83–6
Clofesho, synod of, 165
Cnut, King, 8, 44, 54 f., etc.: laws of, 36, 38, 46, 55, 99, 137, 143, 150, 187
coinage, 120 f.; *see also* mint
Columba, St, 155, 158
compensations, 33, 41–4, 80, 84, 92, 98, 109, 112, 134, 143–5, 147; *see also* wergild
continental influence, 199–201, 232, 234, 237–9
coronation, 50, 53, 113
cotsetlan, 101 f.
Crediton, 71, 93, 184
Cuthbert, Archbishop, 174, 179
Cuthbert, St, 56, 180, 182, 230, 234, 242; lives of, 16, 194 f., 200, 234; stole of, 223, 234, 241
Cuthwine, Bishop of Dunwich, 192, 232
Cynethryth, Queen of Mercia, 120
Cynewulf, King of Wessex, 32, 38, 88, 115
Cynewulf, poems of, 210

Danegeld, 68, 70
Danelaw, 49, 52, 136, 167, 183; conversion of, 181–3, 202; reconquest of, 218
Danes, 7, 59, etc.; treaties with, 98, 110, 122 f., 187

Danish boroughs, 79; *see* Five Boroughs

Danish invasions, 48 f., 54, *et passim*

Danish settlement, 44, 68 f., 76 f., 99, 120, 137, 150 f., 167, 180, 231

Daniel, Bishop, 194

death-penalty, 51, 75, 109, 143 f., 146 f.

Deusdedit, Archbishop, 162, 189

dicing, 91, 186

dioceses, division into, 161–4, 180, 182–4

divorce, 95, 148–51, 183

dogs, 65 f., 92

Domesday Book, 65, 67, *et passim*

Dorchester - on - Thames, 159, 180–2

dress, 95 f., 172

Dunstan, St, 34, 53, etc.: lives of, 202

Dunwich, Suffolk, 118, 164, 181, 192, 232

Durham, 56, 113, 151, 180, 192, 230, 237, 240

Eadbald, King of Kent, 150

Eadberht, King of Kent, 121

Eadberht, King of Northumbria, 60, 172 f., 231

Eadred, King, 52, 56 f., 69

ealdorman, *passim, especially*, 77–82

Ealdred, Archbishop, 176, 237

Eardwulf, King of Northumbria, 175

earl, 77, 80 f., 83, 86, 116, 122, 127, 151

Easby cross, 231

East Anglia, 9 f., 35, *et passim;* Kings of, Aldwulf, Edmund, Eorpwald, Guthrum, Rædwald, Sigeberht

Easter, calculation of, 158, 160–2; name of, 21

Ecgfrith, King of Northumbria, 32, 43, 56, 70, 170

Eddius's *Life of Wilfrid*, 194, 215

Edgar, King, 50, 52 f., *et passim;* laws of, 122, 129, 133, 137, 139, 165

Edith, Queen, 101, 133

Edmund, King of East Anglia, 59; cult of, 181, life of, 34

Edmund I, King, 43 f., 51, 62, 92, 146, 200; laws of, 43, 53, 55

Edmund II, King, 55

Edward the Confessor, King, 8, 52, *et passim*

Edward the Elder, King, 70, 74, 76, 127, 149, 181; laws of, 122

Edward the Martyr, King, 54

Edwin, Earl, 118

Edwin, King of Northumbria, 24, 32–4, 49, 59, 70, 157–9

Egbert, Archbishop, 36, 164 f., 172, 194, 196; *Dialogue* of, 43

Egbert, King of Kent, 162

Egbert, King of Wessex, 120

Elmham, Norfolk, 90, 152, 164, 181

Ely, 89 f., 104, 117, 170, 185, 239

Emma, Queen, 67, 131, 236

Eorpwald, King of East Anglia, 120, 157

Essex, 8, 22, *et passim;* Kings of, Offa, Sigeberht

Ethelbert, Archbishop of York, 196

Ethelbert, King of Kent, 24, 59, 134, 150, 155 f.; laws of, 150, 156, 214

Ethelred the Unready, King, 8, 34, *et passim;* laws of, 42, 129, 143, 146 f., 166

Ethelred, King of Mercia, 173

Ethelred, King of Northumbria, 33, 37

Exeter, 46, 55, 67, 73, 82, 113, 240

exile, voluntary, 31–3, 160, 173 f., 177

Falconers, 65, 105

famine, 69, 103, 112, 198

Felix, St, 158, 189

Felix, Frankish secretary, 58, 199

Felix's *Life of St Guthlac*, 197, 203 215

fertility cults, 19–21

fighting, penalty for, 51, 80, 84, 98, 145

fines, 51 f., 64, 75, 77, 80 f., 84, 109, 112, 141, 144 f., 151, 166
fisheries, 100, 103, 118
Five Boroughs, 136
five-hides unit, 18, 72, 84 f., 98
Fleury-sur-Loire, 62, 185, 201, 236
folkland, 154
folk-moot, 81, 137 f.
forcible entry into houses, 51, 80, 84, 98, 139
foreign craftsmen, 50, 66, 70, 225, 227, 234
foreigners: harbouring of, 122; inheritance after, 64, 114
foreign masons, 16, 161, 225
foreign scholars, 62, 184 f., 201 f., 215
foreign visitors, 58–63, 66
forfeiture, 51, 64, 81 f., 87, 143, 149, 152, 154
fortress building, 64, 75 f., 85
fox-hunting, 91, 172
Frankish influence, 66, 215, 232, 235
Frisian merchants, 120, 124
Frisians, 60, 70, 111, 177, 179 f., 231
furniture, 89 f., 152
Fursey, St, 16, 159, 198

Gebur, 98, 100, 102
geburland, 98
geneat, 98 f., 102
gesith, 29, 83 f., 94
gilds, 46, 132, 175
Glastonbury, 111, 117, 170, 181, 200, 229, 234, 240
Godwine, Earl, 80, 87, 131, 176
Golden Gospels of Stockholm, 232
goldsmiths, 105 f., 133, 208
Greek, 162, 190 f., 192, 222
Gregory the Great, 24, 119, etc.; Dialogues of, 215; life of, 194; Pastoral Care of, 191, 215, 234, 242
Grim's Ditches, 22
Guthlac, St, 25, 170, 241; life of, 197, 203, 220; poem on, 172, 210

Guthrum, King, 60, 122

Hadrian, Abbot, 162, 190 f.
harbouring of outlaws, 46, 50, 84, 123, 139 f.
Harold, Cnut's son, King, 54
Harold, Earl, 88
Harold Fairhaired of Norway, 62
Harthacnut, King, 52, 54, 69
haw, see town-houses
hawking, 65 f., 91 f., 105, 208
hearg, 23
heathen burial customs, 26, 49, 88, 205
heathen religion, 19–28, 48, 138, 156 f., 162, 182 f., 187, 203–5, 223 f.
heriot, 35 f., 97
Hertford, synod of, 149, 162 f.
Hexham, 164, 169, 180, 225 f., 230, 240
hide, 68, 71, 73, 76, 84, 97 f., 140 f., 167
Honorius, Archbishop, 158
horse-racing, 92
hospitality, duty of, 56, 62, 79
hostages, 32, 34, 123
house-carls, 57 f., 69 f., 73
hundred, 24, 69, 71, 116, 123, 137–9, 167
hunting, 91, 103, 208; duties of, 65, 85, 91, 99
huntsmen, 65, 91, 105
Hwætberht, Abbot, 193
Hwicce, 8
Hygeburh, nun of Heidenheim, 197

Icanho, 169 f.
illuminated MSS, 192, 223, 225–7, 232–8, 242; export of, 231 f., 236; import of, 232, 234
incest, 145, 148
Ine, King of Wessex, 50, 172; laws of, 103, 122 f., 134 f., 139, 151, 166, 219
inheritance, 64, 100, 114, 148–54
Irish Church, 158–62, 169 f., 189
iron industry, 116 f.
ivories, 223, 228, 231, 236, 238, 241

James the Deacon, 157, 159

Jarrow, 36, 170, 180, 190, 192, 226, 231

Jellinge style, 237

jewellery, 95 f., 118, 224 f.

John of Beverley, St, 94

John the Old Saxon, 215

jurisdiction, private, 61, 122, 128, 139, 145

Jutes, 11 f., 13, 19

Kenneth, King of Scotland, 56, 60

Kent, 8 f., 13 f., *et passim;* Kings of, Eadbald, Eadberht, Egbert, Ethelbert, Wihtred; laws of, 83, 123, 145, 150 f.

kindred, 37–47, 94, 111 f., 145, 149–53, 173

king, deposition of, 53; election of, 53–5

king's council, 54–6, 136, 153 f., 157, 186

king's farm, 64, 68, 80, 154

king's peace, 51 f., 56, 139, 145, 151

king's priests, 54, 58, 65

king's reeve, *see* reeves

king's writ, 65, 81 f., 139, 168

knights' gild, 132

Læt, 97

land, grants of, 30, 34, 76, etc.; held by title-deed, 85, 153 f.; lease of, 100, 149; services on, 92

Latin scholarship, 172, 200, 219

Laurentius, Archbishop, 150

law, courts of, 137–9, 145; districts of, 136; promulgation of, 137

lawmen, 147

lead-mining, 117

Leofgyth, St, 171, 178; life of, 198

Leofric, Earl, 78, 80

libraries, 191–3, 200

Lichfield, 113, 164, 232 f.

Lincoln, 15, 130–1, 136, 147, 157, 165, 181

Lindisfarne, 164, 169, etc.; bishops of, Aidan, Cuthbert; gospels of, 192, 227, 242

Lindsey, 157, 164, 170, 180, 182, 194

London, 8, 15, *et passim;* bishops of, Mellitus, Theodred; bridge at, 144; councils at, 55, 194; St Pauls at, 72

Lothian, 60

Louis, Emperor, 198

Lul, St, 179, 197, 225, 231 f.

Magonsæte, 8, 171

Maldon, poem on battle of, 34 f., 87, 213

manumission, 82, 86, 94, 107, 112–14

maritime guard, 65, 85

marriage, 42, 45, 59–61, 111 f. 145, 148–53, 162, 183; of clergy, 168, 184, 186

Mayo, English see in, 160

Mellitus, Bishop, 156

merchants, 63, 86, 105, 119, 124 f.; *see also* traders

Mercia, 8 f., 49, *et passim;* ealdormen of, Ælfgar, Ælfhere, Edwin, Leofric; Kings of, Æthelbald, Beorhtwulf, Burgred, Cenred, Ceolred, Ceolwulf, Ethelred, Offa, Penda, Wulfhere; law of, 50, 136

Mercian Register, 21

Middle Angles, 8, 164

minsters, 165 f., 182, 239

minstrelry, 59, 91, 107, 204 f., 209

mints, 82, 120 f., 129 f.

missions: to the continent, 12, 158, 171, 173, 177–80, 187, 192, 197, 209, 230–2, 235, 243; to Scandinavia, 187 f., 243

monasteries, 43, 62, 161, 169–73, 178–81, 184 f., 199, 232; double –, 169 f.; Irish –, 161; private ownership of, 171 f.; reform of, 8, 62, 173, 184 f., 201–3, 217, 219, 234; spurious –, 172 f.

money, purchasing power of, 9, 96, 146

moneyers, 129, 133

Monkwearmouth, 36, 170, 190, 193, 221, 226

Morcar, Earl, 87

morning-gift, 152

murder, 33, 41, 52, 143, 176

mutilation, 143 f.

Northumbria, 7 f., 18, *et passim;* Earls of, Aldred, Morcar, Uhtred, Waltheof; Kings of, Aldfrith, Alhred, Ceolwulf, Eadberht, Eardwulf, Ecgfrith, Edwin, Ethelred, Oswald, Oswiu, Oswulf

Norwich, 66, 128, 130 f.

Oath-helpers, 41, 46, 140 f., 148

oaths, 27, 33, 41, 46, 50, 53, 84, 86, 140 f., 145, 147–9; expressed in hides, 140 f.; in shillings, 141; preliminary –, 140

occupations, 90–5, 132 f.

Oda, Archbishop, 185, 200

Offa, King of the Angles, 48

Offa, King of Essex, 173

Offa, King of Mercia, 31, 48 f., etc.; dyke of, 75

Oftfor, Bishop, 174

Ohthere, voyage of, 13, 59, 63

ordeal, 142 f., 147

Orosius, 59, 191, 215–17

Oswald, Archbishop, 184 f., 201, 239, 241 f.; life of, 201

Oswald, King of Northumbria, 31, 158 f.

Oswiu, King of Northumbria, 36, 68, 159 f., 162, 173

Oswulf, King of Northumbria, 33

outlawry, 46, 140, 149

outlaws, harbouring of, 46, 50, 84, 159 f.

overlordship, 48 f., 55, 59–61, 156, 159, 163

oxen, price of, 9, 51, 96, 100 f., 103, 108

Oxford, 73, 75, 82, 127, 128–31, 187

Parish churches, 164–7

Paulinus, St, 157, 163

Pehtred, book by, 198, 214

penal slavery, 112 f., 144

Penda, King of Mercia, 69, 120, 173

penny, 9, 84, 120

perjury, 141, 145

Peterborough, 170, 185, 218, 239

pilgrimage, 44, 62, 123, 160, 173 f., 176 f., 197, 230

Pippin, King of the Franks, 59, 231

Plegmund, Archbishop, 215

ploughland, 68, 97

poetry, 12, 17 f., *et passim;* aristocratic interest in, 205 f.; diction and metre of, 206–8; MSS. of, 213; nature in, 210 f.

pound, value of the, 9, 75, 108

precious objects, 17, 49, 61, *et passim;* export of, 231; import of, 129, 225–32, 234

prison, 81, 132, 141 f.

prose, vernacular 214–22

protection, breach of, 51, 80, 84, 145

Queen, income of, 67

Rædwald, King of East Anglia, 24, 33, 156

radcniht, 99, 102

Ramsey Abbey, 185, 201, 236, 239

Reculver, 16, 121, 169, 232

reeves, 52, 76, 81 f., etc.; king's –, 64, 80–2, etc.; *see also* town-reeve, sheriff

relics, 58, 61 f., 113, 145, 147

Rhineland, 13, 118, 239 f.

riddles, 111, 193 f., 210

Ringerike style, 238

Rochester, 77, 120 f., 126, 137, 156, 163, 189, 194

Roman Britain, 11–19, 125, 162, 165, 228

Roman Church, usages of, 159–62

Roman influence, 13, 17, 134, 153, 190, 228

Rome, 120, 123 f., 162, 194, 225 f., 241; appeal to, 163, 177; English 'School' at, 175; missionaries from, 155 f., 159, 178; see also pilgrimage

Romsey rood, 236

Rothbury cross, 231

royal estates, 64, 67, 80, 145, 165

royal officials, 67, 77–82, 139; see also ealdorman, earl, reeve, sheriff

runes, 20, 25

Ruthwell cross, 210, 228 f.

Salt, 115 f.

Saxons, 11–13, 19, 78

Saxons, Old or Continental, 12, 48, 177–9, 215; poetry of, 209, 212

Scandinavian influence, 7, 44, 60, 77, 150 f., 229, 237 f.

Scandinavian law, 135, 147

Scandinavian literature, 19, 57

Scandinavian religion, 20–3, 26

schools, 164, 180–91, 196–8, 200–2

sculpture, 17, 227 f., 233 f., 236–8

sculptured crosses, 223, 228–30, 233, 237 f., 241

Selsey, 135, 164

sheep, price of, 9, 96, 100, 146

Sherborne, Dorset, 111, 115, 164

sheriff, 65, 80 f., 106

shilling, value of, 9, 51, 77, 83 f., 97

ships, 62, 69–72, 81, 85 f., 120–2

shipwreck, 121, 125, 175

shire, 78–80

shire-moot, 63, 81, 137–9

Sigeberht, King of East Anglia, 173, 189

Sigeberht, King of Essex, 42

Siric, Archbishop, 175

slaves, 18, 82, 86, 94, 96 f., 99, 101 f., 106, 108–14, 119–21, 144, 167

slave-trade, 111 f., 119 f., 122

smiths, 106, 117

soulscot, 166 f.

Stamford, 136, 147

stepmother, marriage with, 150

stone-quarrying, 117

Streonwald, 35

sulungs, 68

Sunday observance, 121, 198 f.

Sussex, 8, 22 f., 51, etc.

Sutton Hoo, 49, 241

Swein Forkbeard, King, 69, 187

Tacitus, 19 f., 22 f., 27, 29 f., 34, 40, 57, 151, 204

tapestry, 49, 88 f., 223

Tatwine, Archbishop, 193 f.

thanes, 36 f., 43, et passim; twelve leading thanes, 148; gild of, 46

theft, 41, 82, 107, 122, 124, 131–4, 141–9, 152

Theodore, Archbishop, 43, 162–4, 167, 169, 190–2, 196; penitential of, 37, 42, 111 f., 149 f., 196

Theodred, Bishop, 175, 181 f.

three public charges, the, 64 f., 75, 77, 85

tithe, 166 f.

tithing, 46

title-deeds, 85, 148, 153 f.

tolls, 64, 82, 108, 116, 121 f., 123 f., 168

Tostig, Earl, 175, 236 f.

town-houses, 88, 126, 128–9

town-reeve, 81 f.

towns, 81 f., 122, 126–33; see also boroughs

trade, 13, 63, 81 f., 108, 111, 115–26, 128 f.

traders, 81 f., 118–25, 192; see also merchants

treachery to a lord, 30, 33, 38, 50, 53, 143

treasure-giving, 29–31, 35 f., 93

treasury, 58, 66

Uhtred, Earl, 44, 89

Ulfcytel of East Anglia, 35

Ultan, illuminator, 230

Utrecht Psalter, 236

Vengeance, 31–3, 36–43, 45–7, 51, 125, 140, 146, 205
Vespasian Psalter, 232
Viking raid', 7 f., 75, *et passim*
vouching to warranty, 108, 146

Waltheof, Earl, 45
Wansdyke, 22
Wapentake, 137, 147
Watling Street, 180
weapon-smith, 21, 106, 117, 224
Welsh, 8, 18, 32, etc.; 'Welsh expedition', 65
weoh, 23
Werferth, Bishop, 215 f., 220, 252; Gregory's *Dialogues* translated by, 220
wergild, 39–47, 50f., 75, 80, 83–6, 97 f., 108, 112, 114, 143, 151
Wessex, 8 f., 49 f., *et passim;* Kings of, Æthelbald, Æthelwulf, Alfred, Beorhtric, Caedwalla, Genwealh, Cynewulf, Egbert, Ine
Whitby, 107, 169, 171, 190, 194, 206; Synod at, 160, 190
Whithorn, Galloway, 164, 180
widows, 150–2
Wihtred, King of Kent, 123, 134; laws of, 156
Wilfrid, St, 31 f., 90, 159, 163, 169 f., 175, 177, 192, 225 f., 229, 241; Life of, 194; Latin poem on, 200
Willehad, St, 180
William of Malmesbury, 107, 120, 192, 229
Willibald, St, 173; Life of, 197, 228

Willibrord, St, 171, 177; Calendar of, 242; Life of, 196 f.
Winchester, 55, 67, 81, etc.; bishops of, Athelwold, Daniel, Swithin; Newminster (Hyde Abbey) at, 184; Old Minister at, 90, 129
'Winchester School' of art, 234, 236 f.
Winton Domesday, 133
witchcraft, 23, 41, 143
witnesses, 82, 108, 122, 129, 139, 143, 146
women: education of, 192, 198, 201, occupations of, 93 f., 96 106; position of, 45, 87, 93–5, 150–3
wool, 118 f., 121
Worcester, 65, 69, 75, etc.; bishops of, Oftfor, Oswald, Werferth, Wulfstan
Wulfhere, King of Mercia, 49
Wulfric Spott, 86, 185
Wulfrun, foundress of Wolverhampton, 241
Wulfsige, Bishop of Sherborne, 186
Wulfstan, Archbishop of York, 38, 53, 99, etc.
Wulfstan, St, Bishop of Worcester, 45, 112; Life of, 239
Wulfstan, precentor, 202
Wulfstan, traveller to the Baltic, 59, 124
Wynnebald, St, 173, 178; Life of, 197

Yeavering, 88
York, 15, 24, 52 *et passim;* (Arch)bishops of, Ealdred, Egbert, Ethelbert, John, Oswald, Paulinus, Wilfrid, Wulfstan